Practical GitOps

Infrastructure Management Using Terraform, AWS, and GitHub Actions

Rohit Salecha

Apress®

Practical GitOps: Infrastructure Management Using Terraform, AWS, and GitHub Actions

Rohit Salecha
Mumbai, India

ISBN-13 (pbk): 978-1-4842-8672-2 ISBN-13 (electronic): 978-1-4842-8673-9
https://doi.org/10.1007/978-1-4842-8673-9

Managing Director, Apress Media LLC: Welmoed Spahr
Acquisitions Editor: James Robinson-Prior
Development Editor: James Markham
Coordinating Editor: Jessica Vakili

Cover image designed by Freepik (www.freepik.com)

Distributed to the book trade worldwide by Springer Science+Business Media New York, 1 NY Plaza, New York, NY 10004. Phone 1-800-SPRINGER, fax (201) 348-4505, e-mail orders-ny@ springer-sbm.com, or visit www.springeronline.com. Apress Media, LLC is a California LLC and the sole member (owner) is Springer Science + Business Media Finance Inc (SSBM Finance Inc). SSBM Finance Inc is a **Delaware** corporation.

For information on translations, please e-mail booktranslations@springernature.com; for reprint, paperback, or audio rights, please e-mail bookpermissions@springernature.com.

Apress titles may be purchased in bulk for academic, corporate, or promotional use. eBook versions and licenses are also available for most titles. For more information, reference our Print and eBook Bulk Sales web page at http://www.apress.com/bulk-sales.

Any source code or other supplementary material referenced by the author in this book is available to readers on the Github repository: https://github.com/Apress/Practical-GitOps. For more detailed information, please visit http://www.apress.com/source-code.

Printed on acid-free paper

Table of Contents

About the Author

Rohit Salecha is a technology geek who loves to explore anything that runs and understands binary. As a security engineer, he is passionate about learning the length, breadth, and depth of technology.

Being more on the defensive side, he has evangelized secure software development at various organizations for more than a decade.

He is ridiculously driven by the "everything as code" mantra and strongly believes that the security team must strive toward making themselves irrelevant.

In his free time, he is either reading books or watching movies. He is a fitness freak who loves to jog, swim, and cycle on different terrains.

About the Technical Reviewers

Gaurav Raje is a Senior Product Manager at Amazon in the Returns, ReCommerce, and Sustainability group. Previously, he was an Experience Owner Lead at USAA where he led an Agile team and actively monitored the backlog by discussing product features with a cross-functional team including IT, Legal and Compliance, and Leadership. He implemented features that provided automated solutions and reduced the manual dependency on USAA's customer fulfillment centers.

Prior to joining USAA, Gaurav was a Manager at PwC Consulting, where his main projects consisted of performing gap assessments of small Asian banks by reviewing their procedures, resources, and technology and facilitating workshops with client stakeholders as necessary; subsequently, he produced recommendations (procedural enhancements and a technology implementation) to address the gaps; these recommendations resulted in future sales opportunities.

Gaurav holds an MBA from Georgetown University and a BS in electrical and computer engineering from the University of Colorado at Boulder.

Anand Tiwari is an Information Security Professional. He loves to play with open source tools and is more inclined toward defense than offense in the information security domain. He works with the operation and development team, solving challenges between the security and DevOps teams.

Preface

In 2018, I heard the term "Kubernetes" for the first time, and the only understanding I had of AWS was that we can run machines in the cloud that can be accessed from anywhere. Being in the security domain, hearing new technology terms and learning about these technologies has been an undying passion of mine.

It took me two years to understand DevOps, and I created a small hobby project called Practical DevOps lab (`www.rohitsalecha.com/project/practical_devops/`) to help people understand the core underlying technologies that make up the umbrella term.

After completing this, I asked myself what's next?

So I decided to level up, and the result is this book. I wanted to explore cloud and cloud-native technologies like AWS and Kubernetes and how they can be set up using Infrastructure as Code like Terraform.

I wouldn't say that I am an expert at any of these technologies because that was never my aim. My aim was to have a basic hands-on understanding of them, and in this book, I am sharing that limited knowledge that I have because being from the security domain, it's my job to help organizations secure their assets, but if I don't have a basic understanding of what they are, then I wouldn't be doing my job well.

Since this is a totally practical and hands-on book, it would be recommended to use it as an ebook as it'll help in working faster. We'll be dealing with technologies like AWS Route53, AWS EKS (Kubernetes), and AWS ELB, which do not fall under the free tier categories, and hence, there'll be charges (>$15) associated when you execute the code provided in this book.

CHAPTER 1

What Is GitOps?

1.1 The Era of DevOps

Businesses today have expanded into different horizons and industries with the enablement of technology. Today, we have folks delivering food at home by simply placing an order on an application in a hand-held device and streaming your favorite movie/sitcom on whatever device you wish to see. All these have been possible because people are exploring different ways to solve real-world problems with the help of technology.

An interesting question to ask at this juncture is who is pushing whom? Is it that new ways to do business are pushing technology to the edge or is it because we have high-end technology that businesses are thriving? This is a typical chicken-and-egg question as to which came first: the egg or the chicken?

Frankly speaking, it doesn't matter who is pushing whom, but one thing purely common between the two is "agility"; everyone wants things to be done faster. But then going fast can be risky, and hence, people also look for stability. Gone are the days when system administrators would cut-short their holidays to support the festive surges. Thanks to technology platforms like AWS (Amazon Web Services) and the like, which are also popularly known as cloud computing platforms, businesses and technology can achieve speed with resilience and reliability.

© Rohit Salecha 2023
R. Salecha, *Practical GitOps*, https://doi.org/10.1007/978-1-4842-8673-9_1

This culture of being able to deliver software with agility and reliability gave rise to the term which we call "DevOps." The influence that the DevOps methodology has had on the people, process, and technology, the three pillars of success for any organization, is tremendous and revolutionary. DevOps brings about a change in which businesses operate. The IT (information technology) team has sort of broken out of the shackles of being boring, slow, and always taking the blame for failures. Many blogs/personas describe DevOps as a methodology that brings Dev and Ops together, which is certainly true from a technology perspective. However, I believe that DevOps has brought business and technology to become equal stakeholders in the success of organizations. Peter Sondergaard in the Gartner Symposium, 2013, declared that "Every company is a technology company," which implies that the success of every business is tied to the success of your technological processes and tools.

1.1.1 What Problems Is DevOps Addressing?

Before understanding what DevOps is, let's rewind our clocks back and understand how software development functioned a few decades ago. In ancient times of IT, back when we'd just fixed the Y2K bug, the Waterfall model of software development was very popular and most widely accepted. The model was quite simple as illustrated here.

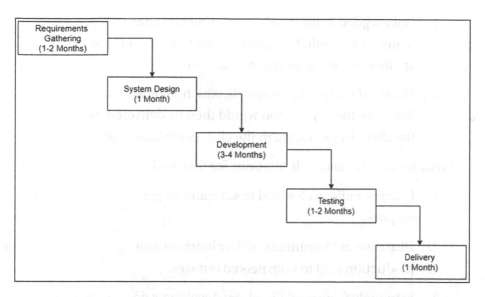

Figure 1-1. *Waterfall SDLC model*

1. A project would be kicked off, and a business analysis team would visit the client and jot down all the requirements, which would take around one to two months.

2. Once all the requirements are captured, the architecture team would convert these requirements into a system design and provide a road map for software development.

3. Based on the preceding two stages, the software development team would then start writing the code and test it out in their local systems, which would easily take a minimum of three to four months to complete. The project management team would track the progress of the development against the requirements specified and also the budget.

4. Once a good majority of the requirements have been done, there would be a pilot testing by deploying the application in a staging environment.

5. Finally, if everything goes well, which seldom happens, the application would then be delivered to the client by deploying in the client's environment.

What are the challenges/limitations for this model?

1. Lengthy build cycles lead to slow and sluggish outputs.

2. Disparate environments of development and production lead to unexpected outages.

3. Extremely focused skills where developers do not wish to interfere in operations and vice versa. This hinders transparency in processes and huge dependencies.

4. The day the software is delivered, everyone involved in that part of the application is expected to be on the floor waiting to quickly identify if something unexpected is observed.

5. Scaling up with manually created infrastructure is a big challenge as downtimes are required.

6. Implementing backup and disaster recovery strategies is expensive as it involves maintaining two copies of infrastructure (maybe a little scaled-down one) and also ensuring syncing of the data between them.

1.2 Introduction to DevOps

DevOps is a methodology that brings together three practices that work in tandem:

- Continuous integration
- Continuous delivery/deployment
- Continuous monitoring

Understanding each of these practices individually will help us understand DevOps, which shall also lay groundwork for explaining the term "GitOps."

1.2.1 Continuous Integration

Continuous integration as described by Martin Fowler (https://martinfowler.com/articles/continuousIntegration.html) is a software development practice where different members of the team integrate changes frequently from at least a one to multiple changes in a day.

There are various tools that can be used for this purpose, namely, Git, CVS, Mercurial, SVN, etc.

The primary purpose of all these tools is to

- Ensure version control of all the objects/files that are saved

- Provide necessary tooling to resolve merge conflicts so as to reduce issues arising owing to integration

- Provide traceability of changes so as to understand its impact on the running systems

- Allow the implementation of a transparent and flexible peer review process

- Accelerate failure detection by implementing automated testing

The preceding diagram illustrates the practice of continuous integration where developers working on different parts of the project, that is, Frontend and Backend, are all checking the application code with the Dockerfiles and Kubernetes administrators checking the Kubernetes Manifests into the repository. The illustration makes use of the tool called "Git," originally developed by Linus Torvalds in 2005, which so far is the most widely used software for version controlling and also the tool of choice for this book. The key element about Git is that it is "distributed," meaning there is a local copy on your machine and a main copy stored somewhere on your remote servers.

In our illustration, the red dot lines signify the developer's machine where the entire source code of the project resides along with the current changes that they have made. The solid lines in the shape of the cloud signify the central repository where the code is finally merged from all the developers. Hence, a copy of the code will always be present in the central repository and in each developer's machine.

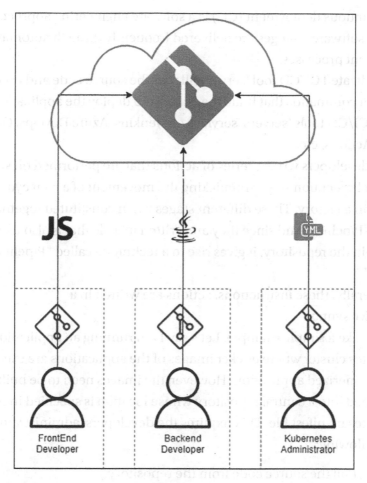

Figure 1-2. *Distributed Git model*

1.2.2 Continuous Delivery/Deployment

Deployment is the practice of pulling the source code from a repository and performing actions that are necessary to package and run the application on a desired system.

7

Continuous deployment (CD) is a software engineering approach in which software changes are delivered frequently through automated deployment processes.

A dedicated CI/CD tool/server will pull the source code and execute a series of commands that build, package, and deploy the application. Popular CI/CD tools/servers/services are Jenkins, Azure DevOps, CircleCI, GitHub Actions, etc.

The developers write a series of actions that are performed on serial or parallel execution stages mimicking the movement of a conveyor belt running in a factory. These different stages when constituted together are called a "Pipeline," and since they are written in a file that is also usually checked in the repository, it gives rise to a technique called "Pipeline as Code."

Generally, these instructions/actions are written in a declarative syntax.

Let's take a simple example. Let's say I am running an application on a Kubernetes cluster where docker images of the applications are executed as a containerized application. However, the images need to be built and pushed into a central repository whose location is specified in the Kubernetes manifest file. This requires the developers/administrators to do the following:

1. Pull the source code from the repository.

2. Perform automated QA/security testing.

3. Build an image with the latest version of the code:

    docker build -t testimage/repository:version.

4. Push the built image into a container repository:

    docker push testimage/repository:version

5. Once the images are pushed into the repository, the Kubernetes administrators apply their manifest files.

This process is called continuous delivery as we are continuously delivering the changes to the central docker repository.

An interesting thing to note here is that in the continuous delivery process, a human intervention is needed to execute the application as indicated in step 5 where an administrator needs to apply the Kubernetes manifest files.

Continuous deployment is a more advanced process where upon thoroughly testing, the changes are directly deployed into the Kubernetes environment without any human intervention, something which we'll explore in more detail.

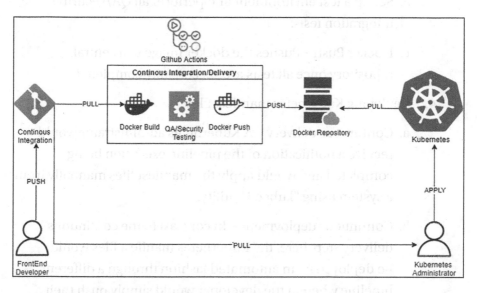

Figure 1-3. *Continuous delivery pipeline*

The preceding image illustrates the complete process where the docker image building is automated as described in the following:

1. Developers push their application code and Kubernetes administrators their Kubernetes manifests into their respective repositories once development and testing are complete.

2. The CI/CD server, GitHub Actions in our case, which is listening for a commit event, pulls the code into a temporary location.

3. Upon receiving the trigger of a commit event, the tool starts the execution of the pipeline, and as described in the figure, we are performing two actions:

   a. Docker Build – Which builds a docker image from the Dockerfile present in the repository.

   b. Set up a test environment and perform all QA/security/integration tests.

   c. Docker Push – Pushes the docker image to a central repository once all tests are successfully completed.

4. Deploying Kubernetes manifest files:

   a. Continuous delivery – A Kubernetes administrator would receive a notification of the pipeline execution being completed and would apply the manifest files manually from a system using "kubectl" utility.

   b. Continuous deployment – In contrast to the continuous delivery step, here, the Kubernetes manifest files would be deployed in an automated fashion through a different pipeline wherein the developer would simply push their Kubernetes manifest files into the source code repository and the deployment pipeline would get triggered. As a matter of fact, this is the core idea that'll be discussed in this book.

1.2.3 Continuous Monitoring

Feedback is one of the most important parts of any process and is certainly a big deal in DevOps. As we deploy faster, we are able to see the new features quickly and rapidly; however, what to do when things go wrong? In the case of an application running in a pod in a Kubernetes environment, there are many things that can go wrong like no taint matching, no node available for scheduling, etc. How do we debug this real time without having to actually SSH into the cluster? How do we know if a node is exhausting its memory, or the CPU is spiking? How can we get all those details real time?

This is where the practice of continuous monitoring becomes an extremely important part of DevOps as it gives real-time feedback on how our infrastructure is behaving.

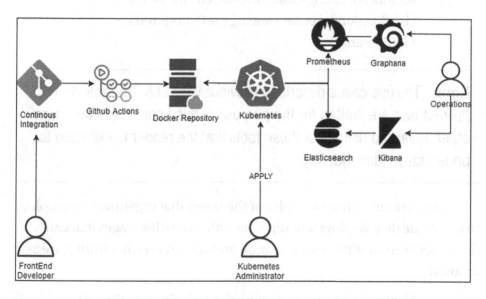

Figure 1-4. *Continuous monitoring using Prometheus, Grafana, and ELK Stack*

11

The preceding image illustrates the idea of continuous monitoring where we are using two popular solutions for monitoring the Kubernetes cluster.

1. Prometheus and Grafana – Primarily used for monitoring performance parameters like memory, CPU utilization, etc. Prometheus is the data store that pulls the requisite information, and Grafana is the dashboarding solution for viewing the information stored in Prometheus.

2. Elasticsearch and Kibana – Primarily used for viewing the log events near real time like access logs, error logs, etc. Elasticsearch is used for storing the unstructured data pushed in through various solutions like Logstash, Filebeat, etc. Kibana is the visualization layer for viewing the data stored in Elasticsearch.

Note   The use cases described previously for ELK, Grafana, and Prometheus are limited for the purpose of this book. There are many other advanced usages of these tools that the reader is expected to understand independently.

These are only a few examples of the stages that organizations employ to automate their deployment pipeline. Other possible stages that can occur between continuous integration and continuous monitoring are as follows:

- Continuous testing – Testing the code changes through automated testing using tools like Selenium.

- Continuous verification – Verifying the results of testing against the acceptance criteria, which are also codified in the pipeline.

- Continuous security – Leveraging the security toolsets like SAST (Static Application Security Testing), SCA (Software Composition Analysis), DAST (Dynamic Application Security Testing), Compliance as Code, Container Scanning, etc., as different stages within the DevOps pipeline to derive a higher level of security assurance before the code hits production. This is also popularly known as the DevSecOps movement.

All in all DevOps tries to answer all the issues that we've observed in the waterfall model of software development. DevOps is a methodology to

- Push our changes faster by reducing the build time

- Create a multi-environment synergy by having least possible differences between the staging and production environments

- Foster a multi-skilled culture where developers and operations understand each other's job

- Reduce dependencies between individuals by attempting to automate as much as is possible

- Ensure scalability of infrastructure without downtimes

- Provide a way to collect and correlate the metrics for our infrastructure so as to take appropriate actions in case of a disaster

1.3 Infrastructure As Code (IaC)

Now that we've got a good understanding of what DevOps is all about, it's important to understand one more key term, which in my opinion is the enabler of DevOps, and that is "Infrastructure as Code." The best way to understand this term is to take a use-case example and understand how this requirement was solved over a period.

Let's say we wish to run a simple HTML page using Apache Web Server on an Ubuntu operating system (OS). The tech stack is quite simple, but let's understand how people managed to execute this over time.

1.3.1 Evolution of Server Infrastructure

Let's start from the time when the client-server architecture started gaining dominance over the mainframe technology.

1995–2005

- Purchase a bare-metal server and place it in a stack in a data center.

- Install the Ubuntu OS by logging in directly from the terminal using a CD drive.

- Once the OS is installed, configure the network and other necessary components.

- Then install Apache using the "apt-get" command.

- Configure the IP address manually and statically and serve the web page on the address.

- All kinds of updates, backups, etc., needed to be done by hand and were extremely tedious.

- Time taken to prepare the server: ~1–2 weeks.

Then in the new decade, virtualization technologies began to shape up the landscape where in a single bare-metal device, multiple OS could be installed and configured. With virtualization, the steps changed a bit.

2005–2015

- Create a virtual machine using your favorite virtualization technology.

- Download the Ubuntu ISO and configure it as a virtual disk to install the virtual machine.

- Once the OS is installed, configure the network, which is slightly easier especially in the virtualization environment as compared to the manual steps.

- Then install Apache using the "apt-get" command and serve the web page on the IP address of the virtual machine.

- Create virtual hosts for serving multiple websites on the same server owing to shrinking IP address space.

- Time taken to prepare the server: ~2–3 days.

In the past decade, people started realizing that it's quite futile to spin up a full-blown server with its own memory, disk, CPU, etc., just for serving a few HTML pages even if it's virtualized. Hence, they started using containerization technology to quickly spin up and tear down containers.

Note   All code files can be cloned from the following repository on GitHub: `https://github.com/Apress/Practical-GitOps/`. Once downloaded/cloned, they'll be accessible as per the chapter number associated with the code. So for accessing the code of Chapter 1, you'll need to open the folder "chapter1"; for accessing the source code of Chapter 2, you'll need to open the folder "chapter2" and so on.

2015–Present

- The following is a sample Dockerfile that takes the base image of the Ubuntu container and installs the necessary components.

Code Block 1-1. Dockerfile for Apache2

```
File: chapter1\Dockerfile

1: FROM ubuntu
2: RUN apt-get update
3: RUN apt-get install -y apache2
4: RUN apt-get install -y apache2-utils
5: RUN apt-get clean
6: EXPOSE 80 CMD ["apache2ctl", "-D", "FOREGROUND"]
```

- Once the Dockerfile is ready, its first build, and a customized image is created, it is then pushed into a central repository.

- Then a container orchestration system like Docker Swarm, Kubernetes, Mesos, etc., is used to execute as a container application. In this manner, thousands and millions of small websites can be containerized and deployed in a matter of seconds.

- Time taken to prepare the container: ~2–5 minutes.

- Organizations also started utilizing cloud computing like AWS wherein in a matter of few clicks, you can get a virtual machine on the Internet with everything pre-configured; all you've got to do is deploy your application.

- As an alternative to clicks on console, you can also utilize tools like Terraform to spin up resources on different cloud platforms. The following sample Terraform code deploys an EC2 instance on the AWS environment.

Code Block 1-2. Terraform code for EC2

```
File: chapter1\ec2.tf

17: resource "aws_instance" "app_server" {
18:    ami             = "ami-00399ec92321828f5"
19:    instance_type = "t2.micro"
20:    tags = {
21:      env = "test"
22:    }
23: }
```

- Time taken to prepare the server: ~5–10 minutes.

The advantage that the new age technology holds, be it either containers or cloud computing, they can all be codified in a simple declarative format as shown in the code snippets. This gives the ability to version control our infrastructure in a declarative manner and be able to track, update, and manage everything from the version control software, for example, "Git," which will be followed in this book.

1.3.2 Tools of Trade – IaC

In the IaC space, we primarily have two types of tools that solve two different problems:

- Infrastructure provisioning tools – This set of tools is primarily used for setting up the base infrastructure

17

like servers with a particular OS, for example, setting
up an Ubuntu OS or a Red Hat OS. Vagrant, Puppet,
Terraform, CloudFormation, and Docker are some
examples of infrastructure provisioning tools that can
spin up a server either locally or remotely (on cloud).

-   Infrastructure configuration tools – This set of tools
    specializes in configuring the infrastructure once it
    is provisioned. For example, we may set up an EC2
    instance on AWS using Terraform, but we'll need to use
    a configuration tool like Ansible, Chef, or basic Shell
    scripts to install the required dependencies like the
    Apache2 server and set up the virtual hosts.

In this book, we'll be exploring Terraform with AWS in much more
detail with chapters dedicated to both topics.

1.3.3 Mutable vs. Immutable Infrastructure

Change being the only constant is bound to happen to our infrastructure
as demanded by our applications' requirements. Hence, when dealing
with infrastructure in a fast-moving DevOps environment, there is a very
important distinction that needs to be made with respect to the life span of
the infrastructure that we are deploying.

However, the degree and frequency of changes required, and the effort
required to implement these changes, is what defines our infrastructure to
be a mutable or an immutable infrastructure.

Mutable Infrastructure

-   Infrastructure that, once provisioned, cannot
    be destroyed owing to various reasons like high
    dependency and explicit manual configurations;
    examples include, but not limited to, Mail, Exchange,
    Identity, and Database servers.

- These systems also undergo very minimal changes throughout their life span. For example, if you need to update a database server, then you don't have to completely destroy and create a new one from scratch. You've just got to update its version by retaining the data.

- Hence, the degree of change needed is very low, frequency of changes is not that often, but the efforts required to implement the changes are generally very high.

Immutable Infrastructure

- Infrastructure that has limited or no dependency on other components that are running; for example, in a microservice architecture, if one service goes down, it doesn't affect the other services.

- Infrastructure that is better to recreate than update. For example, a Front-End reactjs application running in docker needs to update itself to a newer version. It makes no sense to update the code from within the running docker container. It is much better to replace the running container with a newer image containing the updated version.

- Hence, the degree and frequency of changes needed is quite high; however, the efforts required to implement these changes are generally very low.

It is extremely important to understand these terms and be able to visualize their implementation. These terms are also quite commonly elucidated as pets vs. cattle. If you view a server (containerized or virtualized) as something that can be replaced at any time, then it's like a cattle sort of representing tens or thousands of servers performing a similar job. However, if you view a server as an indispensable part of your daily operations, then it's a pet representing something that's done quite uniquely.

Another very practical example is Kubernetes. The master plane components of Kubernetes can be considered as a pet as doing any kind of changes here can lead to drastic effects and hence need to be treated as a mutable infrastructure. The deployments or workloads can be considered as a cattle or an immutable resource, which can be quickly replaced/updated.

We'll explore more about Kubernetes and its AWS equivalent, that is, AWS EKS, in more detail in this book.

1.3.4 State in IaC

State in computer systems is a collection of information about a program or an object stored either in a file or memory. The information represents the current state of the program/object and helps in identifying what future state would look like by diffing between the current and the desired information.

If we are spinning up infrastructure resources using IaC technologies, then it's extremely important to store their state as without that information, we won't know how resources were created and how they would handle changes.

Let's take a simple example of how Terraform manages its state when creating a simple EC2 instance on AWS. (We'll explore Terraform in much more detail in chapters ahead).

A sample *terraform.state* file where Terraform state is stored is shown here.

Code Block 1-3. Terraform state

```
{
  "version": 4,
  "terraform_version": "1.0.7",
```

```
"serial": 1,
"lineage": "2d17ac77-08f2-94d9-e1e5-991fc1e2fe12",
"outputs": {},
"resources": [
  {
    "mode": "managed",
    "type": "aws_instance",
    "name": "app_server",
    "provider": "provider[\"registry.terraform.io/hashicorp/
    aws\"]",
    "instances": [
      {
        "schema_version": 1,
        "attributes": {
          "ami": "ami-00399ec92321828f5",
          "arn": "arn:aws:ec2:us-
          east-2:871811778330:instance/i-0bc3c235e3991243b",
          "associate_public_ip_address": true,
          "availability_zone": "us-east-2c",
          "capacity_reservation_specification": [
            {
XXXXXXXX ---- SNIPPED FOR BREVITY------ XXXXXXXXX
```

This file is created once "terraform apply" is executed and its operation of creating an EC2 instance on AWS is completed as illustrated in Figure 1-5.

The state stores information about the instance ID, network interface ID, and much more details that are required when modifications are to be made to this server or to destroy this instance.

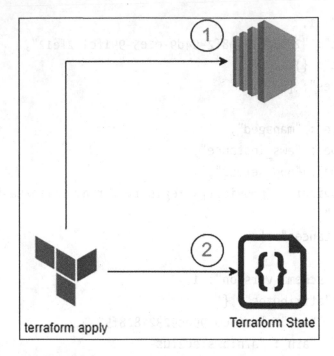

Figure 1-5. *Executing Terraform apply*

When the resource needs to be destroyed or any new resource needs to be added, Terraform will first reference the *terraform.state* file and provide information about what is going to change. Once that is done, it'll then go ahead and execute the necessary changes.

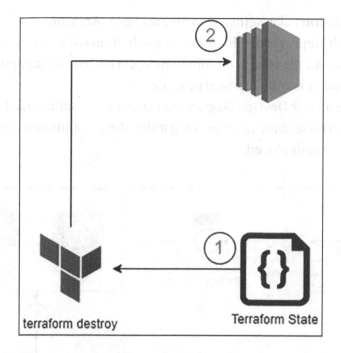

Figure 1-6. *Executing terraform destroy*

We'll discuss in detail how to manage the terraform state in the best possible way; however, for now, understanding the importance of state is extremely necessary from the GitOps perspective.

1.4 Problems with Continuous Delivery

So we saw the difference between continuous deployment and continuous delivery and that in the latter, a manual step is required to reflect the changes in production whereas in the former, an automated pipeline needs to be set up wherein changes are directly pushed without any manual approval.

Most organizations generally start the DevOps movement in continuous delivery and then move up to continuous deployment as a mature automated process needs to be in place for the same.

Organizations like Netflix, Google, Facebook, Amazon, etc., continuously deploy their changes into production without any manual intervention. All the testing for functionality, security, and compliance is added as part of the deployment pipeline.

Let's recall our DevOps diagram that employs a continuous delivery pipeline and raise some questions regarding the environment in which our application gets deployed.

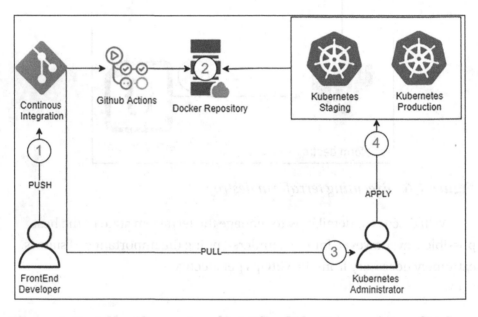

Figure 1-7. *A sample continuous delivery pipeline*

1.   Developers push the code into the source code repository.

2.   Once the code is pushed into the repository, GitHub Action is triggered, which builds and pushes the docker images to the docker repository.

3. Once the pipeline is executed, the Kubernetes administrator will pull the Kubernetes manifest files from the repository.

4. Post pulling the code, they will apply the manifest files into the respective Kubernetes cluster for the environments.

Now let's analyze the potential problems/issues with this approach:

- Manual deployment – As with all activities done manually, there is always an element of human error.

- No state management: In this scenario, the Kubernetes cluster would be created by hand, and all deployments are done by hand, albeit through the manifest files. However, being able to track the actual state with the manifest files would be a big challenge in itself. Hence, there'll be a huge gap between the current state and the desired state, which in many cases leads to uncertainty. Also, not just about the Kubernetes cluster but the entire infrastructure that has been set up on cloud if done through console/CLI will be unmanageable and untraceable.

- CLI vs. cloud: Every Kubernetes administrator will have their own choice of operation; some would want to manage through CLI, while others would be comfortable with the GUI. This will lead to inconsistencies in the way the cluster and its resources are managed, leading to confusion.

If manual processes exist especially in managing the IT infrastructure resources, there'll always be inconsistencies leading to possible outages/issues.

1.5 Introduction to GitOps

As we saw, DevOps is more of a combination of culture, tools, and processes to develop and deliver business applications faster. GitOps is a more technical term that encourages everything to have the "Git" as the single source of truth. By everything, I mean your application as well as your infrastructure must be deployed from Git. For teams following DevOps, their application code is already maintained in Git; however, their infrastructure is more or less deployed by hand.

Hence, GitOps stresses more on having your infrastructure deployed directly from Git, providing flexibility to developers to be able to choose their own deployment strategies and taking the load off the system administrators to manage and deploy complex environments like staging, production, backup, and disaster recovery.

GitOps is a process to manage your infrastructure deployments in an auditable, repeatable, version-controlled, and reliable manner. GitOps will help you create a "snapshot" of your infrastructure in the form of a "state," allowing you to make decisions while designing and deploying changes. It'll help you scale up/scale in whenever required and manage almost all aspects of your cloud infrastructure through a few lines of code.

The following are some mandatory requirements to implement a GitOps process for the infrastructure that is responsible for running business applications:

- Your infrastructure must be defined in a declarative format and stored in a version-controlled system.

- The state of the infrastructure must be recorded in a well-defined format.

- All infrastructure changes must be done through code only.

- Any new changes in the infrastructure must be approved by identifying the difference between the current state and the desired state.

– Drifts in state changes that occur owing to manual infrastructure modifications must be identified and reconciled.

In a typical GitOps process, the entire infrastructure should be captured in Git and deployed through a CI/CD process. The application deployment should also trigger the Kubernetes manifest files being applied without human intervention. The following image captures the "raw" idea of how this can be in an automated fashion.

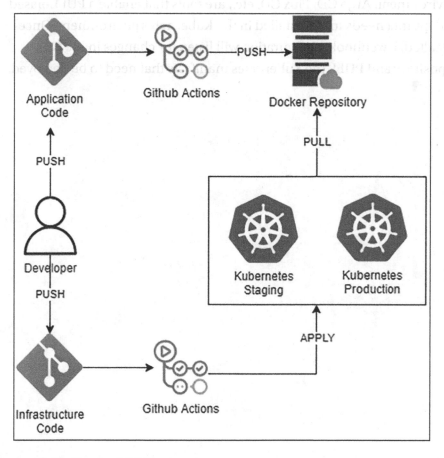

Figure 1-8. *Typical GitOps process*

Running in parallel to the DevOps pipeline, the GitOps pipeline is responsible for initializing, creating, and managing the infrastructure on which the applications are being deployed in an auditable, repeatable, and reliable manner.

What we are discussing here is a PUSH-based GitOps wherein GitHub Actions is being used to PUSH the changes into the deployment environment like AWS or GCP.

However, there exists a PULL-based GitOps that is governed by an operator that is listening for changes and then deploys them in the environment. Argo CD, Flux CD, etc., are tools that enable a PULL-based GitOps that needs to be installed in the Kubernetes environment. Once installed, a webhook configuration will listen for changes in the Git repository and PULL the Kubernetes manifests that need to be deployed.

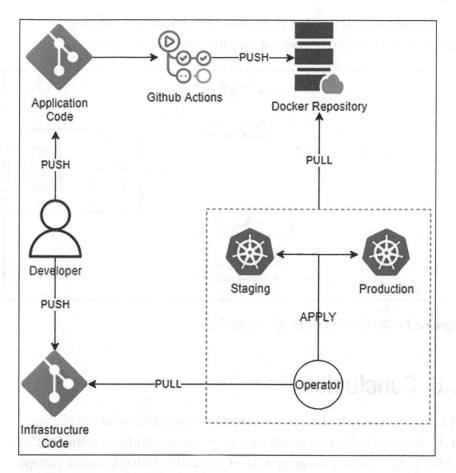

Figure 1-9. PULL-based GitOps

These PULL-based GitOps tools are more suitable for an exclusive Kubernetes-based environment only. Some of these tools can also deploy an entire Kubernetes cluster in an environment of your choice, that is, on premises, AWS, GCP, etc.

In this book, I'll, however, be discussing a PUSH-based approach using Terraform, GitHub Actions, and AWS EKS wherein we'll not only be managing Kubernetes resources in code but also the supporting AWS infrastructure like a PostgreSQL database, DNS configurations, HTTPS certificates, Load Balancer, and many more.

The following is the GitOps pipeline we shall build and also understand the different components in different chapters.

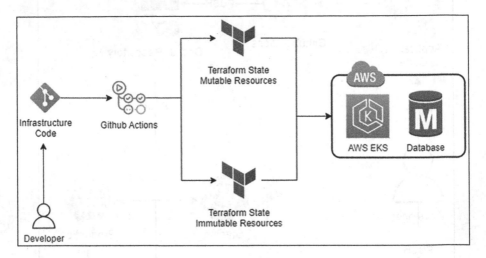

Figure 1-10.   *Complete GitOps pipeline*

1.6 Conclusion

In this chapter, we looked at what DevOps is and how it has solved some of the biggest challenges in software development. Infrastructure as Code added to the speed and agility of DevOps, and to utilize it better, GitOps movement was started. GitOps helps in creating a continuous deployment pipeline to deploy the changes faster, reliably, and efficiently.

In the next chapter, we'll look at how we can create an EC2 instance on AWS using Console as well as CLI to elaborate how easy it has now become to spin up a server on AWS.

CHAPTER 2

Introduction to AWS

2.1 Prerequisites

AWS CLI will be explored in this chapter, and hence, to log in using the
CLI, we'll need to install the **awscli** tool, which can be installed on your
favorite operating system by following the instructions provided on the
official AWS documentation:

- https://docs.aws.amazon.com/cli/latest/user-guide/install-cliv2.html
- I am currently using **AWS CLI Version 2.7.9**.

Note   All the code in this book will work only on AWS CLI Version 2.X
and above.

2.2 Introduction to AWS

In this chapter, we'll introduce ourselves to AWS (Amazon Web Services),
one of the most popular cloud service providers. This chapter will help us
build context for the next chapter as well; hence, even if you're familiar
with AWS, do at least skim through this chapter.

© Rohit Salecha 2023
R. Salecha, *Practical GitOps*, https://doi.org/10.1007/978-1-4842-8673-9_2

I love history, and hence, before I tend to explain a topic, I'd like to provide a historical overview of what happened before using this new technology/technique as, in my opinion, it helps to understand things better. In the previous chapter, we learned about the evolution of the IT infrastructure from a bare-metal server to a docker container and an EC2 instance running on the AWS cloud. We also discussed the challenges faced with the bare-metal infrastructure or even the virtualization of the infrastructure resources. However, here, I'd like to specifically talk about one of the most important challenges with infrastructure resources, which is **scalability**.

Imagine you are the infrastructure director of an e-commerce site that is selling some amazing products. This e-commerce site owing to its popularity has a high demand during the daytime, and by nightfall, the demand reduces considerably. To put it in numbers , during the day, roughly seven to eight servers are needed to serve the load, whereas by nightfall, only two to three servers are enough to keep the site up and running. How do you scale with such a demand? Purchasing ten servers and keeping them operational only for 12 hours? This can be expensive operationally and from a capital expenditure perspective, both.

Now let's say some organization living up in the sky gives you a sort of a magic wand that gives you the ability to spin up and tear down servers with a single whoosh (or maybe a command). You've just got to log in into their console, do some clicks, or fire some commands (we'll see both in this chapter) and voilà, you have your servers ready for deployment!

This is the power of what is popularly known as "cloud computing." This capability helps in making our demands more **scalable** wherein we can spin up and tear down as many servers as needed being charged only for the consumption.

AWS (Amazon Web Services) is one of the most popular "cloud computing" service providers wherein one of the major services that they provide is **Elastic Compute Cloud** or popularly known as **EC2**, which is a very well-thought-out name. EC2 machines can be configured with an operating system of our choice, a range of CPU, memory, and plenty of other configurations.

Let's jump right in and start creating our own EC2 machine on AWS using the AWS GUI and through the CLI interface. Why are we using both? As stated earlier, there is a specific set of information that I require to capture to proceed with writing our Terraform scripts in the next chapter. I'd like you to get sensitized to that information so that it'll become easier for you to write terraform scripts.

2.2.1 Create an AWS Account

Let's first go ahead and create our AWS account. If you already have an account, feel free to skip this section. Navigate to the URL https://aws .amazon.com/free and create a new account using an email address and strong password. Using the free account will provide us $300 of free credit for a period of 12 months albeit certain services that we may use like AWS EKS and AWS Route53. While signing up, you'll be required to enter your credit card details as well.

Note   Providing a cost estimation at this stage will be a bit difficult as I am not sure how much time you'd keep the resources on. All resources have an hourly rate, and hence, it all depends on how many hours you keep your EKS/RDS on. Let's assume that you'd be running along with the book and quickly delete the resources once you're done exploring. In such a scenario, it should cost you roughly about $15 or more.

> **Tip** You can manage multiple AWS accounts using different email
> addresses. If you are concerned about the number of mailboxes to
> monitor, many email providers allow you to create aliases for the
> same mailbox. For example, if you use Gmail, you can create an
> account using the Email Sub Addressing trick like someone+gitops@
> gmail.com, which is a new account for AWS, but all communication
> will land on someone@gmail.com, helping you manage multiple
> accounts with a single inbox.

Once you've created an account, you'll be signed in as a **root** user in
AWS. It is strongly recommended to apply two-factor authentication on
your root account and create a separate user with the requisite permissions.
Figure 2-1 is the expected screen with best practices being followed upon
browsing the URL https://console.aws.amazon.com/iamv2/home#/home.

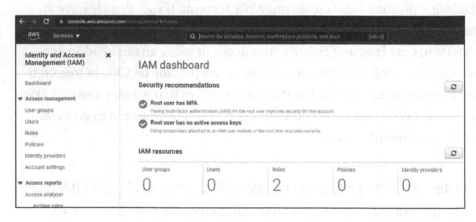

Figure 2-1. *Expected IAM dashboard*

One more very important feature to enable is the **Cost Explorer**,
which can be enabled by browsing to https://console.aws.amazon.com/
billing/home?#/tags and clicking **Enable Cost Explorer** as shown in the
following. Though we are in a free tier account, this will help us analyze the
expenditure in much more detail.

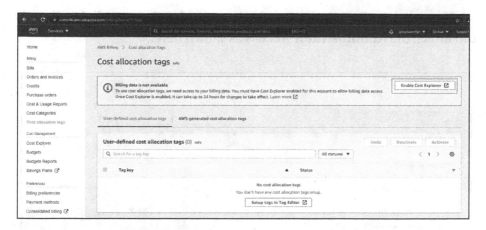

Figure 2-2. *Enable Cost Explorer*

Create a new user by navigating to `https://console.aws.amazon` `.com/iamv2/home#/users` and clicking **Add Users**. Ensure to enable the programmatic and password access as shown here.

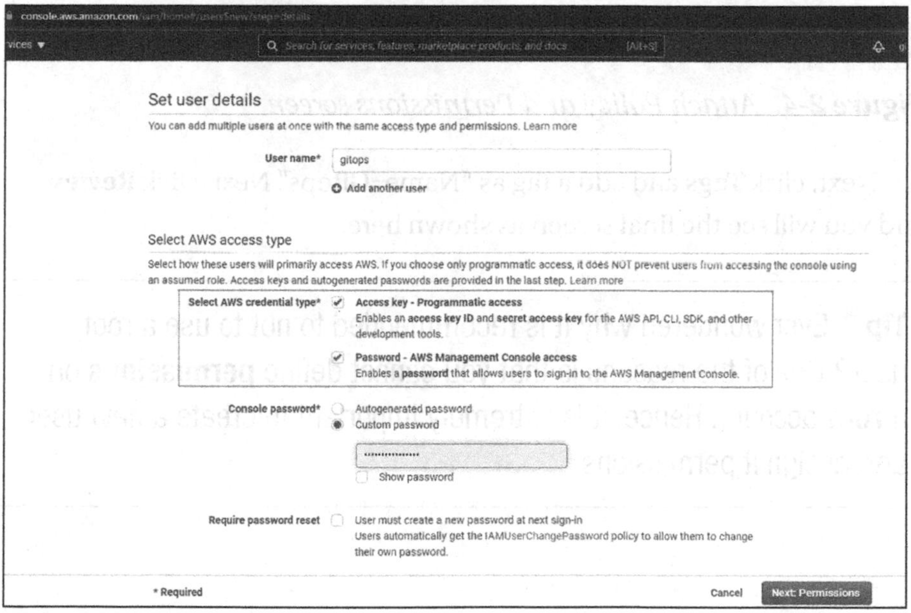

Figure 2-3. *Add User screen*

Next, click on **Permissions** and select **Attach existing policies directly** and attach the **Administrator Access** as shown here.

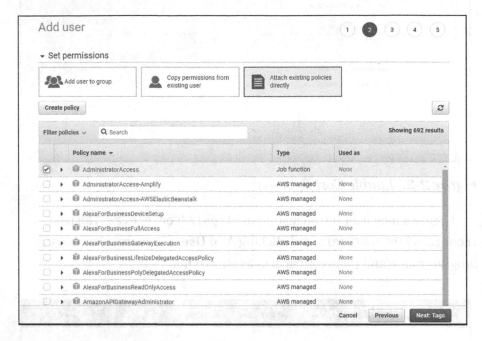

Figure 2-4. *Attach Policy and Permissions screen*

Next, click **Tags** and add a tag as "Name=Gitops". Next, click **Review** and you will see the final screen as shown here.

Tip   Ever wondered why it is recommended to not to use a root user? One of the reasons is that you cannot define **permissions** on a **root** account. Hence, it is extremely important to create a new user and assign it permissions.

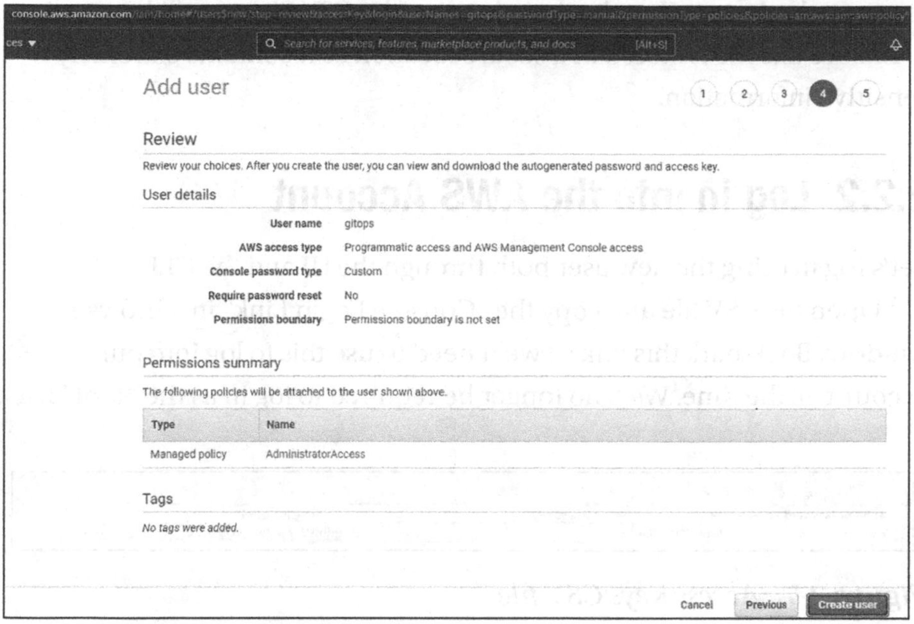

Figure 2-5. *Create User Final screen*

Finally, click **Create User** to complete the setup. You should be able to see a screen as shown here.

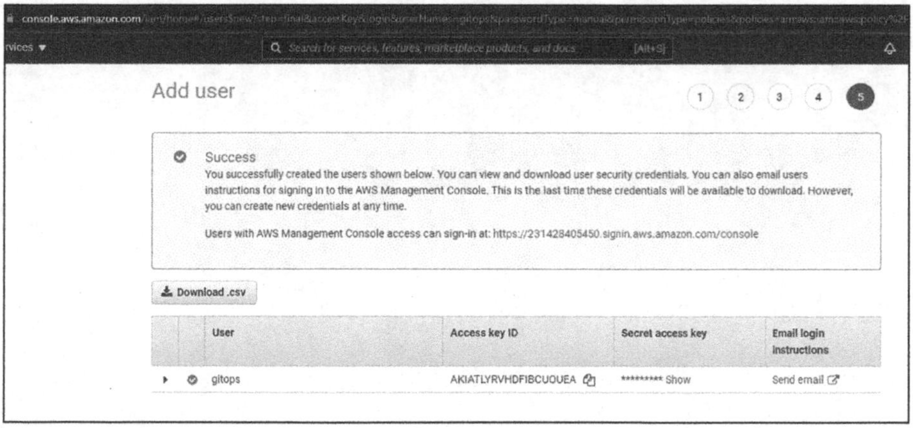

Figure 2-6. *Access Keys Download screen*

Save the **Access Keys** by downloading the CSV file as we'll be needing it. Ensure this file is stored in a secure location as it contains extremely sensitive information.

2.2.2 Log in into the AWS Account

Let's log in using the new user both through the UI and the CLI.

Open the CSV file and copy the "Console Login Link" in a browser window. Bookmark this link as we'll need to use this to log into our account all the time. We'll no longer be required to log in as the "root" user.

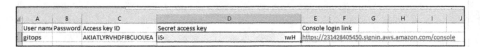

A	B	C	D	E	F	G	H	I	J
User name	Password	Access key ID	Secret access key	Console login link					
gitops		AKIATLYRVHDFIBCUOUEA	is‹ wH	https://231428405450.signin.aws.amazon.com/console					

Figure 2-7. *Access Keys CSV file*

Sign into the AWS account using the credentials created.

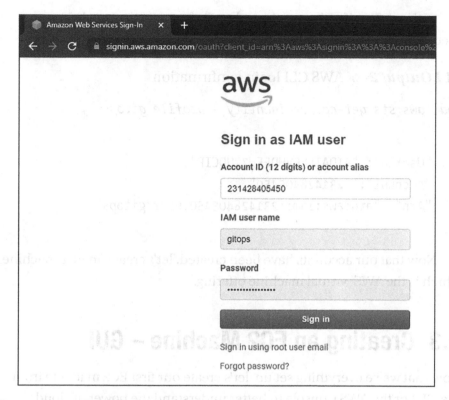

Figure 2-8. AWS Sign-In screen

Let's configure our AWS CLI profile by executing the command and entering the information as shown here using the CSV file we downloaded earlier.

CLI Output 2-1. AWS CLI profile configuration

```
cmd> aws configure --profile gitops
AWS Access Key ID [None]: AKIATLYRVHDFIBCUOUEA
AWS Secret Access Key [None]: XXXXXXXXXXXXXXXXXXXXXXXXXXXXXXXX
XXXXXXXXXX
Default region name [None]: us-east-2
Default output format [None]: json
```

Let's confirm if we've configured our information correctly by executing the following command.

CLI Output 2-2. AWS CLI login confirmation

```
cmd> aws sts get-caller-identity --profile gitops
{
    "UserId": "AIDATLYRVHDFFW7RHDCIP",
    "Account": "231428405450",
    "Arn": "arn:aws:iam::231428405450:user/gitops"
}
```

Now that our accounts have been created, let's create an EC2 machine, which is the AWS' virtual machine offering.

2.3 Creating an EC2 Machine – GUI

Now that we've everything set up, let's create our first EC2 machine from the GUI or the AWS Console to better understand the power of cloud computing.

2.3.1 Default Region Selection

In AWS, selecting a region is very important for most services. All instructions in the book will be provided for **Ohio (us-east-2)** as the default region. So ensure you select the region as Ohio from the drop-down box on the top-right corner as shown in the following before moving into any of the steps.

Note AWS Region selection is completely arbitrary as all the services that we'll be exploring in this book are available in all the regions. It totally depends on the user to select which region they are comfortable with; however, once you do select, please continue to use it as services like AWS EKS, RDS, OpenSearch, etc., are region specific.

Figure 2-9. AWS Default Region Selection screen

Once logged in, enter the term **ec2** in the search bar on top as shown here.

Figure 2-10. AWS Search Bar EC2 screen

You'll be greeted with an EC2 launch console where you can click on the Launch Instance button as shown here.

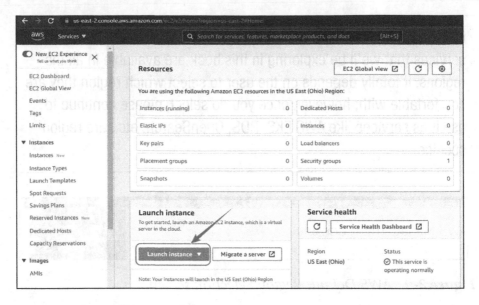

Figure 2-11. *AWS Launch Instance screen*

The page will navigate to a section where you can select the base operating system that is required for spinning up our VM as shown here.

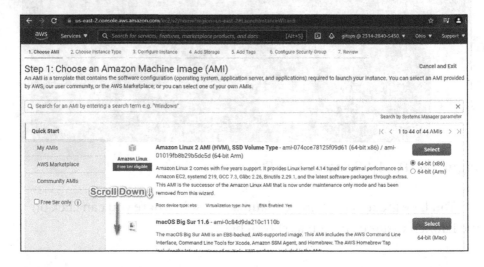

Figure 2-12. *Selecting Base Operating System screen*

2.3.2 Instance Type Selection

Scroll down below till you see the **Ubuntu** image and then click **Select** as shown here.

One information to note, as highlighted in yellow, is the AMI ID, which is **ami-00399ec92321828f5**.

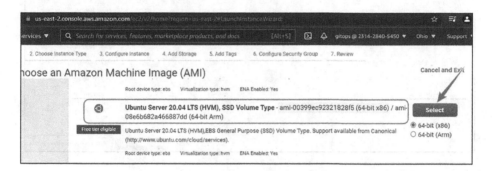

Figure 2-13. *Selecting Ubuntu OS screen*

On the next screen, we'll be asked to choose the configuration of the virtual machine. For now, to save money, we'll go ahead with the **t2. micro** instance as shown in the following and then click **Next: Configure Instance Details**.

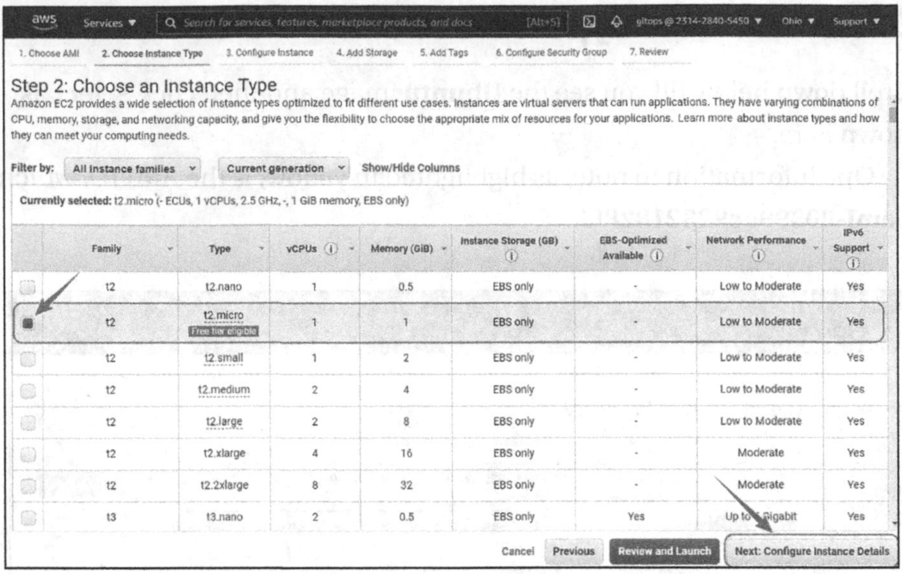

Figure 2-14. *Instance Selection screen*

Tip   In AWS, CPU selection is the most important aspect as RAM and bandwidth depend on it. The higher the CPU, the higher is the RAM and bandwidth. However, you might find certain instances that are memory optimized not following this rule.

2.3.3 Instance Configuration

In this screen, we can configure the instance-level details like which network it'll belong to and what it needs to install at startup. As can be seen in the following screenshot, the default VPC (virtual private cloud) is configured for the instance's deployment.

No action needed here; we just need to scroll down to a very important section.

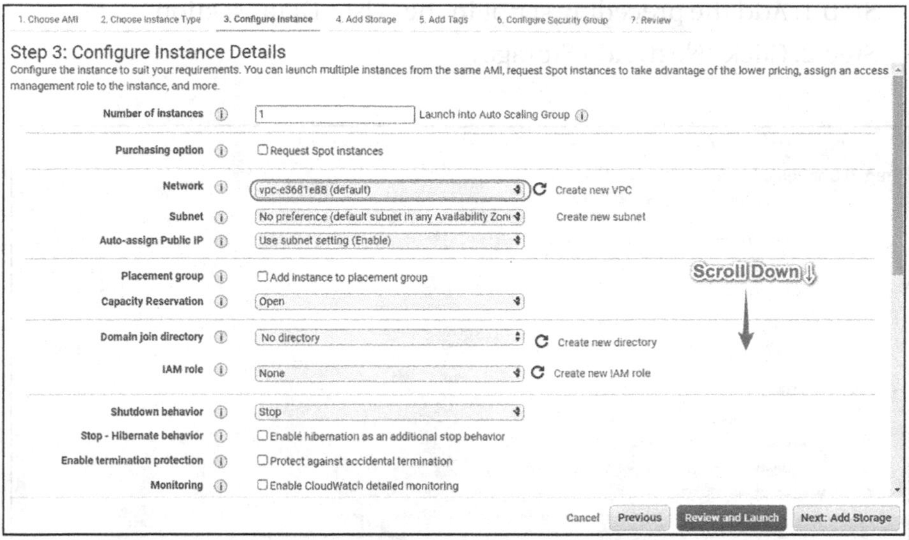

Figure 2-15. *VPC Selection screen*

Now we need to configure the instance to run an Apache2 web server on port 80 upon launch. This can be done by adding our commands to set up an Apache2 server in the "User Data" section using the script as shown in Figure 2-16.

Tip   The "User Data" section is a place where you can "bootstrap" your servers with necessary dependencies using scripts for the respective operating systems. Bash for *nix and PowerShell for Windows.

Code Block 2-3.   User data script

File: chapter2\user_data.sh

```
1: #!/bin/bash
2:
3: sudo apt update -y
4: sudo apt install apache2 -y
```

Step 1: Add the preceding script in the "User Data" section.

Step 2: Click "Next: Add Storage".

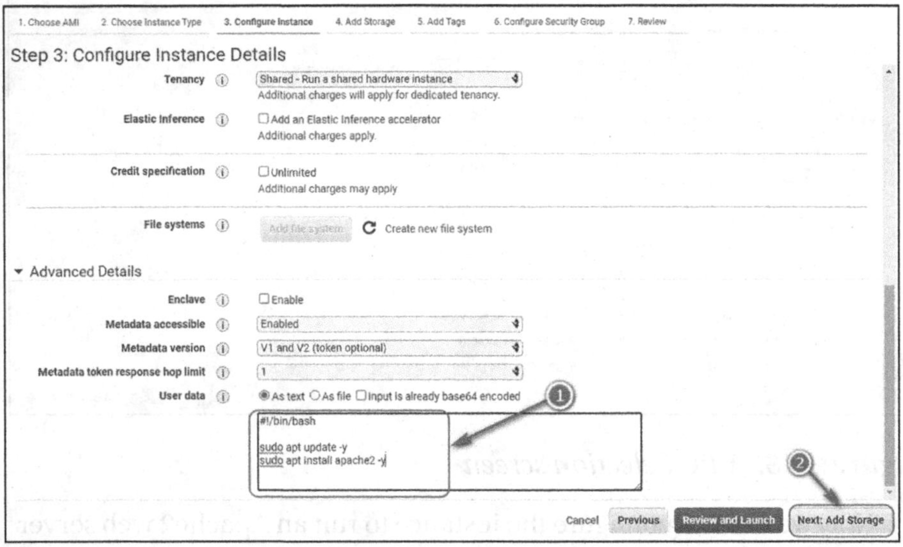

Figure 2-16. User Data Script Configuration

2.3.4 Instance Storage

The next section is to add **Storage**, that is, adding a separate disk to store any data. We'll keep the defaults here and then click **Next: Add Tags**.

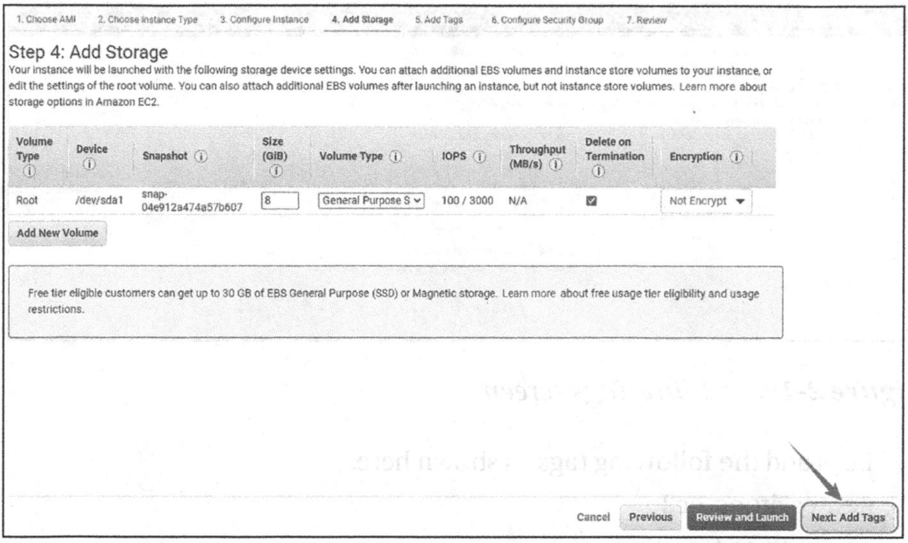

Figure 2-17. *Storage Configuration screen*

2.3.5 Tags

Adding tags is very important especially when you're working in a cloud environment. If you remember when we created a new account, I asked you to enable a setting called **Enable: Cost Explorer**. This functionality relies heavily on tags to provide us proper billing information.

Aside from billing, tags help us perform granular selections that can then be applied for authentication, authorization, configuration, and termination. So let's click **Add Tag** and add a simple tag.

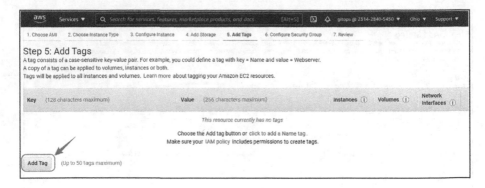

Figure 2-18. *Adding Tags screen*

Let's add the following tags as shown here.

name: gitops-ec2

environment: testing

After adding the tags, click **Next: Configure Security Group**.

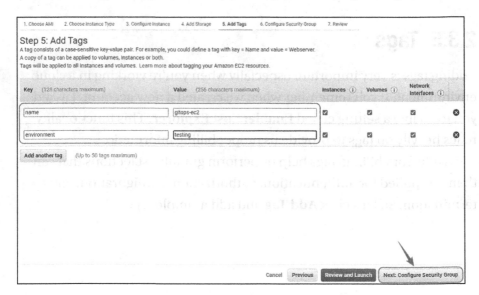

Figure 2-19. *Adding name and environment tags screen*

2.3.6 Security Groups

Next is a very important section from security perspective wherein we configure which ports/services we would like to configure on our EC2 machine. The following screenshot shows that AWS is suggesting opening the SSH port for remote login.

Tip   If you're familiar with **Windows Firewall** in Windows or **iptables** in Linux wherein we are restricting only certain ports to be listening on our machine, security groups are almost similar in functionality. It is AWS' way of ensuring that no insecure services are running **by default**.

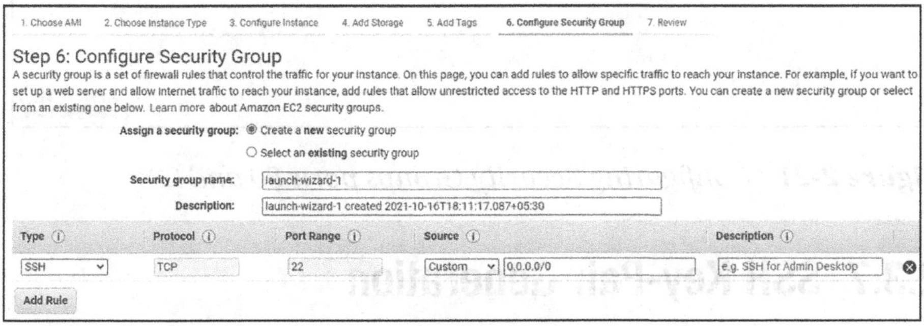

Figure 2-20. Adding Security Groups screen

However, we are installing an Apache2 web server, and by default, it runs on port 80. Hence, we need to allow port 80 to be listening as well for which we'll need to add a rule to allow port 80 as well.

Step 1: Add a good name to the security group, let's call it **gitops-ec2-external**.

Step 2: Add a rule to allow port **80** from all IPs **0.0.0.0/0**; just select **HTTP** from the drop-down box.

Step 3: Click **Review and Launch**.

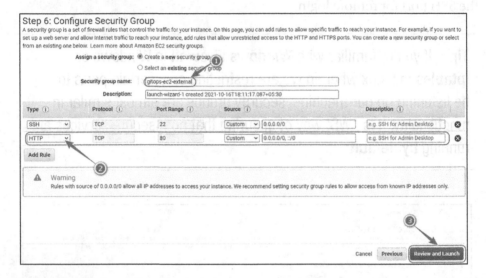

Figure 2-21. *Configuring Security Groups ports 80 and 22*

2.3.7 SSH Key-Pair Generation

This is the final review screen where we can review all the information which we've configured so far. Once all information has been reviewed, you can click **Launch** as shown here.

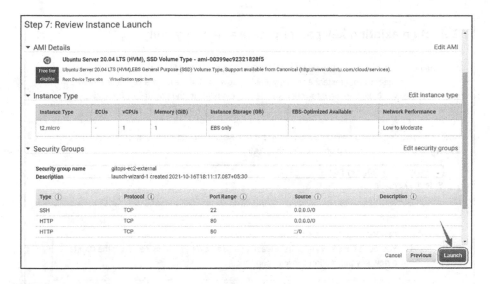

Figure 2-22. *Final Review screen*

Upon clicking **Launch**, you'll be asked to create an SSH key pair as shown here. This key will be needed to log in to the EC2 machine we've launched. Hence, it's also very important and needs to be performed.

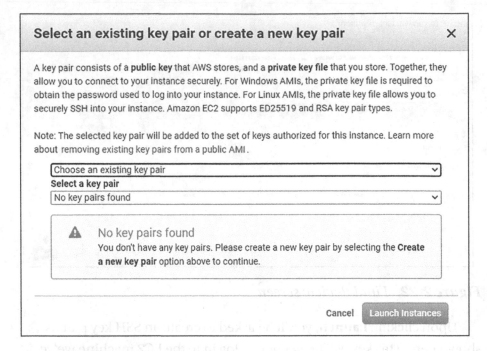

Figure 2-23. *SSH Key Pair creation screen*

From the drop-down that says **Choose an existing key pair**, select **Create a new key pair** and add a name as **gitops.**

Step 1: Create a new key pair.

Step 2: Enter a name as **gitops**, keeping the key-pair type as default, that is, RSA.

Step 3: Click **Download Key Pair**.

Note   Please keep the downloaded key pair safe and secure. Also, do make a note of the name of this key pair as it'll be required to reference in the future.

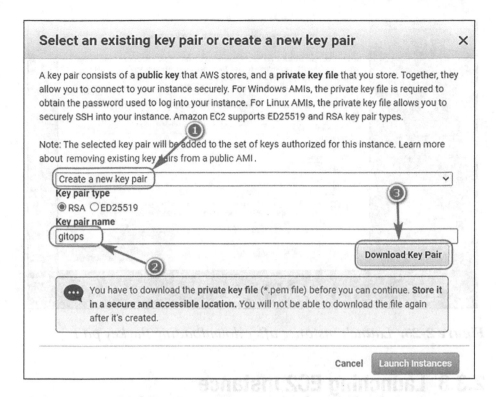

Figure 2-24. *Configure Key Pair Name and Download screen*

Once the key pair has been downloaded, click on **Launch Instances** to finally launch the instance.

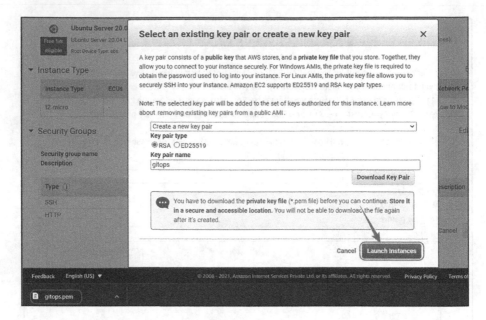

Figure 2-25. *Launch Instance after downloading the key pair*

2.3.8 Launching EC2 Instance

It takes about one to two minutes for the instance to launch and get configured properly. Let's click **View Instance** to view the details like the **IP Address** of the instance.

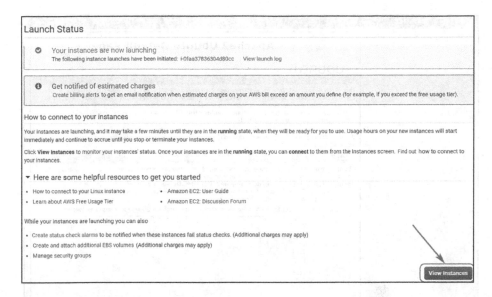

Figure 2-26. *Launch Status screen*

Upon clicking **View Instance**, you'll be redirected to the page where all the information about the instance can be seen. One detail that we require is the **IP Address**, which you can view by scrolling a bit toward the right.

Figure 2-27. *Copy the IP address*

Let's copy the IP and paste it into our browser and see the magic unfold! We've successfully launched an Ubuntu system with Apache2 server running with a few clicks that would take anywhere between 10 and 15 minutes! This is the power of cloud computing!

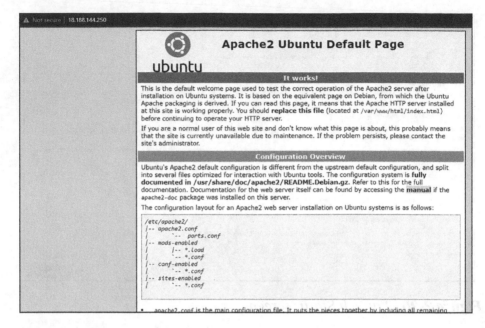

Figure 2-28. *Accessing EC2 from the browser*

2.3.9 Terminating EC2 Instance

Let's terminate this instance by following these steps:

Step 1: Click on "Instance State".

Step 2: Click on "Terminate Instance".

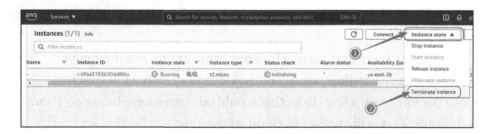

Figure 2-29. *Terminating EC2 Instance*

Note   It'll take about five minutes to terminate the instance.

2.4 Creating an EC2 Machine – CLI

We saw how it is possible to spin up a virtual machine on AWS cloud with an Ubuntu OS and an Apache2 web server with a few clicks. Not only was it easy but the entire process is also very much parameterized where you can simply specify the parameters and spin up a system of your choice. However, doing via GUI has its own limitation, the most important one being **lacking automation**. To automate this process of creating an EC2 instance, we need the AWS CLI tool that was used to configure the access keys.

2.4.1 Configuring CLI Environment

The base command to create a running EC2 machine on AWS is the following.

CLI Output 2-4. Configuring CLI environment

```
cmd> export AWS_PROFILE=gitops
cmd> aws ec2 run-instances
```

When working with multiple profiles, it is a good practice to either initialize the CLI environment by exporting the AWS_PROFILE variable or adding –profile, for example, *aws ec2 run-instances --profile*.

Now there are five parameters that we need in order to execute the same Apache2 virtual machine that we spun up on AWS through the GUI in the earlier section. They are

- AMI ID – ami-00399ec92321828f5

- Instance Type – t2.micro

- Key Name – gitops

- User Data – chapter2\user_data.sh

- Security Group ID – We'll need to fetch

- Network/Subnet ID – We'll need to fetch

2.4.2 Fetching Security Group ID

So first, let's fetch the security group ID which we'd created in the earlier section.

CLI Output 2-5. Fetching security group ID

```
cmd> aws ec2 describe-security-groups --query
'SecurityGroups[*].[GroupName,GroupId]'
[
    [
        "gitops-ec2-external",
        "sg-085db3a64b72894be"
    ],
    [
        "default",
        "sg-f687edba"
    ]
]
```

Using the ***aws ec2 describe-security-groups*** command, we are getting the details of all the security groups that are configured for the account in the default region, that is, us-east-2. However, we are only interested in the security group ID, and hence, we've formatted the output using the *--query* parameter of AWS CLI to fetch only the **GroupName** and the **GroupID**.

2.4.3 Fetching Subnet ID

Next, in a similar manner, let's retrieve the **SubnetID** of the subnet where we need to deploy our EC2 instance. A subnet is a logical grouping of networks within a single VPC. AWS creates a subnet per zone as can be seen in the following. The **US-East** region has three zones, and hence, we are having three different subnets. We can, however, select any of the subnets to deploy our EC2 machine in.

CLI Output 2-6. Fetching subnet ID

```
cmd> aws ec2 describe-subnets --query 'Subnets[*].
[SubnetId,AvailabilityZone]'

[
    [
        "subnet-79b62812",
        "us-east-2a"
    ],
    [
        "subnet-060bdf7b",
        "us-east-2b"
    ],
    [
        "subnet-49764905",
        "us-east-2c"
    ]
]
```

So far, we've got the following information:

- AMI ID – ami-00399ec92321828f5

- Instance Type – t2.micro

- Key Name – gitops

- Security Group ID – sg-085db3a64b72894be

- Network/Subnet ID – subnet-79b62812

- User Data – chapter2\user_data.sh

2.4.4 Launching EC2 Instance

Now we are ready to run the command that will create our EC2 instance from the CLI!

CLI Output 2-7. Launching EC2 from CLI

```
cmd> aws ec2 run-instances --image-id ami-00399ec92321828f5
--count 1 \
    --instance-type t2.micro --key-name gitops \
    --security-group-ids sg-085db3a64b72894be \
    --subnet-id subnet-79b62812 --user-data file://chapter2/
    user_data.sh

{
    "Groups": [],
    "Instances": [
        {
            "AmiLaunchIndex": 0,
            "ImageId": "ami-00399ec92321828f5",
            "InstanceId": "i-06adc4012f2b88810",
            "InstanceType": "t2.micro",
```

```
        "KeyName": "gitops",
        "LaunchTime": "2021-10-23T13:28:22.000Z",
        "Monitoring": {
            "State": "disabled"
        },
        "Placement": {
            "AvailabilityZone": "us-east-2a",
            "GroupName": "",
            "Tenancy": "default"
        },
        "PrivateDnsName": "ip-172-31-5-130.us-east-2.
        compute.internal",
        "PrivateIpAddress": "172.31.5.130",
        "ProductCodes": [],
        "PublicDnsName": "",
        "State": {
            "Code": 0,
            "Name": "pending"
        }
--------SNIP-----------------
    }
```

Take note of the "instance-id", which is "**i-06adc4012f2b88810**", which we'll need to query the IP address of our server.

2.4.5 Accessing EC2 Instance

Now here, we need to query for the IP address of a specific instance using the instance ID we received. The following command applies the "-filter" flag against two attributes, that is, instance-state and instance-id, with their respective values and then queries for the **PublicIpAddress** field.

CLI Output 2-8. Obtain the IP address through describe instances

```
cmd> aws ec2 describe-instances
--filters \
"Name=instance-state-name,Values=running" \
"Name=instance-id,Values=i-06adc4012f2b88810" \
--query 'Reservations[*].Instances[*].[PublicIpAddress]' \
--output text

18.217.95.186
```

Let's run a curl command to verify if the instance is indeed running. As shown here, the same is verified.

CLI Output 2-9. Curl the IP address

```
cmd> curl -I http://18.217.95.186

HTTP/1.1 200 OK
Date: Sat, 23 Oct 2021 17:01:56 GMT
Server: Apache/2.4.41 (Ubuntu)
Last-Modified: Sat, 23 Oct 2021 13:29:27 GMT
ETag: "2aa6-5cf051de7a237"
Accept-Ranges: bytes
Content-Length: 10918
Vary: Accept-Encoding
Content-Type: text/html
```

2.4.6 Terminating EC2 Instance

Let's destroy the instance that we started earlier using the following command by first querying for the instance ID and then running the terminate-instances command.

CLI Output 2-10. Terminating the EC2 instance through CLI

```
cmd> aws ec2 describe-instances \
--filters \
"Name=instance-state-name,Values=running" \
--query 'Reservations[*].Instances[*].[InstanceId]' \
--output text

i-06adc4012f2b88810

cmd> aws ec2 terminate-instances --instance-id
i-06adc4012f2b88810

{
    "TerminatingInstances": [
        {
            "CurrentState": {
                "Code": 32,
                "Name": "shutting-down"
            },
            "InstanceId": "i-06adc4012f2b88810",
            "PreviousState": {
                "Code": 16,
                "Name": "running"
            }
        }
    ]
}
```

2.5 Clean-Up

Just to ensure that we don't end up getting billed unnecessarily, you visit the EC2 console on the AWS GUI and double-check if everything is deleted. **The Instances (running) field should show 0 and ensure you've selected the correct region.** If it's still showing, execute the commands specified in CLI Output 2-10.

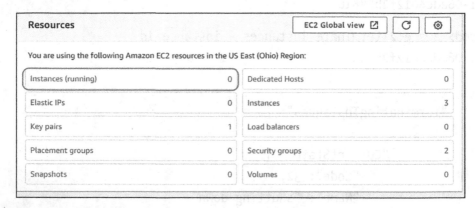

Figure 2-30. *EC2 Instances running is zero*

Note   Always double-check the region; we've been following us-east-2 in this chapter.

2.6 Conclusion

In this way, we saw how AWS makes it easy to set up infrastructure in a matter of minutes in case of GUI and seconds in case of using CLI. It may, however, be easy to perform the preceding actions, but when it comes to setting up a production-grade environment, it cannot be (or rather should not be) done using either GUI or using CLI as it is difficult to keep track of what's running and while doing interconnections with the different systems, etc.

At times, running infrastructure in the cloud can get expensive if you don't know what exactly is running as against what is needed. Hence, in the next chapter, we'll introduce ourselves to a tool called Terraform, which will make our lives a lot easier as it'll help us in not only creating the infrastructure but also in managing the state as well as facilitating interconnections between different systems and AWS services.

CHAPTER 3

Introduction to Terraform

In the previous chapters, we looked at how an EC2 machine can be created using the GUI as the CLI interface. In this chapter, we'll understand what Terraform is and how using Terraform we'll create the exact same EC2 machine with the exact same configuration without using CLI/GUI consoles.

3.1 Prerequisites

From here onward, I'll be showing a lot of code snippets that can be downloaded from the GitHub link shared earlier. It is recommended that you get hold of the following before moving ahead as all will be required henceforth if you wish to follow along with the book:

- A code editor. I am using Visual Studio Code (VS Code), which can be downloaded and installed from the following link:

  - https://code.visualstudio.com/Download

- Terraform plugin by HashiCorp for VS Code can be installed from here or from within VS Code itself:

  - https://marketplace.visualstudio.com/
    items?itemName=hashicorp.terraform

- Terraform binary installed in the path. The following link can be used to download and install terraform amd add terraform binary in the path. The code discussed in the book currently supports Terraform >= 1.2.0:

  - www.terraform.io/downloads.html

3.2 Introduction to Terraform

When we wish to set up something, there are primarily two aspects to it: provisioning and configuring. We provision a home using bricks and mortar and then configure it using different pieces of furniture like bed, sofa, etc.

In the infrastructure world, when we say we need to create an Apache2 web server, we first need to provision an underlying operating system and its binaries and then configure the server so that it can run as expected.

Tools like Terraform, Ansible, Chef, Puppet, SaltStack, AWS CloudFormation, etc., help us in provisioning and configuring infrastructure resources in the cloud (and on premises, e.g., OpenShift) through simple lines of declarative code. Declarative programming is a method of writing instructions that define the goal of the program. It doesn't involve itself on the how part. For example, in terraform, the following few lines simply say that we want an EC2 instance to be up and running. We don't know or rather we don't really care **how** it'll be done.

Code Block 3-1. Iteration1 code for spinning up an EC2 machine

```
File: chapter3\infra\iteration1\main.tf

19: resource "aws_instance" "apache2_server" {
20:   ami           = "ami-00399ec92321828f5"
21:   instance_type = "t2.micro"
```

```
22:    user_data = << EOF
23:         #!/bin/bash
24:         sudo apt update -y
25:         sudo apt install apache2 -y
26:      EOF
27:    tags = {
28:      env = "dev"
29:    }
30: }
```

Terraform as a tool is developed in Go and has three main components as shown here.

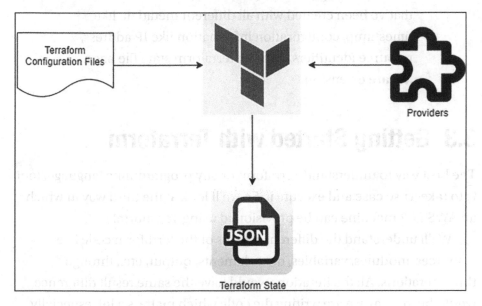

Figure 3-1. *Terraform Core Components*

- Terraform Configuration Files – Files containing the HCL formatted declarative code providing instructions of what needs to be done. These files have the *.tf* extension.

- Providers – They are plugins that terraform relies on to interact with the APIs of different IaaS (Infrastructure as a Service) providers like AWS, GCP, and Azure or even SaaS (Software as a Service) providers like Datadog or PaaS (Platform as a Service) providers like Kubernetes, which we'll explore in detail in this book. Information on how to start/stop/destroy the different resources/ services is baked into these providers.

- Terraform State – After taking inputs from the configuration files and the providers, terraform creates a *state* file that is a pure JSON document wherein it maps the complete infrastructure resources that've been created with all different metadata like timestamp, configuration information like IP address, resource identifiers, etc. The terraform state file has a **.tfstate** extension.

3.3 Getting Started with Terraform

The best way to understand Terraform or any programming language/tool is to take a use case and execute it. So we'll look at the third way in which an AWS EC2 machine can be provisioned using Terraform!

We'll understand the different aspects of the terraform code like resources, modules, variables, data elements, output, etc., through three iterations. All the iterations would have the same result difference would be the way we are writing the code which matters a lot, especially when you are writing in declarative format. Each iteration would be an improvisation over the previous one with the third iteration being the best, most independent, scalable, and conformant with best practices.

Before we begin, let's confirm a few things.

A. You've downloaded the code repository. You should've the following folder format and you'll need to open the specific chapter that we are learning.

CLI Output 3-2. Code folders

```
cmd> tree -d -L 1
├── chapter1
├── chapter2
├── chapter3
├── chapter4
├── chapter5
├── chapter6
├── chapter7
├── chapter8
├── chapter9
├── chapter10

10 directories
```

B. You've installed Terraform version 1.0.0 or greater and authenticated with AWS as shown here.

CLI Output 3-3. Terraform Getting Started

```
cmd> terraform --version

Terraform v1.0.7
on linux_amd64

cmd> export AWS_PROFILE=gitops
cmd> aws sts get-caller-identity
{
    "UserId": "AIDATLYRVHDFFW7RHDCIP",
```

```
    "Account": "231428405450",
    "Arn": "arn:aws:iam::231428405450:user/gitops"
}
```

3.4 Iteration #1

The following 26 lines of code will spin up an EC2 server for us on AWS using all the defaults. Here, it can be seen that we've not provided the VPC ID; hence, Terraform will query the default VPC in AWS and set up the server in it.

CLI Output 3-4. main.tf for iteration1

```
File: chapter3\infra\iteration1\main.tf

01: # Setting and locking the Dependencies
02: terraform {
03:   required_providers {
04:     aws = {
05:         source  = "hashicorp/aws"
06:         version = "4.10"
07:     }
08:   }
09:
10:   required_version = ">= 1.1.0"
11: }
12:
13: # AWS Provider configuration
14: provider "aws" {
15:   region = "us-east-2"
16: }
17:
```

```
18: # AWS EC2 Resource creation
19: resource "aws_instance" "apache2_server" {
20:   ami             = "ami-00399ec92321828f5"
21:   instance_type = "t2.micro"
22:   user_data = "${file("user_data.sh")}"
23:   tags = {
24:     env = "dev"
25:   }
26: }
```

L02-11: Sort of the primary starting point of execution, like ***main()*** where the provider dependencies are checked and downloaded. As stated, earlier providers are nothing but plugins that fit into the terraform architecture. Here, we are declaring that this code will run only for Terraform version >= 1.1.0, and we are going to use the AWS provider for the specific version. If we were to use GCP, then we'd add the GCP-related information. We'll be adding many more providers as we proceed ahead.

L14-16: Every provider needs some information for configuration. The AWS provider needs information about the region, access keys, tokens, etc. The complete documentation of the AWS provider is available here: https://registry.terraform.io/providers/hashicorp/aws/latest/docs.

For our requirement, we only need to set the region as we've already configured the AWS CLI and authenticated using it; we only need to export the environment variable AWS_PROFILE before running terraform.

L19-30: In terraform, every resource needs to be configured separately. Here, we're configuring the AWS EC2 machine with all the information that we'd seen earlier like the AMI ID, instance type, and the user data startup script that is being loaded using the file function of Terraform. When we start building on terraform, we'll be mainly working on these resources, and you can imagine each resource to be a Lego piece. The entire Lego will be built by juxtaposition of these pieces.

3.4.1 Terraform Working Directory

Let's now run this code and explore the different terraform commands. Before running any terraform command, it is important to understand what terraform considers as the **root** of the project or the terraform working directory. As shown in the following, we must first change into the directory that contains the terraform code, which is the *iteration1* directory for us.

All the *.tf* files in this directory will be **clubbed** and executed together by terraform, and hence, this directory becomes the **root** directory or the terraform working directory.

CLI Output 3-5. Terraform's current working directory

```
cmd> cd chapter3/infra/iteration1
cmd> ls -l
total 4
-rw-r--r-- 1 ubuntu ubuntu  476 Oct 30 11:57 main.tf
-rw-r--r-- 1 ubuntu ubuntu   59 Oct 30 11:57 user_data.sh
```

Terraform doesn't apply recursively; for example, if we had a folder called child under the iteration1 folder and we apply terraform on the iteration1 folder, then any *.tf* files inside the child directory will not apply!

CLI Output 3-6. Terraform applies to only *.tf files in a single folder

```
cmd> cd chapter3/infra/iteration1
cmd> tree -a iteration1
iteration1              <------ Root Directory
├── child               <------ Child Directory
│   └── child.tf        <------ Terraform will not include
└── main.tf             <------ Terraform will include
└── user_data.sh

1 directory, 3 files
```

Tip   You can, however, use the flag *-chdir* to change the root directory to something else; for example, the ***terraform -chdir=child apply*** command will consider the *child* directory as the root directory. But still, it'll not read the ***.tf** files in the parent directory!

3.4.2 Terraform init

Let's now execute the first command, which is **terraform init**, as shown here.

Tip   Always export the profile using the AWS_PROFILE environment variable as it becomes easy to follow which AWS environment we are working on. The values in the environment variables have taken the highest precedence in terraform's execution.

CLI Output 3-7. Output for terraform init

```
cmd> export AWS_PROFILE=gitops
cmd> cd chapter3/infra/iteration1
cmd> terraform init

Initializing the backend...

Initializing provider plugins...
- Finding hashicorp/aws versions matching "~> 3.27"...
- Installing hashicorp/aws v3.63.0...
- Installed hashicorp/aws v3.63.0 (signed by HashiCorp)
```

Terraform has created a lock file .terraform.lock.hcl to record the provider selections it made previously. Include this file in your version control repository so that Terraform can guarantee to make the same selections by default when you run "terraform init" in the future.

Terraform has been successfully initialized!

You may now begin working with Terraform. Try running "terraform plan" to see any changes that are required for your infrastructure. All Terraform commands should now work.

If you ever set or change modules or backend configuration for Terraform, rerun this command to reinitialize your working directory. If you forget, other commands will detect it and remind you to do so if necessary.

terraform init initializes the entire terraform ecosystem by downloading and installing the dependencies. As can be seen from the preceding command output, it basically downloads the AWS provider of the specific version and creates a *.terraform.lock.hcl* file, which contains the information about all the dependencies and their hashes. *Terraform init* command also creates a *.terraform* folder where the actual dependency is installed as shown in the following in the output of the tree command.

CLI Output 3-8. Folder structure after terraform init

```
cmd> tree -a
.
├── .terraform
│   └── providers
│       └── registry.terraform.io
│           └── hashicorp
│               └── aws
│                   └── 4.10.0
│                       └── linux_amd64
│                           └── terraform-provider-aws_
                                v4.10.0_x5
```

```
├── .terraform.lock.hcl
└── main.tf
└── user_data.sh
```

7 directories, 4 files

3.4.3 Terraform Plan

Now that our project has been initialized, let's execute the next command, that is, **terraform plan**.

The terraform plan command provides a detailed output about all the resources that are going to be added, removed, or updated with appropriate signs:

> + – The plus symbol indicates that a resource will be added.
>
> - – The hyphen indicates that the resource will be destroyed.
>
> ~ – The tilde indicates that the resource will be updated.

In the preceding plan execution, we can only see + symbol since this is the very first time we've applied the plan.

CLI Output 3-9. Terraform Plan output

```
cmd> terraform plan

Terraform used the selected providers to generate the following
execution plan. Resource actions are indicated with the
following symbols:
  + create
```

```
Terraform will perform the following actions:

  # aws_instance.apache2_server will be created
  + resource "aws_instance" "apache2_server" {
   + ami                                  = "ami-00399ec92321828f5"
   + arn                                  = (known after apply)
   + associate_public_ip_address          = (known after apply)
   + availability_zone                    = (known after apply)
   + cpu_core_count                       = (known after apply)
   + cpu_threads_per_core                 = (known after apply)
   + disable_api_termination              = (known after apply)
   + ebs_optimized                        = (known after apply)
   + get_password_data                    = false
   + host_id                              = (known after apply)
   + id                                   = (known after apply)
   + instance_initiated_shutdown_behavior = (known after apply)
   + instance_state                       = (known after apply)
   + instance_type                        = "t2.micro"
   + ipv6_address_count                   = (known after apply)
   + ipv6_addresses                       = (known after apply)
   + key_name                             = (known after apply)
   + monitoring                           = (known after apply)
   + outpost_arn                          = (known after apply)
   + password_data                        = (known after apply)
   + placement_group                      = (known after apply)
   + placement_partition_number           = (known after apply)
   + primary_network_interface_id         = (known after apply)
   + private_dns                          = (known after apply)
   + private_ip                           = (known after apply)
   + public_dns                           = (known after apply)
   + public_ip                            = (known after apply)
   + secondary_private_ips                = (known after apply)
```

```
+ security_groups                    = (known after apply)
+ source_dest_check                  = true
+ subnet_id                          = (known after apply)
+ tags                               = {
    + "env" = "dev"
  }
+ tags_all                           = {
    + "env" = "dev"
  }
+ tenancy                            = (known after apply)
+ user_data                          = "7bdaf2f31b227
                                         2f40c05104fc1ce
                                         987cdcdbafd5"

+ user_data_base64                   = (known after apply)
+ vpc_security_group_ids             = (known after apply)

+ capacity_reservation_specification {
    + capacity_reservation_preference = (known after apply)

    + capacity_reservation_target {
        + capacity_reservation_id = (known after apply)
      }
  }

+ ebs_block_device {
    + delete_on_termination = (known after apply)
    + device_name           = (known after apply)
    + encrypted             = (known after apply)
    + iops                  = (known after apply)
    + kms_key_id            = (known after apply)
    + snapshot_id           = (known after apply)
    + tags                  = (known after apply)
    + throughput            = (known after apply)
    + volume_id             = (known after apply)
```

```
      + volume_size           = (known after apply)
      + volume_type           = (known after apply)
    }

  + enclave_options {
      + enabled = (known after apply)
    }

  + ephemeral_block_device {
      + device_name  = (known after apply)
      + no_device    = (known after apply)
      + virtual_name = (known after apply)
    }

  + metadata_options {
      + http_endpoint                = (known after apply)
      + http_put_response_hop_limit = (known after apply)
      + http_tokens                  = (known after apply)
    }

  + network_interface {
      + delete_on_termination = (known after apply)
      + device_index          = (known after apply)
      + network_interface_id  = (known after apply)
    }

  + root_block_device {
      + delete_on_termination = (known after apply)
      + device_name           = (known after apply)
      + encrypted             = (known after apply)
      + iops                  = (known after apply)
      + kms_key_id            = (known after apply)
      + tags                  = (known after apply)
```

```
    + throughput              = (known after apply)
    + volume_id               = (known after apply)
    + volume_size             = (known after apply)
    + volume_type             = (known after apply)
    }
  }

Plan: 1 to add, 0 to change, 0 to destroy.
```

Note: You didn't use the -out option to save this plan, so Terraform can't guarantee to take exactly these actions if you run "terraform apply" now.

> **Tip**   Terraform plan outputs can run into hundreds and even thousands of lines; hence, if you wish to save the output, then you can use the command ***terraform plan -out plan.tfplan*** to save the plan that is not readable by a traditional editor but does contain all the configuration information.

From the plan, it's quite discernable that terraform is not only creating the AWS EC2 instance but also creating everything associated with it like the EBS volume, root volume, and network interfaces just to name a few.

3.4.4 Terraform Apply

Let's now look at the final command: ***terraform apply***. Upon firing the ***terraform apply*** command, it'll spool out the entire plan first and then wait for our input as shown here.

Let's enter *yes* to execute our plan.

CLI Output 3-10. Terraform apply output

```
cmd> terraform apply

XXXXXXXXXXXXX---SNIPPED----XXXXXXXXXXXXX

Do you want to perform these actions?
  Terraform will perform the actions described above.
  Only 'yes' will be accepted to approve.

  Enter a value: yes

aws_instance.apache2_server: Creating...
aws_instance.apache2_server: Still creating... [10s elapsed]
aws_instance.apache2_server: Still creating... [20s elapsed]
aws_instance.apache2_server: Still creating... [30s elapsed]
aws_instance.apache2_server: Creation complete after 35s
[id=i-0a2a8acd8cd1385c5]

Apply complete! Resources: 1 added, 0 changed, 0 destroyed.
```

That's it, our EC2 instance has now been created with just a few lines of code! That is the power of infrastructure as code.

3.4.5 Terraform State File

We can now see that a new file has been created called **terraform.state** whose contents are as follows. The ***tfstate*** file stores all the information about the resources that we need and terraform requires to store to perform any other actions like update or deletion. Feel free to scroll through the next two pages as I just wanted to share here what the terraform state looks like.

CLI Output 3-11. Terraform tfstate file

```
cmd> cat terraform.tfstate

{
  "version": 4,
  "terraform_version": "1.1.0",
  "serial": 1,
  "lineage": "1c277ed5-56d2-74b8-5037-026d4dac8a76",
  "outputs": {},
  "resources": [
    {
      "mode": "managed",
      "type": "aws_instance",
      "name": "apache2_server",
      "provider": "provider[\"registry.terraform.io/hashicorp/
      aws\"]",
      "instances": [
        {
          "schema_version": 1,
          "attributes": {
            "ami": "ami-00399ec92321828f5",
            "arn": "arn:aws:ec2:us-
            east-2:XXXXXXXXXXXX:instance/i-0a2a8acd8cd1385c5",
            "associate_public_ip_address": true,
            "availability_zone": "us-east-2b",
```

```
"capacity_reservation_specification": [
    {
        "capacity_reservation_preference": "open",
        "capacity_reservation_target": []
    }
],
"cpu_core_count": 1,
"cpu_threads_per_core": 1,
"credit_specification": [
  {
    "cpu_credits": "standard"
  }
],
"disable_api_termination": false,
"ebs_block_device": [],
"ebs_optimized": false,
"enclave_options": [
  {
    "enabled": false
  }
],
"ephemeral_block_device": [],
"get_password_data": false,
"hibernation": false,
"host_id": null,
"iam_instance_profile": "",
"id": "i-0a2a8acd8cd1385c5",
"instance_initiated_shutdown_behavior": "stop",
"instance_state": "running",
"instance_type": "t2.micro",
"ipv6_address_count": 0,
```

```
"ipv6_addresses": [],
"key_name": "",
"launch_template": [],
"metadata_options": [
  {
    "http_endpoint": "enabled",
    "http_put_response_hop_limit": 1,
    "http_tokens": "optional"
  }
],
"monitoring": false,
"network_interface": [],
"outpost_arn": "",
"password_data": "",
"placement_group": "",
"placement_partition_number": null,
"primary_network_interface_id":
"eni-038a548d78778b9c6",
"private_dns": "ip-172-31-16-189.us-east-2.compute.
internal",
"private_ip": "172.31.16.189",
"public_dns": "ec2-34-209-221-82.us-east-2.compute.
amazonaws.com",
"public_ip": "34.209.221.82",
"root_block_device": [
  {
    "delete_on_termination": true,
    "device_name": "/dev/sda1",
    "encrypted": false,
    "iops": 100,
    "kms_key_id": "",
```

```
          "tags": {},
          "throughput": 0,
          "volume_id": "vol-01e32fc3ab4908837",
          "volume_size": 8,
          "volume_type": "gp2"
        }
      ],
      "secondary_private_ips": [],
      "security_groups": [
        "default"
      ],
      "source_dest_check": true,
      "subnet_id": "subnet-3abb6842",
      "tags": {
        "env": "dev"
      },
      "tags_all": {
        "env": "dev"
      },
      "tenancy": "default",
      "timeouts": null,
      "user_data":
      "7bdaf2f31b2272f40c05104fc1ce987cdcdbafd5",
      "user_data_base64": null,
      "volume_tags": null,
      "vpc_security_group_ids": [
        "sg-f32c11d8"
      ]
    },
```

```
        "sensitive_attributes": [],
        "private": "XXXXXXXXXXXXXXXXXXXXXXXXXXXXXXXXXXXXXXXXXX"
      }
    ]
  }
]
}
```

We can also find the IP address of the EC2 machine by querying using the following command.

CLI Output 3-12. Querying for public IP address from tfstate

```
cmd> cat terraform.tfstate | grep "public_ip"

"associate_public_ip_address": true,
"public_ip": "34.209.221.82",
```

3.4.6 Terraform Destroy

Let's now destroy the EC2 machine and everything else created with it using a simple command: ***terraform destroy***.

CLI Output 3-13. Terraform Destroy command output

```
cmd> terraform destroy

aws_instance.apache2_server: Refreshing state...
[id=i-0a2a8acd8cd1385c5]
```

Terraform used the selected providers to generate the following execution plan. Resource actions are indicated with the following symbols:
  - destroy

Terraform will perform the following actions:

```
# aws_instance.apache2_server will be destroyed
- resource "aws_instance" "apache2_server" {
    - ami                                   = "ami-00399ec923
                                              21828f5" -> null

    - arn                                   = "arn:aws:ec2:us-
                                              east-2:87181177
                                              8330:instance/
                                              i-0a2a8acd8
                                              cd1385c5"
                                              -> null

    - associate_public_ip_address          = true -> null
    - availability_zone                    = "us-east-2b"
                                              -> null

    - cpu_core_count                       = 1 -> null
    - cpu_threads_per_core                 = 1 -> null
    - disable_api_termination              = false -> null
    - ebs_optimized                        = false -> null
    - get_password_data                    = false -> null
    - hibernation                          = false -> null
    - id                                   = "i-0a2a8acd8cd13
                                              85c5" -> null

    - instance_initiated_shutdown_behavior = "stop" -> null
    - instance_state                       = "running" ->
                                              null

    - instance_type                        = "t2.micro" -> null
    - ipv6_address_count                   = 0 -> null
    - ipv6_addresses                       = [] -> null
    - monitoring                           = false -> null
    - primary_network_interface_id         = "eni-038a548d78
                                              778b9c6" -> null
```

```
    - private_dns                         = "ip-172-31-16-
                                            189.us-east-2.
                                            compute.
                                            internal"
                                            -> null
    - private_ip                          = "172.31.16.189"
                                            -> null
    - public_dns                          = "ec2-34-209-221-
                                            82.us-east-2.
                                            compute.
                                            amazonaws.com"
                                            -> null
    - public_ip                           = "34.209.221.82"
                                            -> null
    - secondary_private_ips               = [] -> null
    - security_groups                     = [
      - "default",
      ] -> null
    - source_dest_check                   = true -> null
    - subnet_id                           = "subnet-3abb6842"
                                            -> null
    - tags                                = {
      - "env" = "dev"
      } -> null
    - tags_all                            = {
      - "env" = "dev"
      } -> null
    - tenancy                             = "default" ->
                                            null
```

```
    - user_data                         = "7bdaf2f31b227
                                          2f40c05104fc1ce
                                          987cdcdbafd5"
                                          -> null

    - vpc_security_group_ids            = [
        - "sg-f32c11d8",
      ] -> null

XXXXXXXXXXXXXXX------SNIPPED-------XXXXXXXXXXXXXXXXXXXXX

Plan: 0 to add, 0 to change, 1 to destroy.

Do you really want to destroy all resources?
  Terraform will destroy all your managed infrastructure, as
  shown above.
  There is no undo. Only 'yes' will be accepted to confirm.

  Enter a value: yes

aws_instance.apache2_server: Destroying...
[id=i-0a2a8acd8cd1385c5]
aws_instance.apache2_server: Still destroying...
[id=i-0a2a8acd8cd1385c5, 10s elapsed]
aws_instance.apache2_server: Still destroying...
[id=i-0a2a8acd8cd1385c5, 20s elapsed]
aws_instance.apache2_server: Still destroying...
[id=i-0a2a8acd8cd1385c5, 30s elapsed]
aws_instance.apache2_server: Destruction complete after 37s

Destroy complete! Resources: 1 destroyed.
```

Note   From now onward, to save the environment and to avoid making you turn multiple pages just to skip the output of terraform commands, I shall be omitting them (terraform output commands) altogether except for a few places where required.

Tip   We can use the *--auto-approve* flag to avoid manually entering *yes,* each time running terraform apply and destroy. The following are the full commands:

terraform apply --auto-approve
terraform destroy --auto-approve

3.5 Iteration #2

Now that we've seen the complete execution of the first iteration including terraform init, plan, apply, and destroy, let's try to understand what the problems are associated with this iteration. The problems in the first iteration are as follows:

A.   We must use an extra command to identify the IP address of the machine.

B.   Our machine is still not accessible over the public Internet as we did not apply the security groups.

C.   All the values like the region, instance type, and environment are being hard-coded, and if we wish to change them, then we'll have to modify the main code, which is not recommended.

D.   We'd also like to have a common naming
     convention for all resources such that it's easier
     to identify which region and environment they
     belong to.

E.   Currently, the AMI ID that we are using is also
     hard-coded, and we'd like to fetch the latest version
     of Ubuntu for which we need to access the AWS
     documentation, which is quite a manual process.

How will we solve the preceding problems? The following are the
answers to the corresponding questions in the same order:

A.   We'll be using output variables of terraform.

B.   We'll create new security groups.

C.   We'll be using a separate file called **terraform.auto.
     tfvars** to store our variables.

D.   We'll make use of *local* variables where we can
     combine multiple variables and use the expression
     language syntax to have a uniform naming
     convention.

E.   We'll use the *data* element in terraform to fetch the
     latest Ubuntu AMI.

Let's view the code! Since the code blocks are getting bigger, I shall
break them down.

3.5.1 Terraform Variables

Just like every programming language, terraform also supports variables
that can hold values. There are multiple ways in which we can pass the
variables to terraform through ***.tfvars** file and the variable declaration
syntaxes as shown here.

Code Block 3-14. terraform.auto.tfvars file with variables and values

File: chapter3\infra\iteration2\terraform.auto.tfvars

```
1: environment   = "dev"
2: region        = "us-east-2"
3: instance_type = "t2.micro"
```

Code Block 3-15. main.tf file containing variable declarations

File: chapter3\infra\iteration2\main.tf

```
01: # Variable Declaration
02: variable "environment" {
03:   description = "The environment e.g uat or prod or dev"
04:   type        = string
05: }
06:
07: variable "region" {
08:   description = "The region where we wish to deploy to"
09:   type        = string
10: }
11:
12: variable "instance_type" {
13:   description = "EC2 instance type"
14:   type        = string
15: }
16:
17: locals {
18:   name-suffix = "${var.region}-${var.environment}"
19: }
```

L01–15: We are now declaring the variables of different types in main.tf and their values in a file called **terraform.auto.tfvars**. If we wish to modify attributes like EC2 instance type or environment or region, we only need to modify the **terraform.auto.tfvars** file. This file is imported automatically when the *terraform apply* command is executed; hence, we don't need to specify anything on the command line.

Terraform supports various variable formats like number, lists, maps, and boolean.

L17–19: If we wish to add an expression to a variable like adding a suffix/prefix, then we can make use of a *locals* declaration wherein we can declare variables that support expression syntaxes. Here, we've declared a variable called *name-suffix*, which is a concatenation of region and environment with a hyphen.

3.5.2 Terraform Data Source

While working with terraform, there can arise multiple instances where we may need to read data from an already-existing resource or a repository. The **data** is what we need to declare in order to perform any such read operation.

Code Block 3-16. The usage of the data declaration for a read operation

File: chapter3\infra\iteration2\main.tf

```
38: # Data element fetching the AMI ID of Ubuntu 20.04
39: data "aws_ami" "ubuntu" {
40:   most_recent = true
41:   filter {
42:     name    = "name"
43:     values = ["ubuntu/images/hvm-ssd/ubuntu-focal-20.04-
           amd64-server-*"]
44:   }
```

```
45:    filter {
46:      name   = "virtualization-type"
47:      values = ["hvm"]
48:    }
49:    # AWS ID of Canonical organisation
50:    owners = ["099720109477"]
51: }
```

L38-51: Using the *resources* element, we can perform Create/Update/Delete operations in terraform, but what about Read? As discussed earlier, there may arise situations where during the terraform execution, we may be required to *read* data of existing resources in the cloud provider. This can be achieved using the *data* element that is applied on a resource called ***aws_ami***. Since AWS has hundreds of AMI (Amazon Machine Images) IDs, we are applying a filter to narrow down to what we need using the *filter* and the *owner* elements.

3.5.3 Terraform Resource

Resources are the actual infrastructure objects that need to be declared in terraform and are at the heart of the entire tool. Here, we are declaring two resources: Security Groups and an EC2 Instance.

Code Block 3-17. Security group resource creation definitions

File: chapter3\infra\iteration2\main.tf

```
53: # Creating Security Group with ingress/egress rules
54: resource "aws_security_group" "public_http_sg" {
55:   name = "public_http_sg-${local.name-suffix}"
56:
```

```
57: # Allow all inbound traffic to port 80
58:    ingress {
59:       from_port   = 80
60:       to_port     = 80
61:       protocol    = "tcp"
62:       cidr_blocks = ["0.0.0.0/0"]
63:    }
64:
65: # Allow EC2 to be connected from internet
66:    egress {
67:       from_port   = 0
68:       to_port     = 65535
69:       protocol    = "tcp"
70:       cidr_blocks = ["0.0.0.0/0"]
71:    }
72:
73:    tags = {
74:       "Environment" = var.environment
75:       "visibility"  = "public"
76:    }
77: }
```

L53-77: We are declaring the resource for creating a security
group, which is declaring two rules: an ingress rule to allow inbound
communication on port 80 from anywhere in the world and an egress rule
for the EC2 machine to connect to the outside world. It's only through
this rule that we've been able to access our EC2 machine from over the
Internet. You might find it difficult to understand why I have added the
egress rule. Why would the EC2 machine want to communicate with
the outside world? The simple answer is to contact the Ubuntu package
repository to download the Apache2 server packages!

Code Block 3-18. AWS EC2 instance creation

File: chapter3\infra\iteration2\main.tf

```
79: # AWS EC2 Resource creation
80: resource "aws_instance" "apache2_server" {
81:   ami                    = data.aws_ami.ubuntu.id
82:   instance_type          = var.instance_type
83:   vpc_security_group_ids = [aws_security_group.public_
                                http_sg.id]
84:   user_data = "${file("user_data.sh")}"
85:   tags = {
86:     env  = var.environment
87:     Name = "ec2-${local.name-suffix}"
88:   }
89: }
```

L80-89: The resource definition for EC2 was discussed earlier; however, there is a slight change here where we've modified the way we pass the value to the *ami* parameter on L81. We are now populating the value with AMI ID from the data source declared earlier. We've also added reference to the security group ID on L83 that we've added earlier.

3.5.4 Terraform Output

The output variable allows us to retrieve any attribute about any resource that has been created using the terraform script.

Code Block 3-19. Terraform output declaration with public IP

File: chapter3\infra\iteration2\main.tf

```
91: # Output the Public IP Address
92: output "ip_address" {
93:    value = aws_instance.apache2_server.public_ip
94: }
```

L91-94: Here, we are retrieving the value of the ***public_ip*** variable in the terraform state that we've seen earlier.

Let's execute this terraform script using the following commands and test if everything is working as expected. Only output pertaining to the section needed is being shown here for brevity.

CLI Output 3-20. Execution of iteration #2 script

```
cmd> export AWS_PROFILE=gitops
cmd> terraform init
cmd> terraform plan
cmd> terraform apply --auto-approve

XXXXXXXXXXXXXXX------SNIPPED-------XXXXXXXXXXXXXXXXXXXXX

Apply complete! Resources: 2 added, 0 changed, 0 destroyed.

Outputs:

ip_address = "52.13.99.15"

cmd> curl -I http://34.217.31.143

HTTP/1.1 200 OK
Date: Wed, 03 Nov 2021 14:29:54 GMT
Server: Apache/2.4.41 (Ubuntu)
Last-Modified: Wed, 03 Nov 2021 14:27:59 GMT
ETag: "2aa6-5cfe33780883b"
```

```
Accept-Ranges: bytes
Content-Length: 10918
Vary: Accept-Encoding
Content-Type: text/html
```

```
cmd> terraform destroy --auto-approve
```

Hence, we are now able to access our EC2 machine and improvise the code a little with terraform variables, data sources, and terraform output!

3.6 Iteration #3

In the second iteration, we were able to make it a little better from a coding perspective; however, there have been a few things that were missing and some best practices that we need to instill. The following are the issues and suggestions that we'll need to implement:

A. We are still missing the SSH rule in the security group, because of which, we can't SSH into your EC2 instances.

B. The security group resource code is getting repetitive, and a lot of the information remains common or not much used. Hence, it's best if there is a way that we can abstract that information and focus on only what is needed. The abstraction should be such that it is reusable as well.

C. Till now, we've been using a single *.tf* file to add all the functionality; however, as we keep adding additional functionality, our code will grow, and keeping everything in a single file will become problematic.

D. We need to ensure that the security groups
    are always created before the EC2 instance is
    instantiated because our startup script ***user_data.sh***
    won't work if the security groups are not defined.

How will we solve the preceding problems? The following are the
answers to the corresponding questions in the same alphabetical order:

A. We'll need to create a new SSH security group with
    port mappings to the SSH port 22.

B. Since we are now repeating the creation of security
    groups, we can **modularize** it. Terraform allows a
    common functionality to be loaded as a module,
    which is nothing but a very crude equivalent of a
    function. A function takes inputs and spools out
    output. We'll see how a terraform module also does
    almost the same thing.

C. We'll need to segregate the code into different files
    as a best practice if we need to continue to add more
    functionality.

D. By using the input variables and module outputs, we
    can define dependencies implicitly. In Terraform,
    we can define dependencies in two ways implicitly
    and explicitly:

    – Using input/output variables, dependencies can be
      made implicit.

    – Using the depends_on keyword, we can make depen-
      dencies more explicit to influence the order of execu-
      tion. We'll be exploring the role of this keyword in
      more detail through practical examples in upcoming
      chapters.

The new set of changes is not just code-level changes but a completely different structure in which we've written the code. So let's view the structure that is shown here.

CLI Output 3-21. New structure for iteration #3

```
cmd> cd chapter3/infra/iteration3
cmd> tree -a
.
├── main.tf
├── modules
│   └── securitygroup
│       ├── main.tf
│       ├── output.tf
│       └── variables.tf
├── output.tf
├── providers.tf
├── scripts
│   └── user_data.sh
├── terraform.auto.tfvars
└── variables.tf

3 directories, 9 files
```

- The ***variables.tf*** and ***terraform.auto.tfvars*** files contain the input variables and their values.

- The ***output.tf*** contains all the output variables that need to be seen on the CLI output.

- The ***provider.tf*** contains the provider definitions and the dependencies information.

- The ***main.tf*** file contains the actual implementation of our requirements using the different resources and data elements.

- The ***modules*** folder contains the different modules that we've defined. Each module consists of the following files:

    - ***main.tf*** – Contains the implementation and declaration of the resources that need to be created

    - ***variables.tf*** – Contains the input variable declarations for the variables being defined in *main.tf*

    - ***output.tf*** – The output information that may be needed like the ***id*** number of the resource

- The scripts folder contains the startup/user data scripts that are needed to be executed.

3.6.1 Terraform Modules

Modules in terraform can be considered as a raw equivalent of functions in imperative languages. We combine a set of common resource creation functionality into one single unit for reusability. It is the only way to make terraform reusable.

In terraform for module declaration, it is mandatory to have the ***module*** in lieu of the resource keyword and the ***source***, which can take various different values like folder/directory path, GIT URL, HTTP/HTTPS URL, or any FQDN (fully qualified domain name) syntax. Here, we are feeding the values to the input variables.

Let's have a closer look at the ***main.tf*** file and the files under the ***module*** directory to understand the changes that have been made.

Code Block 3-22. Module declarations and invocation

File: chapter3\infra\iteration3\main.tf

```
XXXXXXXXXXXXXXX------SNIPPED-------XXXXXXXXXXXXXXXXXXXXX
19:
20: # HTTP Ingress Security Group Module
21: module "http_sg_ingress" {
22:    source        = "./modules/securitygroup"
23:
24:    sg_name       = "http_sg_ingress"
25:    sg_description = "Allow Port 80 from anywhere"
26:    environment   = var.environment
27:    type          = "ingress"
28:    from_port     = 80
29:    to_port       = 80
30:    protocol      = "tcp"
31:    cidr_blocks   = ["0.0.0.0/0"]
32: }
33:
34: # Generic Egress Security Group Module
35: module "generic_sg_egress" {
XXXXXXXXXXXXXXX------SNIPPED-------XXXXXXXXXXXXXXXXXXXXX
46: }
47:
48: # SSH Ingress Security Group Module
49: module "ssh_sg_ingress" {
XXXXXXXXXXXXXXX------SNIPPED-------XXXXXXXXXXXXXXXXXXXXX
60: }
61:
```

```
62: # AWS EC2 Resource creation
63: resource "aws_instance" "apache2_server" {
64:    ami             = data.aws_ami.ubuntu.id
65:    instance_type = var.instance_type
66:    vpc_security_group_ids = [module.http_sg_ingress.sg_id,
67:       module.generic_sg_egress.sg_id,
68:    module.ssh_sg_ingress.sg_id]
69:    key_name   = var.ssh_key_name
70:    user_data = file("scripts/user_data.sh")
71:    tags = {
72:       env   = var.environment
73:       Name = "ec2-${local.name-suffix}"
74:    }
75:
76:    depends_on = [
77:       module.generic_sg_egress
78:    ]
79: }
```

L21–32: Since the security group resource is going to be invoked multiple times, we've created a module and specified the location of the module using the *source* keyword on **L22.**

L66–68: The output of the security group modules, that is, the security group ID, is being fed to the EC2 resource.

L69: Adding the name of the SSH key that we created in the previous chapter from the GUI. The variable *ssh_key_name* holds the name of the key, and the value is defined in the *terraform.auto.tfvars* file.

L76–78: Declaration of the *depends_on* meta-variable where we are explicitly setting the dependency on the *module.generic_sg_egress* module as we need the egress rules to be created before the server starts up.

Next, let's look at the ***main.tf*** file of the security groups module, which contains the complete implementation of security group creation.

Code Block 3-23. Module implementation code

File: chapter3\infra\iteration3\modules\securitygroup\main.tf

```
01: # AWS Security Group definition
02: resource "aws_security_group" "security_group" {
03:    name        = var.sg_name
04:    description = var.sg_description
05:    tags = {
06:       "Environment" = var.environment
07:    }
08: }
09:
10: # AWS Security Group Rules definition
11: resource "aws_security_group_rule" "security_group_rule" {
12:    type            = var.type
13:    from_port       = var.from_port
14:    to_port         = var.to_port
15:    protocol        = var.protocol
16:    cidr_blocks     = var.cidr_blocks
17:    security_group_id = aws_security_group.security_group.id
18: }
```

L02–08: In contrast to the original code for creating the security groups that we'd seen here, we are declaring two resources instead of a single resource. This is a terraform best practice as it helps in easy decoupling where we are declaring the security group and the rules of that security group separately. So here, we are first declaring the security group alone.

L11–18: We are declaring the rules for the said security group and assigning references to the security group created on **L17**.

The ***variables.tf*** and ***outputs.tf*** files contain the input and output variables for this module, respectively.

Let's get to action and execute this terraform script using the following commands.

Note   Before firing the following commands, ensure you have the key that was created in the previous chapter as we'll be needing it to SSH into our EC2 instance.

CLI Output 3-24.   Executing code of iteration #3

```
cmd> export AWS_PROFILE=gitops
cmd> cd chapter3/infra/iteration3
cmd> terraform init
cmd> terraform plan
cmd> terraform apply --auto-approve

XXXXXXXXXXXXXXX------SNIPPED-------XXXXXXXXXXXXXXXXXXXXXX

Apply complete! Resources: 7 added, 0 changed, 0 destroyed.

Outputs:

ip_address = "18.222.72.137"

cmd> curl -I http://18.222.72.137

HTTP/1.1 200 OK
Date: Mon, 08 Nov 2021 09:40:48 GMT
Server: Apache/2.4.41 (Ubuntu)

XXXXXXXXXXXXXXX------SNIPPED-------XXXXXXXXXXXXXXXXXXXXXX

cmd> chmod 600 gitops.pem
cmd> ssh -i gitops.pem ubuntu@18.222.72.137
```

```
The authenticity of host '18.222.72.137 (18.222.72.137)' can't
be established.
ECDSA key fingerprint is SHA256:xucxKFUDtOz+dCxJ3R+SMONcEANaosT
tGLLUV8Tlcgc.
Are you sure you want to continue connecting (yes/no/
[fingerprint])? yes

Welcome to Ubuntu 20.04.3 LTS (GNU/Linux 5.11.0-1020-
aws x86_64)

XXXXXXXXXXXXXXX------SNIPPED-------XXXXXXXXXXXXXXXXXXXXXX
```

3.7 Selective Destroy

There may arise situations where we do not wish to destroy the entire infrastructure, but rather just a small part of it. For example, in our previous example, we wish to destroy the EC2 instance that we've created without destroying the security groups that are declared.

The best way to be able to do this is to comment out the portion we wish to destroy and then perform *terraform apply*.

Note   // and # are the acceptable comment characters for terraform compilers.

Let's run through a practical example to understand how this would work. Open the main.tf file in the iteration3 folder and comment out the **apache2_server** resource from the main.tf file and the output variable from the output.tf file as shown here.

Code Block 3-25. Commenting out EC2 declaration

File: chapter3\infra\iteration3\main.tf

```
XXXXXXXXXXXXXXX------SNIPPED-------XXXXXXXXXXXXXXXXXXXXXX
61:
62: # AWS EC2 Resource creation
63: // resource "aws_instance" "apache2_server" {
64: //    ami             = data.aws_ami.ubuntu.id
65: //    instance_type = var.instance_type
66: //    vpc_security_group_ids = [module.http_sg_ingress.sg_id,
67: //      module.generic_sg_egress.sg_id,
68: //    module.ssh_sg_ingress.sg_id]
69: //    key_name  = var.ssh_key_name
70: //    user_data = file("scripts/user_data.sh")
71: //    tags = {
72: //      env  = var.environment
73: //      Name = "ec2-${local.name-suffix}"
74: //    }
75:
76: //    depends_on = [
77: //      module.generic_sg_egress
78: //    ]
79: // }
```

Code Block 3-26. Commenting out terraform output declaration

File: chapter3\infra\iteration3\output.tf

```
1: // # Output the Public IP Address
2: // output "ip_address" {
3: //   value = aws_instance.apache2_server.public_ip
4: // }
```

Next, follow the following commands and observe that the EC2 machine will get destroyed after we run *terraform apply*.

CLI Output 3-27. Executing code after commenting the EC2 instance

```
cmd> export AWS_PROFILE=gitops
cmd> cd chapter3/infra/iteration3
cmd> terraform apply --auto-approve

XXXXXXXXXXXXXXX------SNIPPED-------XXXXXXXXXXXXXXXXXXXXXX

Terraform used the selected providers to generate the following
execution plan. Resource actions are indicated with the
following symbols:
  - destroy
Terraform will perform the following actions:

  # aws_instance.apache2_server will be destroyed
  - resource "aws_instance" "apache2_server" {
XXXXXXXXXXXXXXX------SNIPPED-------XXXXXXXXXXXXXXXXXXXXXX
    }

Plan: 0 to add, 0 to change, 1 to destroy.

Changes to Outputs:
  - ip_address = "13.58.114.103" -> null
aws_instance.apache2_server: Destroying...
[id=i-03ad2902551bfd91d]
aws_instance.apache2_server: Still destroying...
[id=i-03ad2902551bfd91d, 10s elapsed]
aws_instance.apache2_server: Still destroying...
[id=i-03ad2902551bfd91d, 20s elapsed]
aws_instance.apache2_server: Still destroying...
[id=i-03ad2902551bfd91d, 30s elapsed]
```

```
aws_instance.apache2_server: Destruction complete after 35s

Apply complete! Resources: 0 added, 0 changed, 1 destroyed.
```

From the preceding output, it is clearly visible that Terraform destroyed our EC2 instance without destroying the security groups that were associated with it.

Let's finally destroy everything so that we don't end up getting billed unnecessarily.

CLI Output 3-28. Terraform destroys everything

```
cmd> cd chapter3/infra/iteration3
cmd> terraform destroy --auto-approve
```

3.7.1 Terraform Destroy Protection

Destroying a terraform resource is a one-way street; there is absolutely nothing one can do once it is destroyed other than spinning it up again. That generally is not a problem for immutable resources like EC2 servers or docker containers; in fact, they are designed to be flexible in all scenarios, even accidental deletion.

However, certain mutable resources like a Database server **must be protected from accidental deletion**. There are multiple ways possible to do this using AWS CLI and the GUI console, but how can this be done using terraform?

The answer is by using the life cycle meta-argument as shown in the following, **L80–82**.

Note   This code is not available in the repository; it is only for demonstration purposes here.

Code Block 3-29. Terraform prevent destroy life cyle
meta-argument

```
63: resource "aws_instance" "apache2_server" {
64:    ami             = data.aws_ami.ubuntu.id
65:    instance_type = var.instance_type
66:    vpc_security_group_ids = [module.http_sg_ingress.sg_id,
67:      module.generic_sg_egress.sg_id,
68:    module.ssh_sg_ingress.sg_id]
69:    key_name     = var.ssh_key_name
70:    user_data = file("scripts/user_data.sh")
71:    tags = {
72:      env  = var.environment
73:      Name = "ec2-${local.name-suffix}"
74:    }
75:
76:    depends_on = [
77:      module.generic_sg_egress
78:    ]
79:
80:    lifecycle {
81:      prevent_destroy = true
82:    }
83:
84: }
```

Here, when we do ***terraform destroy***, terraform refuses to destroy
our EC2 instance because of the life cycle meta-argument as shown in the
following output.

CLI Output 3-30. Deletion protection terraform apply

```
cmd> terraform destroy --auto-approve

XXXXXXXXXXXXXXX------SNIPPED-------XXXXXXXXXXXXXXXXXXXXXX


| Error: Instance cannot be destroyed
|
|   on main.tf line 63:
|   63: resource "aws_instance" "apache2_server" {
|
| Resource aws_instance.apache2_server has lifecycle.prevent_
destroy set, but the plan calls for this resource to be
destroyed. To avoid this error and continue with the
| plan, either disable lifecycle.prevent_destroy or reduce the
scope of the plan using the -target flag.
```

To delete the resource, we'll need to flip the boolean from true to false: ***prevent_destroy = false***.

Hence, in this manner, accidental deletions can be avoided.

3.8 Terraform Drift

Drift means moving away from the normal state, which very well resonates with the concept of **terraform drift**. When we hit apply, we are moving our desired state defined in *.tf files to current state stored in ***.tfstate** file. Anything that is managed and defined in ***.tf** files can be managed by terraform, but what about changes that are happening to resources outside of terraform on the resources that are created using terraform? For example, if we have an EC2 instance with security groups created using terraform and we edit one of the security groups to add one more rule from GUI. How would terraform behave in this scenario?

Terraform will attempt to reconcile with the state that is currently stored in the **.tfstate** file and the actual configuration that is created in the cloud.

Let's take a practical example to understand how exactly Terraform will do this reconciliation.

For this, we'll need access to the AWS GUI, and we'll also need to spin up the EC2 machine using the iteration #3 code.

Let's first spin up our EC2 machine using terraform by executing the following commands.

CLI Output 3-31. Executing terraform for iteration #3

```
cmd> export AWS_PROFILE=gitops
cmd> cd chapter3/infra/iteration3
cmd> terraform apply --auto-approve
```

Now let's head to our AWS GUI console and search and navigate to the Security Groups section as shown here.

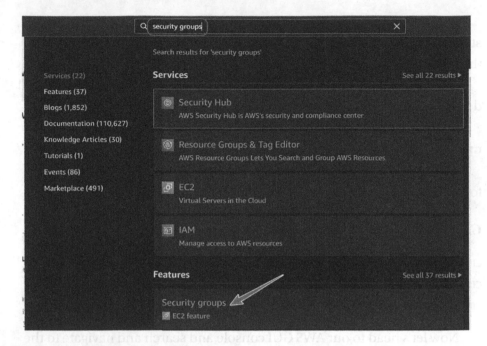

Figure 3-2. *Accessing Security Groups in AWS GUI*

In this section, we can see all the rules that were created by terraform. We now need to edit the http group.

1. Select the http_sg_ingress rule.

2. Click on the Actions tab and then click Edit inbound rules.

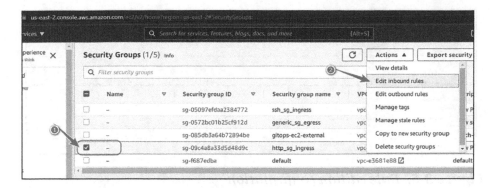

Figure 3-3. *Editing Security Groups from AWS GUI*

In the edit screen:

1. Click Add rule.

2. Select Custom TCP and enter the port number as 8080 and CIDR as 0.0.0.0/0.

3. Click Save rules.

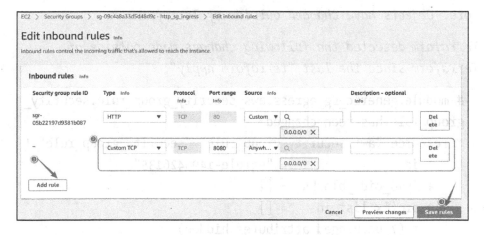

Figure 3-4. *Adding port 8080 as an additional security group rule*

Let's confirm that our rule has been added by viewing the screen here.

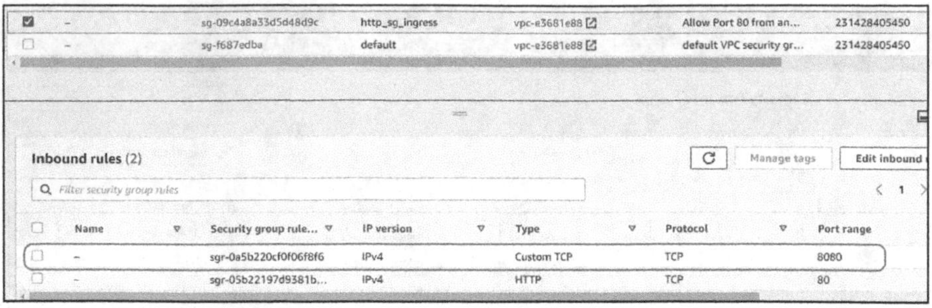

Figure 3-5. *Rule edition confirmation*

This addition was done manually from the GUI. Let's head back to our terminal and now execute ***terraform plan*** as shown here.

CLI Output 3-32. Terraform plan for reconciliation with changes made in AWS GUI

```
cmd> terraform plan

XXXXXXXXXXXXXXX------SNIPPED-------XXXXXXXXXXXXXXXXXXXXXX

Note: Objects have changed outside of Terraform

Terraform detected the following changes made outside of
Terraform since the last "terraform apply":

  # module.generic_sg_egress.aws_security_group_rule.security_
  group_rule has been changed
  ~ resource "aws_security_group_rule" "security_group_rule" {
        id                 = "sgrule-1495426135"
      + ipv6_cidr_blocks  = []
      + prefix_list_ids   = []
        # (7 unchanged attributes hidden)
    }
```

```
# module.http_sg_ingress.aws_security_group.security_group
has been changed
~ resource "aws_security_group" "security_group" {
      id                        = "sg-064becd5995aae1bb"
    ~ ingress                   = [
        + {
            + cidr_blocks       = [
                + "0.0.0.0/0",
              ]
            + description       = ""
            + from_port         = 8080
            + ipv6_cidr_blocks  = []
            + prefix_list_ids   = []
            + protocol          = "tcp"
            + security_groups   = []
            + self              = false
            + to_port           = 8080
          },
        + {
            + cidr_blocks       = [
                + "0.0.0.0/0",
              ]
            + description       = ""
            + from_port         = 80
            + ipv6_cidr_blocks  = []
            + prefix_list_ids   = []
            + protocol          = "tcp"
            + security_groups   = []
            + self              = false
            + to_port           = 80
          },
      ]
```

```
    name                        = "http_sg_ingress"
    tags                        = {
        "Environment" = "dev"
    }
    # (7 unchanged attributes hidden)
}
XXXXXXXXXXXXXXXX------SNIPPED-------XXXXXXXXXXXXXXXXXXXXX
```

Terraform detected that a new rule has been added with port 8080, and hence, it provided a plan to reconcile those changes. Before we reconcile, let's check if the current **terraform.tfstate** file contains the changes that we've made.

CLI Output 3-33. Terraform shows command grepping for port 8080.

```
cmd> terraform show | grep 8080
```

As can be seen, the preceding output is empty, which means that our current state doesn't have the new security group whereas terraform detected some changes that we performed manually from the AWS GUI.

Let's run ***terraform apply*** to reconcile the changes, and if we execute **terraform show** and grep for port 8080, we can see that the state has been reconciled.

CLI Output 3-34. Reconciliation with terraform apply

```
cmd> terraform apply --auto-approve
cmd> terraform show | grep 8080
          from_port        = 8080
          to_port          = 8080

cmd> terraform destroy --auto-approve
```

Tip   driftctl is an excellent tool that detects, tracks, and alerts on infrastructure drifts (`https://driftctl.com/`).

AWS Config is also a very good service provided by AWS to monitor, detect, and alert on cloud infrastructure changes (`https://aws.amazon.com/config`).

3.9 Clean-Up

Just to ensure that we don't end up getting billed unnecessarily, execute the following commands to confirm that we've deleted all the resources.

CLI Output 3-35. Terraform destroy commands for complete clean-up

```
cmd> export AWS_PROFILE=gitops

cmd> cd chapter3/infra/iteration1
cmd> terraform destroy --auto-approve

cmd> cd chapter3/infra/iteration2
cmd> terraform destroy --auto-approve

cmd> cd chapter3/infra/iteration3
cmd> terraform destroy --auto-approve
```

It is also highly recommended that you visit the EC2 console on the AWS GUI and double-check if everything is deleted. **The Instances (running) field should show 0.**

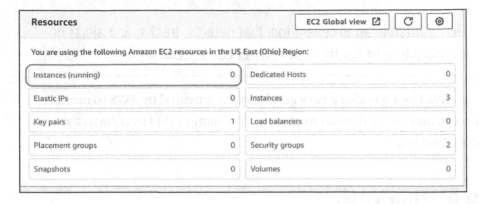

Figure 3-6. *EC2 instance dashboard screen showing zero running instances*

Note   Always double-check the region; we've been following us-east-2 in this chapter.

3.10 Terraform Commands Reference

Listing some terraform commands for reference

Table 3-1. *Terraform Commands Reference*

Command	Description
terraform init	Initializes the terraform code by downloading the dependencies
terraform plan	Shows the details about the CRUD (create, read, update, and delete) operations that will be performed on the cloud infrastructure. Uses the *-out filename.tfplan* flag to output the plan into a file
terraform apply	Accepts and applies the changes that were discussed in the earlier stage that perform all the CRUD operations. Uses the *--auto-approve* flag to automate
terraform destroy	Destroys all the resources that were defined. Uses the *--auto-approve* flag to automate
terraform fmt	Formats the terraform code by applying the rules to all the *.tf* files under the root directory. Uses the *-recursive* flag to apply to all *.tf* files in the subdirectories
terraform validate	Validates the terraform configuration files
terraform show	Shows the contents of the .tfstate file in a more readable manner

3.11 Conclusion

In this chapter, we learned how to create an EC2 server hosting an SSH and an HTTP service on AWS cloud using Terraform and also learned its nuances in the process. Terraform is a declarative syntax language, and it is slightly difficult to formulate our ideas especially when we come from a background coding in Java, Python, etc. Hence, we learned what are the best ways to organize our program and the different syntaxes like the meta-arguments, output variables, modules, and so on. We also learned how to manipulate the terraform state by selectively destroying resources and reconcile the state in case of a drift with the actual deployed configuration.

In the next chapter, we'll look at how the terraform state can be managed remotely rather than storing it locally as local creation inhibits collaboration and is extremely risky.

CHAPTER 4

Introduction to Terraform Cloud and Workspaces

In the previous chapter, we were introduced to Terraform using a simple example of spinning up an EC2 machine on AWS. We also learned about a few best practices of writing a Terraform code through three different iterations. However, what we learned in the previous chapter was suitable for individual testing and development as the terraform state that stores all the information about the cloud infrastructure that has been set up is stored locally in the developer's machine.

Terraform state, as we'll learn in more detail, is an extremely sensitive and critical file, and it is certainly not advisable to have it stored in the local machine. Hence, in this chapter, we'll explore how we can store the terraform state in Terraform Cloud, which is an offering by the creators of terraform. In Terraform Cloud, it is more readily accessible, and we can very well avoid the trauma of accidental deletion/modification so as to protect the integrity of the whole Infrastructure-as-Code operation. We'll also look at how we can deploy the same terraform code in multiple environments with minimal tweaking.

© Rohit Salecha 2023
R. Salecha, *Practical GitOps*, https://doi.org/10.1007/978-1-4842-8673-9_4

4.1 Prerequisites

In addition to the previous chapters, the following is the prerequisite for this chapter:

- Terraform Cloud account – For remote management of the terraform state. Please sign up and create a free account.

    - `https://app.terraform.io/signup/account`

4.2 Terraform State Management

When you hit ***terraform apply***, terraform creates/updates/deletes your infrastructure in the cloud in conformance with the instructions that are provided. Once the ***apply*** operation is completed, it also creates a file called ***terraform.tfstate*** detailing all the information about the resources that currently exist in your infrastructure. A different way to put it, ***terraform.tfstate*** reflects the implementation of the ***desired*** state of your cloud infrastructure. It's a huge JSON file that we've seen in the previous chapters and is **one of the most important** files in the entire terraform operation process. This file is always created in the root folder where ***terraform apply*** has been executed.

The file must follow the CIA triad of security, that is, confidentiality, integrity, and availability.

- Confidentiality – The terraform state file is a clear-text JSON file and hence should be kept in a location where access is limited to a few people. Any secret if embedded in the terraform file will also be shown in clear text here.

- Integrity – Don't ever try to modify the state file by hand as it contains details about your cloud infrastructure. Hence, only the terraform binary must be allowed to edit it.

- Availability – Terraform while executing plan, apply, and destroy needs to be able to read that file; hence, it should be made available to the terraform binary.

Terraform binary while operating on the *terraform.tfstate* file **locks** it when in use. During this time, it doesn't allow anyone to view/edit or even delete the file. This is Terraform's way to manage the CIA of the **tfstate** file on your local machine as illustrated in the following diagram.

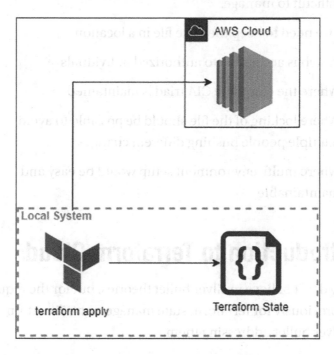

Figure 4-1. *Terraform state when saved locally*

By now, you must've realized why we should not operate terraform from our local machines when spinning up cloud infrastructure especially for production environments. Let's elaborate some of the reasons why:

— Managing the **tfstate** file locally makes it less collaborative. If you're working in a team, then you'd have to manually share the **tfstate** file, which is not scalable.

— Storing the state in the local machine can certainly make it susceptible to accidental deletions and modifications, dismantling the CIA triad.

— In case of a multi-environment setup, we need to maintain multiple state files locally, which makes it extremely difficult to manage.

Hence, we need to keep the state file in a location

— Which is accessible to authorized individuals

— Where the complete CIA triad is maintained

— Where locking of the file should be possible to avoid multiple people pushing different changes

— Where multi-environment setup would be easy and maintainable

4.3 Introduction to Terraform Cloud

I personally don't believe in silver bullet theories, but for the requirements discussed previously for terraform state management, Terraform Cloud is indeed a silver bullet addressing them.

Note Prior to 2019, developers would store terraform state in cloud storage solutions like S3 buckets in AWS, Cloud Storage in GCP, and so on. This practice is still prevalent even today as it helps in solving the preceding problems; however, we are exploring Terraform Cloud to access various other features like API automation and VCS linking, which we'll explore in the upcoming chapters.

By configuring your local terraform workspace with Terraform Cloud, all operations like plan, apply, destroy, etc., are now delegated completely to Terraform Cloud. Your state as well gets stored securely in Terraform Cloud as illustrated here.

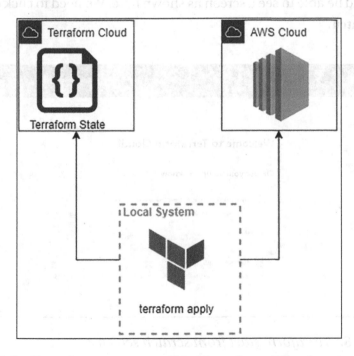

Figure 4-2. *Terraform state stored in Terraform Cloud*

In Terraform Cloud, in order to store the state, we need to make **workspaces**, which help in logically segregating all aspects of terraform operation. We can define workspaces for specific environments like staging, prod, etc., and also assign specific configurations for these environments. Hence, workspaces make it extremely easy to seamlessly create separate environments by leveraging the same code base.

4.4 Terraform Cloud – Getting Started

4.4.1 Creating a Workspace

Once you've signed up for a free Terraform Cloud account and logged in, you should be able to see a screen as shown here. We need to click on **Start from scratch.**

Figure 4-3. *Terraform start from scratch screen*

Note   Terraform Cloud UI is constantly changing. The screenshots you'll see are as of May 11, 2022.

In Terraform Cloud, the first thing that we need to create is an **Organization**, so enter a suitable organization name and your email address and then click **Create Organization** as shown here.

Note   Here, possibly, you'll need to create a unique name for your organization as **practicalgitops** may not work.

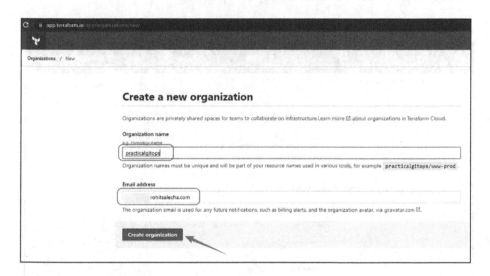

Figure 4-4.   *Create Organization screen*

On the next screen, it'll redirect you to select from the three options:

- Version control workflow – Execute terraform directly from GitHub. Terraform Cloud installs the terraform application in the repository that we wish to connect. Triggers are executed whenever there is a git push.

- CLI-driven workflow – Execute terraform from your CLI. Connect the CLI terraform binary with terraform cloud. Manual commands need to be fired as a trigger.

- API-driven workflow – Execute terraform using Terraform API. Supply the terraform cloud token and access the terraform cloud environment. Triggers can be customized to a very high degree.

One common functionality in all the preceding options is that the terraform state is stored in the Terraform Cloud application.

In this chapter, we'll do a deep dive into the **CLI-driven workflow**, and in Chapter 5, we'll look at the other two options.

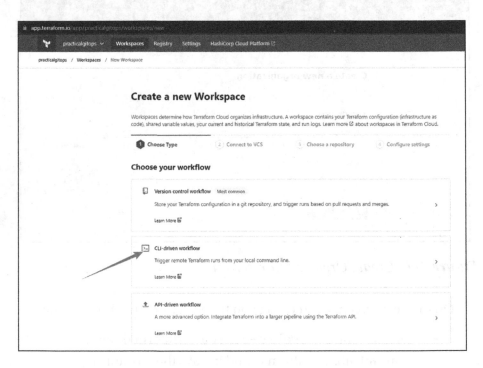

Figure 4-5. *Selecting CLI-driven workflow*

On the next screen, add the workspace name as **dev** with a suitable description and then click **Create workspace.**

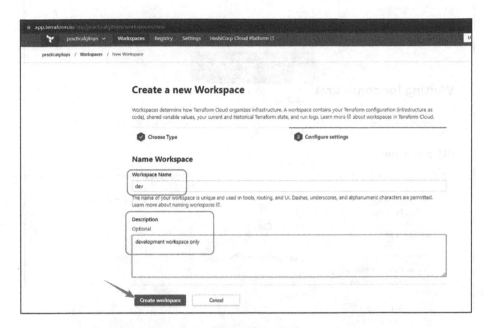

Figure 4-6. *Creating a workspace called dev*

4.4.2 Configure Workspace

We've got the workspace created but not completely configured; hence, let's click **Settings ➤ General** as shown here.

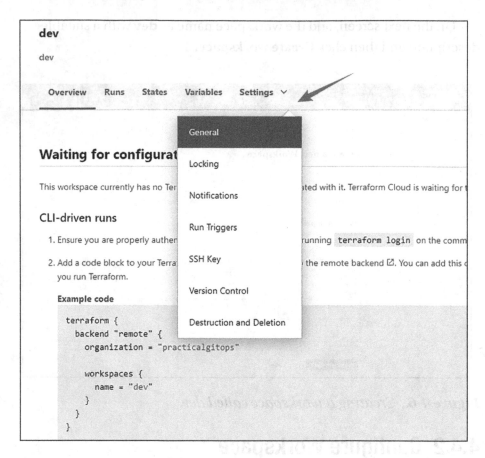

Figure 4-7. *Access workspace settings*

Here, we just need to change one setting as shown in the following. However, in the next chapter, we'll need to add an additional setting of the "Terraform Working Directory."

– Lock the Terraform version to **1.0.0**

Click **Save settings.**

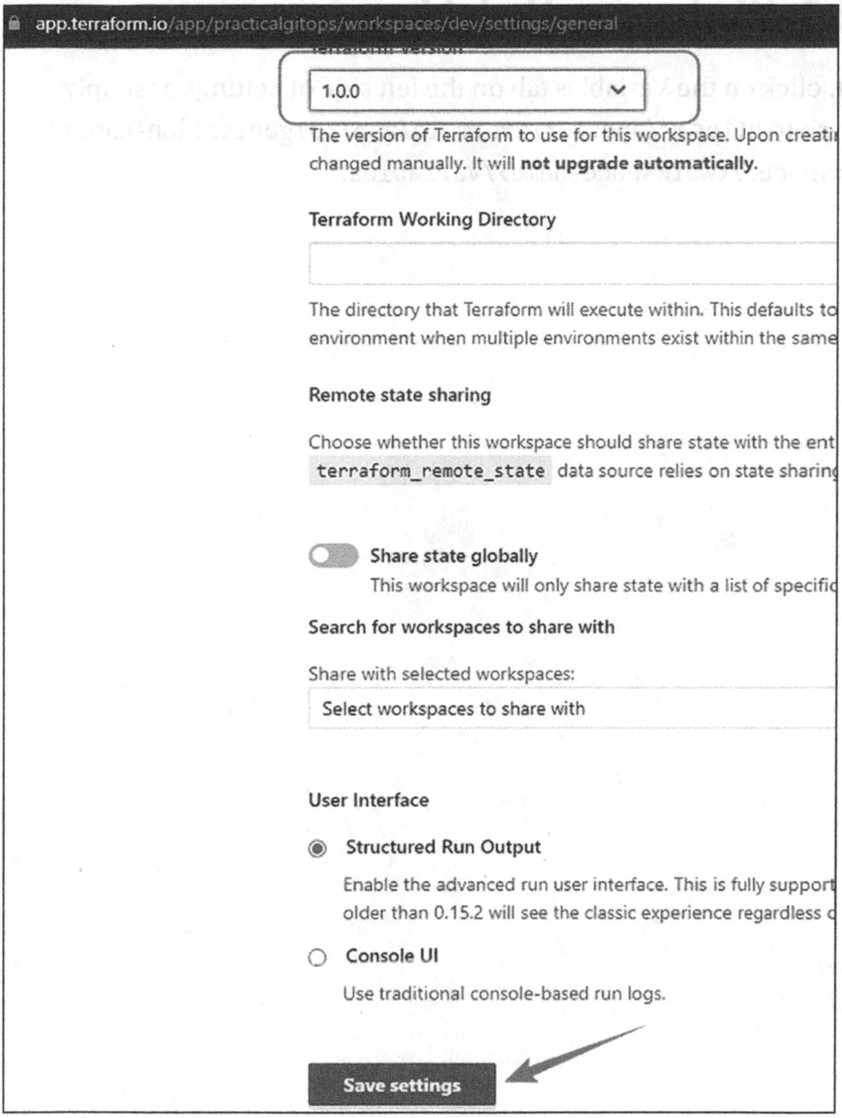

Figure 4-8. *Modifying Terraform version*

4.4.3 Workspace Variables

Next, click on the Variables tab on the left side of Settings or simply browse to `https://app.terraform.io/app/<organisation-name>/workspaces/<workspace-name>/variables`.

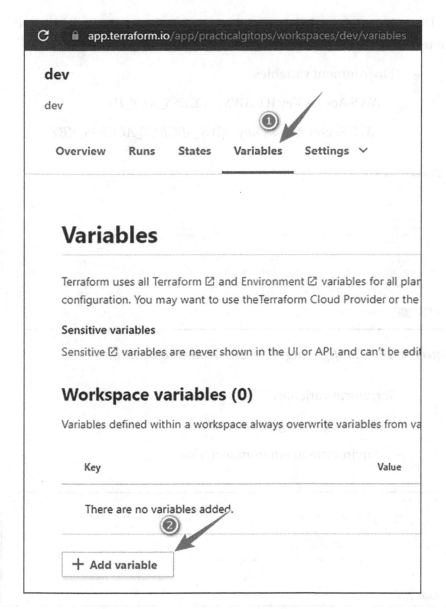

Figure 4-9. *Accessing the Terraform Variables section*

Here, we need to add four variables: two environment variables and two terraform variables.

- Environment variables

  - AWS Access Key ID: *AWS_ACCESS_KEY_ID*

  - AWS Secret Access Key: *AWS_SECRET_ACCESS_KEY*

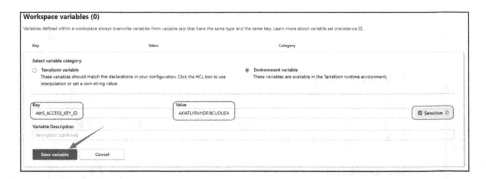

Figure 4-10. *Configuring AWS environment variables*

- Terraform variables

  - AWS Region: *region: us-east-2*

  - Environment: *environment: dev*

Figure 4-11. *Configuring terraform variables*

Your Variables page should have the following details.

Workspace variables (4)			
Variables defined within a workspace always overwrite variables from variable sets that have the same type and the same key. Learn more about variable set precedence ☑.			
Key	Value	Category	
AWS_ACCESS_KEY_ID SENSITIVE	Sensitive - write only	env	···
AWS_SECRET_ACCESS_KEY SENSITIVE	Sensitive - write only	env	···
region	us-east-2	terraform	···
environment	dev	terraform	···
+ Add variable			

Figure 4-12. *Terraform Cloud all variables configured*

Environment variables are utilized by Terraform for configuring the environment in which terraform needs to be run. For example, we've provided the AWS Access Keys as an environment variable to set up the AWS environment just the way we used the AWS_PROFILE variable in the previous chapters.

Terraform variables consist of data that terraform requires for its execution and can be configured in the workspace.

4.4.4 Terraform Login

Next, we need to move our focus on the terminal to fire a very important command. So yank up your terminal window where Terraform is installed and execute the command ***terraform login*** and follow these steps:

1. Execute the command ***terraform login.***

2. It'll ask for your permission to store the token in a file called **credentials.tfrc.json.**

3. Once you enter "Yes", it'll open your browser and navigate to the following link: https://app. terraform.io/app/settings/tokens?source=terr aform-login

asking for your permission to create an API token. Provide any name to the token and click **Create API token.**

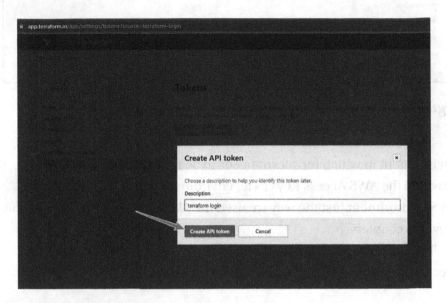

Figure 4-13. *Create API token screen*

4. Copy the generated token.

Figure 4-14. *Copying the generated token*

5. Paste it in the command line where the cursor is
    waiting for your input.

```
ubuntu → infra terraform login
Terraform will request an API token for app.terraform.io using your browser.

If login is successful, Terraform will store the token in plain text in
the following file for use by subsequent commands:
    /home/ubuntu/.terraform.d/credentials.tfrc.json

Do you want to proceed?
  Only 'yes' will be accepted to confirm.

  Enter a value: yes


------------------------------------------------------------------------

Terraform must now open a web browser to the tokens page for app.terraform.io.

If a browser does not open this automatically, open the following URL to proceed:
    https://app.terraform.io/app/settings/tokens?source=terraform-login


------------------------------------------------------------------------

Generate a token using your browser, and copy-paste it into this prompt.

Terraform will store the token in plain text in the following file
for use by subsequent commands:
    /home/ubuntu/.terraform.d/credentials.tfrc.json

Token for app.terraform.io:
  Enter a value:

Retrieved token for user practicalgitops

------------------------------------------------------------------------
```

Figure 4-15.   *Pasting the Terraform API token*

We've now successfully connected our CLI with Terraform Cloud!

Note   This is a very sensitive operation; hence, you need to ensure that access to this file is limited. **This is needed only for this chapter;** you can then discard the value by deleting this file.

4.4.5 Running Terraform in Terraform Cloud

Now let's execute the code that we developed in the third iteration in the previous chapter not locally but on Terraform Cloud!

However, before we jump into the execution part, there is a small change that needs to be explained. We've added three new files: **backend. tf**, **dev.hcl,** and **prod.hcl**.

CLI Output 4-1. Chapter4 directory structure

```
cmd>cd chapter4/infra
cmd> tree -a
.
├── backend.tf
├── dev.hcl
├── main.tf
├── modules
│   └── securitygroup
│       ├── main.tf
│       ├── output.tf
│       └── variables.tf
├── output.tf
├── prod.hcl
├── providers.tf
├── scripts
│   └── user_data.sh
├── terraform.auto.tfvars
└── variables.tf

3 directories, 12 files
```

The **backend.tf** file informs terraform that the state needs to be stored remotely and the exact location of the states is provided in the **dev. hcl** and **prod.hcl** files for the development and production workspaces, respectively.

Code Block 4-2. backend.tf file

File: chapter4/infra/backend.tf

```
1: terraform {
2:    backend "remote" {}
3: }
```

Code Block 4-3. dev.hcl file

File: chapter4/infra/dev.hcl

```
1: workspaces { name = "dev" }
2: hostname     = "app.terraform.io"
3: organization = "practicalgitops"
```

Through this new configuration file, we are basically telling terraform to store the **terraform.tfstate** file in the **dev** workspace that was created in the **practicalgitops** organization earlier through the GUI on app. terraform.io.

Let's now run our Terraform commands.

Code Block 4-4. Running terraform init

```
cmd> cd chapter4/infra
cmd> terraform init -backend-config=dev.hcl

Initializing modules...
- generic_sg_egress in modules/securitygroup
- http_sg_ingress in modules/securitygroup
- ssh_sg_ingress in modules/securitygroup

Initializing the backend...

Successfully configured the backend "remote"! Terraform will automatically
use this backend unless the backend configuration changes.
```

XXXXXXXXXXXXXXX------SNIPPED-------XXXXXXXXXXXXXXXXXXXXXX

There are three interesting things to note here:

1. The ***terraform init*** command takes an additional
    argument (***-backend-config=dev.hcl***) specifying the
    details about the *remote* backend configuration.

2. Everything is now being initialized in Terraform
    Cloud, and the state file will also be stored there as is
    evident from the message ***Successfully configured
    the backend "remote"***.

3. Last but most importantly, we are no longer
    specifying the AWS Profile credentials! The
    command to export the AWS_PROFILE variable
    is not needed anymore because terraform will be
    utilizing the AWS Credentials stored as environment
    variables in Terraform Cloud! Hence, we can get
    rid of the AWS credentials from our local machines!
    This is happening because of ***terraform login***.

Let's view the output for ***terraform plan*** as shown here.

Code Block 4-5. Running terraform plan

```
cmd> terraform plan

Running plan in the remote backend. Output will stream here.
Pressing Ctrl-C
will stop streaming the logs, but will not stop the plan
running remotely.

Preparing the remote plan...
```

The remote workspace is configured to work with
configuration at
dev relative to the target repository.

Terraform will upload the contents of the following directory,
excluding files or directories as defined by a
.terraformignore file
at /chapter4/infra/.terraformignore (if it is present),
in order to capture the filesystem context the remote workspace
expects:
    /chapter4/infra

To view this run in a browser, visit:
https://app.terraform.io/app/practicalgitops/dev/runs/run-
a3a6RtaP35qttEwj

XXXXXXXXXXXXXXX------SNIPPED-------XXXXXXXXXXXXXXXXXXXXXX

Let's understand what exactly is happening here.

1. Terraform will bundle our entire working directory
    that is everything under the **dev** directory into
    Terraform Cloud, and hence, it is asking to
    add **.gitignore** equivalent **.terraformignore**
    in case we wish to avoid leakage of sensitive or
    unnecessary data.

2. Next, once the code is uploaded, it'll execute
    terraform plan in the cloud and stream the logs
    here. We can alternatively also view the live logs
    in the link provided: https://app.terraform.
    io/app/practicalgitops/dev/runs/run-
    a3a6RtaP35qttEwj (ensure your authenticated).

Note   You would be having a slightly different link depending on
the organization and workspace name. Also, each run has a globally
unique number.

So let's open the link and view what it looks like. Terraform Cloud is
spooling the exact same information as we saw in the CLI but in a much
prettier interface.

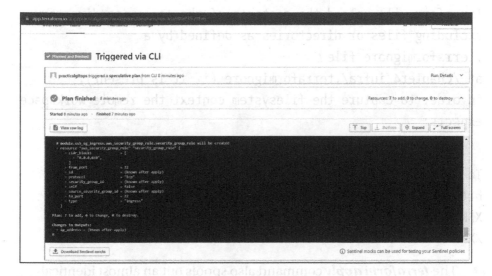

Figure 4-16. *Terraform plan output on Terraform Cloud*

Next, let's execute ***terraform apply*** and see what happens.

CLI Output 4-6. Running terraform apply

```
cmd> terraform apply
```

Running apply in the remote backend. Output will stream here.
Pressing Ctrl-C

will cancel the remote apply if it's still pending. If the
apply started it
will stop streaming the logs, but will not stop the apply
running remotely.

Preparing the remote apply...

The remote workspace is configured to work with
configuration at
dev relative to the target repository.
Terraform will upload the contents of the following directory,
excluding files or directories as defined by a
.terraformignore file
at /chapter4/infra/.terraformignore (if it is present),
in order to capture the filesystem context the remote workspace
expects:
    /chapter4/infra

To view this run in a browser, visit:
https://app.terraform.io/app/practicalgitops/dev/runs/run-
XPKVvP68Xk4pEB33
XXXXXXXXXXXXXXX------SNIPPED-------XXXXXXXXXXXXXXXXXXXXXX

The **terraform apply** command also spools out an almost identical
output on the CLI; however, if we open the browser link https://app.
terraform.io/app/practicalgitops/dev/runs/run-XPKVvP68Xk4pEB33
(ensure your authenticated), it looks a bit different.

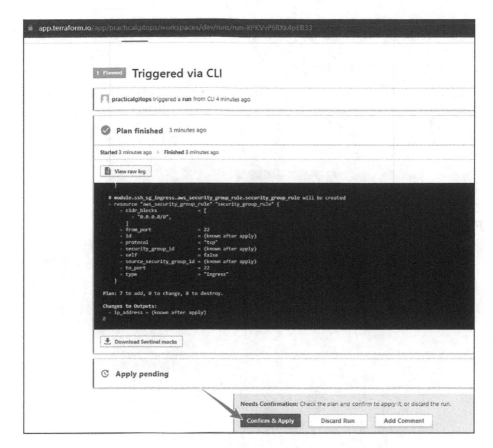

Figure 4-17. *Output of terraform apply on Terraform Cloud*

What's happening here is that Terraform is awaiting our approval on the GUI, that is, on the browser to **confirm and apply** the plan. Earlier we were getting a cursor on the CLI (which we do get now as well, but it is recommended to apply from cloud); however, here, it is asking for approval on the Terraform Cloud portal.

So let's go ahead and click **Confirm & Apply** and see what happens. When you hit the Confirm & Apply button, it'll ask for a comment; just add any appropriate comment and click **Confirm Plan** as shown here.

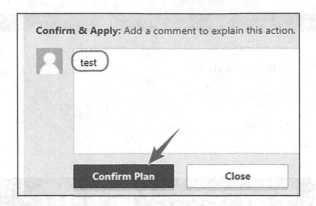

Figure 4-18. *Comment before applying*

We can see that the plan is being applied as shown here.

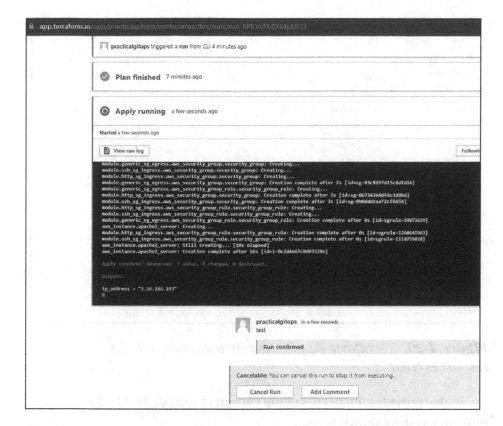

Figure 4-19. *Output of terraform apply on Terraform Cloud*

Once the plan is applied successfully, navigate to the Overview tab and you should be able to see a very nicely formatted output of everything that has been created in this plan as shown here.

NAME	PROVIDER	TYPE	MODULE	UPDATED ↓
ubuntu	hashicorp/aws	data.aws_ami	root	Nov 11 2021
apache2_server	hashicorp/aws	aws_instance	root	Nov 11 2021
security_group	hashicorp/aws	aws_security...	generic_sg_egress	Nov 11 2021
security_group_rule	hashicorp/aws	aws_security...	generic_sg_egress	Nov 11 2021
security_group	hashicorp/aws	aws_security...	http_sg_ingress	Nov 11 2021
security_group_rule	hashicorp/aws	aws_security...	http_sg_ingress	Nov 11 2021
security_group	hashicorp/aws	aws_security...	ssh_sg_ingress	Nov 11 2021
security_group_rule	hashicorp/aws	aws_security...	ssh_sg_ingress	Nov 11 2021

Resources **8**   Outputs **1**   Current as of the most recent state versio...

Filter resources

Figure 4-20. *Terraform Apply Overview showing all resources created*

It also provides the details of the Output in the tab next to the Resources tab as shown here.

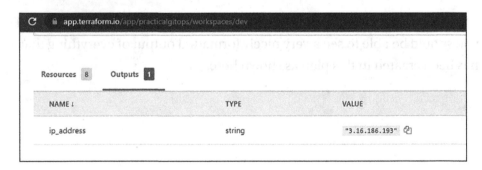

NAME ↕	TYPE	VALUE
ip_address	string	"3.16.186.193"

Resources 8   Outputs 1

Figure 4-21. *Terraform Output field value on Terraform Cloud*

Interestingly, the same output is also streamed in our CLI as shown here.

```
Do you want to perform these actions in workspace "dev"?
  Terraform will perform the actions described above.
  Only 'yes' will be accepted to approve.

  Enter a value: approved using the UI or API

module.generic_sg_egress.aws_security_group.security_group: Creating...
module.ssh_sg_ingress.aws_security_group.security_group: Creating...
module.http_sg_ingress.aws_security_group.security_group: Creating...
module.generic_sg_egress.aws_security_group.security_group: Creation complete after 2s [id=sg-03c9b57d15c8dfd16]
module.generic_sg_egress.aws_security_group_rule.security_group_rule: Creating...
module.http_sg_ingress.aws_security_group.security_group: Creation complete after 2s [id=sg-067343b4df4c1d8b6]
module.ssh_sg_ingress.aws_security_group.security_group: Creation complete after 2s [id=sg-0b0ddd1ea72cf665b]
module.http_sg_ingress.aws_security_group_rule.security_group_rule: Creating...
module.ssh_sg_ingress.aws_security_group_rule.security_group_rule: Creating...
module.generic_sg_egress.aws_security_group_rule.security_group_rule: Creation complete after 0s [id=sgrule-59872629]
aws_instance.apache2_server: Creating...
module.http_sg_ingress.aws_security_group_rule.security_group_rule: Creation complete after 0s [id=sgrule-1260645963]
module.ssh_sg_ingress.aws_security_group_rule.security_group_rule: Creation complete after 0s [id=sgrule-1118759020]
aws_instance.apache2_server: Still creating... [10s elapsed]
aws_instance.apache2_server: Creation complete after 16s [id=i-0c2d4e67c8d03329e]

Apply complete! Resources: 7 added, 0 changed, 0 destroyed.

Outputs:

ip_address = "3.16.186.193"
```

Figure 4-22. *Terraform Cloud output streamed on CLI*

Great! So we are executing Terraform commands from the CLI, and all operation is happening on Terraform Cloud! Now, we can share this same source code with other team members. They can then make changes to the terraform code and deploy them from their machine, and the terraform state remains shared between them.

Whenever a team member runs ***terraform apply***, the state is first checked remotely and then updated in the cloud.

Let's now destroy by using the ***terraform destroy*** command as shown in the following. We can use the ***--auto-approve*** flag to override the manual approval in Terraform Cloud for destruction as well as apply.

CLI Output 4-7. Running terraform destroy

```
cmd> terraform destroy --auto-approve
```

Running apply in the remote backend. Output will stream here. Pressing Ctrl-C

will cancel the remote apply if it's still pending. If the
apply started it
will stop streaming the logs, but will not stop the apply
running remotely.

Preparing the remote apply...

The remote workspace is configured to work with
configuration at
dev relative to the target repository.

Terraform will upload the contents of the following directory,
excluding files or directories as defined by a
.terraformignore file
at /chapter4/infra/.terraformignore (if it is present),
in order to capture the filesystem context the remote workspace
expects:
    /chapter4/infra

To view this run in a browser, visit:
https://app.terraform.io/app/practicalgitops/dev/runs/run-gkkgV
av4xNCdcKQU

4.4.6 Terraform Cloud Run and States

We also get a full log of all the terraform commands executed on the
workspace in the Runs tab as shown in the following with the latest being
shown first. This is something we'll never get if we run from CLI directly.
This helps in understanding how, when, and what is happening to our
infrastructure, something difficult to decipher when using cloud storage as
a remote backend unless we develop our own solution.

Figure 4-23. *Terraform Cloud Run log*

The state is now stored in the Terraform Cloud and can be viewed by navigating to the **States** tab as shown here.

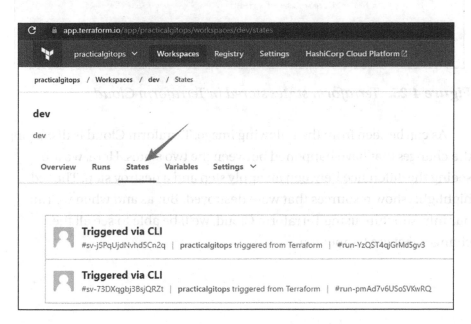

Figure 4-24. *Terraform states log in Terraform Cloud*

All state changes are versioned, and we can view the difference in the state configurations between two consecutive runs. Let's click on the first state to view the changes.

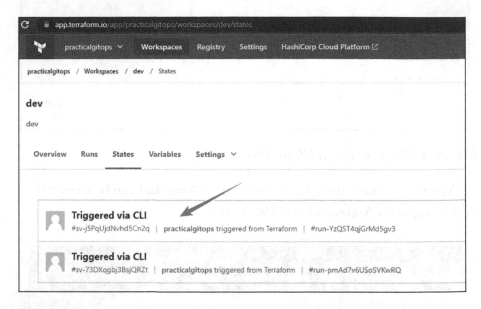

Figure 4-25. *Terraform states stored in Terraform Cloud*

As can be seen from the following image, Terraform Cloud is displaying the changes that have happened between the two states. Here, we are seeing the difference between an apply step and a destroy step. The red highlights show resources that were destroyed. But as and when we run our infrastructure using Terraform Cloud, we'll be able to see all the changes that are happening.

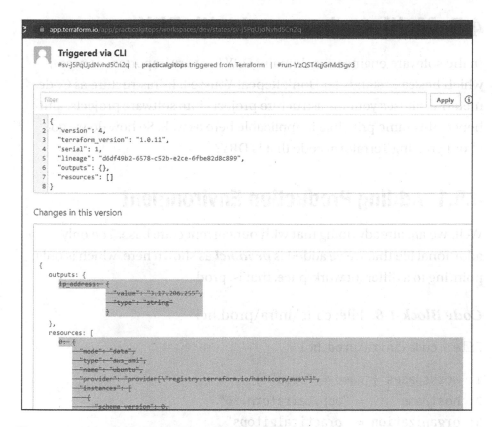

Figure 4-26. *Terraform Cloud state diff*

These exceptional features of having a log of every run and displaying of state information per run and the difference between runs provide wonderful insights into our infrastructure changes. If we store our state in a cloud storage backend, then we won't get all this information out of the box. We'll probably have to upload the state files in a separate software to view all this information. However, in Terraform Cloud, we get all this out of the box.

4.5 Multi-environment with DRY

In the software engineering domain, DRY is a very important concept, which basically stands for Don't Repeat Yourself. Infrastructure as Code metamorphoses your infrastructure projects into software projects, and hence, this same principle is applicable here as well. So how do we go about creating Terraform code that is DRY?

4.5.1 Adding Production Environment

Well, we are already doing that with our current code base. The only additional file that we've added is **prod.hcl** as shown here, which is only pointing to a different workspace, that is, prod.

Code Block 4-8. File: code\infra\prod.hcl

```
File: code\infra\prod.hcl

1: workspaces { name = "prod" }
2: hostname     = "app.terraform.io"
3: organization = "practicalgitops"
```

Let's follow the same steps as provided in the "Creating a Workspace" section to create a new prod workspace.

Tip   It is strongly recommended here to use AWS organizations to create different environments to achieve proper segregation between dev and prod accounts. We'll learn about it in more detail in Chapter 8 where we'll be set up and discuss AWS organizations with a multi-account strategy completely using Terraform.

Keeping all the steps the same as we did for the **dev** workspace, the only difference in this new **prod** workspace is an additional variable that we are adding in the Terraform Cloud, that is, ***instance_type*** variable, and providing it a value of **t3.small**. We are also changing the environment variable value to prod. We could also change the region.

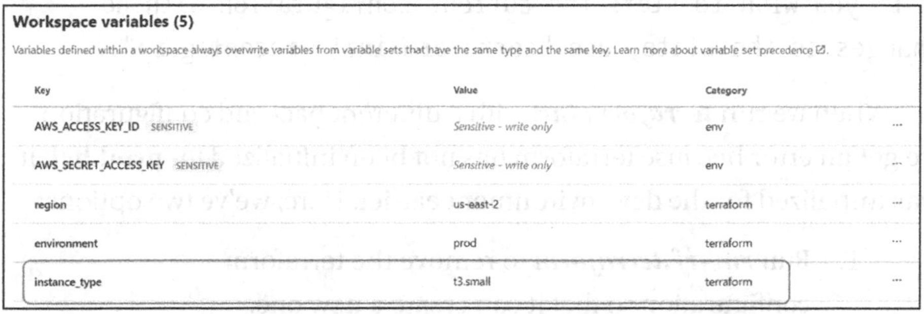

Workspace variables (5)

Variables defined within a workspace always overwrite variables from variable sets that have the same type and the same key. Learn more about variable set precedence ☑.

Key	Value	Category	
AWS_ACCESS_KEY_ID SENSITIVE	Sensitive - write only	env	...
AWS_SECRET_ACCESS_KEY SENSITIVE	Sensitive - write only	env	...
region	us-east-2	terraform	...
environment	prod	terraform	...
instance_type	t3.small	terraform	...

Figure 4-27. *Terraform Cloud variables*

Why are we doing this? Because our production system needs a little more higher configuration machine. Hence, we can override the value of any variable specified in the ***terraform.auto.tfvars*** file by specifying the same here in Terraform Cloud.

Let's run the terraform code in our new production environment by specifying a different backend configuration file this time around.

CLI Output 4-9. Running terraform init error

```
cmd> cd chapter4/infra
cmd> terraform init -backend-config=prod.hcl

Initializing modules...

Initializing the backend...

|
| Error: Backend configuration changed
```

| A change in the backend configuration has been detected,
which may require migrating existing state.

| If you wish to attempt automatic migration of the state, use
"terraform init -migrate-state".
| If you wish to store the current configuration with no
changes to the state, use "terraform init -reconfigure".

When we run ***terraform init*** with a different backend configuration,
we get an error because terraform has not been initialized for **prod.hcl**; it
was initialized for the dev environment earlier. Here, we've two options:

1. Run ***rm -rf .terraform*** to remove the terraform
   configuration so that it can create a new one.

2. Run ***terraform init -backend-config=prod.hcl
   -reconfigure***, which we'll reconfigure the state.

We'll, however, proceed with the nondestructive one, that is,
reconfiguring the state as shown here.

CLI Output 4-10. Terraform init reconfigure

```
cmd> terraform init -backend-config=prod.hcl -reconfigure
cmd> terraform plan

Running plan in the remote backend. Output will stream here.
Pressing Ctrl-C
will stop streaming the logs, but will not stop the plan
running remotely.

XXXXXXXXXXXXXXXX------SNIPPED-------XXXXXXXXXXXXXXXXXXXXXX

  # aws_instance.apache2_server will be created
  + resource "aws_instance" "apache2_server" {
```

```
    + ami                                = "ami-06c7d6c0
                                            987eaa46c"
XXXXXXXXXXXXXXXX------SNIPPED-------XXXXXXXXXXXXXXXXXXXXXX
    + instance_type                      = "t3.small"
    + ipv6_address_count                 = (known after
                                            apply)
    + ipv6_addresses                     = (known after
                                            apply)
    + key_name                           = "gitops"
XXXXXXXXXXXXXXXX------SNIPPED-------XXXXXXXXXXXXXXXXXXXXXX

cmd> terraform apply --auto-approve
```

4.5.2 TF Variables Overriding

An interesting observation to note here is that our terraform variables in the cloud for the *instance_type* have been successfully overridden.

Terraform Variable has the following order of precedence with the decreasing order of priority:

1. Terraform Cloud declaration/environment variables

2. Passing variables in CLI, for example, *terraform apply -var "instance_type=t3.small"*

3. Passing variable value in the **terraform.auto. tfvars** file

4. Passing variable value as "default" in **.tf* files

When the *terraform apply* completes execution, you'll be able to see a new EC2 instance launched in the production environment.

In this manner, by configuring a different workspace for different environments and tweaking the terraform/environment variables, we can deploy various different environments using the same code base as is illustrated in the following figure.

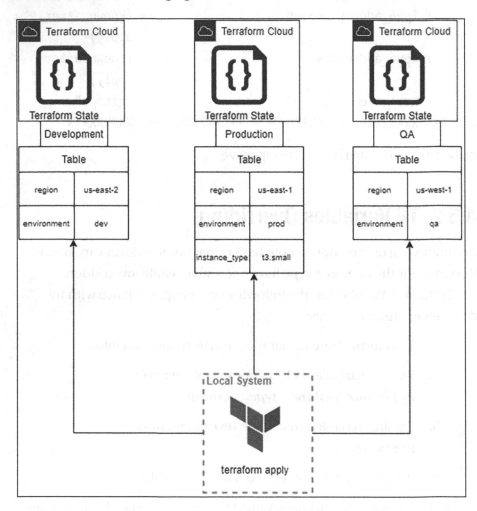

Figure 4-28. *Terraform Cloud with different workspaces*

4.6 Clean-Up

Just to ensure that we don't end up getting billed unnecessarily, execute the following commands to confirm that we've deleted all the resources.

CLI Output 4-11. Running terraform destroy

```
cmd> export AWS_PROFILE=gitops

cmd> cd chapter4/infra
cmd> terraform destroy --auto-approve
```

It is also highly recommended that you visit the EC2 console on the AWS GUI and double-check if everything is deleted. **The Instances (running) field should show 0.**

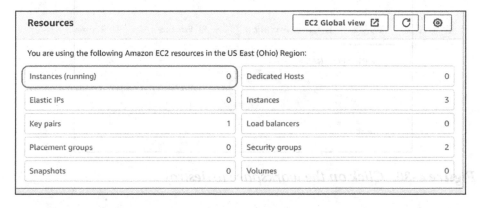

Figure 4-29. *EC2 running instances status*

Note   Always double-check the region; we've been following us-east-2 in this chapter.

4.6.1 Destroying Terraform Cloud Workspaces

It may for some reason or other be necessary to destroy a workspace,
maybe to change the workflow or maybe some sensitive information has
been accidentally committed.

The following steps illustrate how we can go about doing the same.

1.   Click on a workspace that you'd like to destroy.

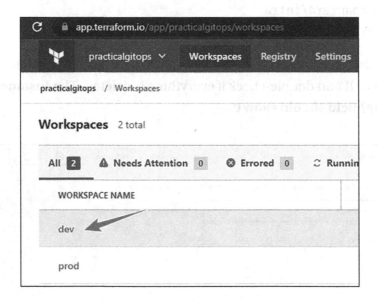

Figure 4-30.   *Click on the workspace to destroy*

2.   Then click **Settings** and then **Destruction and
      Deletion** as shown here.

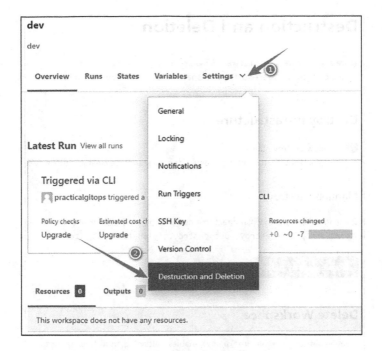

Figure 4-31. *Click on destruction and deletion*

3. Scroll down and click **Delete from Terraform Cloud**.

Figure 4-32. *Workspace deletion*

4. You'll be asked to confirm the deletion by entering the name of the workspace you're deleting. Enter the name and then click **Delete workspace** as shown here.

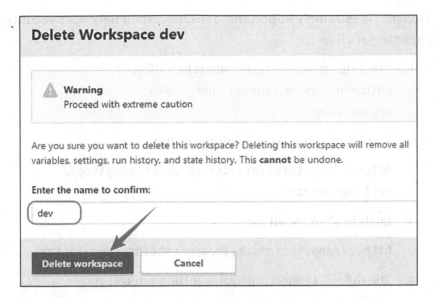

Figure 4-33. *Delete workspace confirmation*

5. Your workspace will then be deleted along with all the runs and state information.

6. Similarly destroy your prod workspace as well.

4.7 Terraform Cloud Security Best Practices

Terraform Cloud is now not only storing your state but is also provisioning your AWS infrastructure. It hence becomes an extremely critical asset for the organization.

If an adversary gains access to your Terraform Cloud account, they can

1. Gain read-only access to your GitHub repository

2. Delete Cloud workspaces

3. View sensitive information (if any) stored in your terraform state files

Hence, it is extremely important to ensure certain necessary security best practices such as

1. Creating separate organizations for different environments on a similar note as AWS organizations

2. Providing access to only limited users:

   `https://app.terraform.io/app/practicalgitops/settings/users`

3. Enabling 2FA for all users:

   `https://app.terraform.io/app/settings/two-factor`

4. The default session timeout is 20160 minutes; you might want to reduce it:

   `https://app.terraform.io/app/practicalgitops/settings/authentication`

5. Monitoring VCS events:

   `https://app.terraform.io/app/practicalgitops/settings/vcs-events`

6. Monitoring active sessions of users:

   `https://app.terraform.io/app/settings/sessions`

7. Setting a strong password:

   `https://app.terraform.io/app/settings/password`

8. Creating tokens per user and also regularly monitoring their usage:

   `https://app.terraform.io/app/settings/tokens`

These are some of the best practices that can be followed from a security perspective.

4.8 Conclusion

In this chapter, we looked at how we can utilize the Terraform Cloud utility to store the terraform space in a remote and secure environment. Terraform Cloud also provides versioning to our terraform state, thereby allowing us to determine the changes between the previous states, thereby enabling us to properly version control the infrastructure changes. It also helps in creating workspaces that are mutually independent of each other and hence can be used to set up different environments using the same code base. Finally, we also saw how we can destroy the workspaces created in the Terraform Cloud as a necessary action in certain unforeseen conditions.

In this chapter, we saw all about how terraform state can be stored remotely; however, we needed to fire the commands to execute terraform. In the next chapter, we'll look at two different ways in which we can leverage Terraform Cloud to execute the commands for us by tying it with our GitHub repository.

CHAPTER 5

Terraform Automation with Git

In the previous chapter, we looked at how terraform state can be stored remotely to allow for collaboration with a larger team. However, just having the state configured remotely won't help much as we also need the teams to collaborate with their code changes. We need a mechanism wherein the developers can push their code into an SCM (Source Code Management) repository and view/approve each other's changes before executing terraform. Git allows for full collaborative workflows; hence, in this chapter, we'll look at two different methods using GitHub and GitHub Actions. We can enable collaboration between developers by taking away their responsibility of manually executing terraform commands from CLI by leveraging the VCS driven-workflow and the Terraform API-driven workflow provided by Terraform Cloud, thus automating the entire terraform workflow. We'll also finally look at the drawbacks of using the VCS workflow and why GitHub Actions is a preferable setup.

© Rohit Salecha 2023
R. Salecha, *Practical GitOps*, https://doi.org/10.1007/978-1-4842-8673-9_5

5.1 Prerequisites

In addition to the previous chapters, the following are the prerequisites for this chapter:

- Git installed and accessible from the command line.

    - `https://git-scm.com/book/en/v2/Getting-Started-Installing-Git` provides installation steps for almost all major operating systems.

    - It is also assumed that you've basic working knowledge of git commands and managing remote git repositories.

- GitHub account; we'll be creating a number of repositories from this chapter onward to keep learning clean.

    - `https://github.com/signup`

- You've connected GitHub with SSH (optional)

    - I'll be using git mainly from the CLI, and hence, whenever performing ***git push***, you'll be asked to enter your GitHub credentials; if you wish to avoid that, then you can configure your Git with SSH.

    - `https://docs.github.com/en/authentication/connecting-to-github-with-ssh` is a guide providing instructions to set up the same across all major operating systems.

- DockerHub account

    - `https://hub.docker.com/signup`

5.2 Terraform Automation with GitHub

Till now we've been manually executing the commands **terraform init**, **terraform plan**, and **terraform apply**. In Terraform Cloud, you could trigger a terraform plan by simply committing into your git repository! There are absolutely no commands that need to be fired from the command line other than checking your code into your repository. This can be accomplished using the VCS (Version Controlled System) feature of Terraform Cloud where we need to integrate our repository with it and then everything is managed from Terraform Cloud.

5.2.1 Setting Up the GitHub Repository

Let's start by first setting up a GitHub repository. Assuming you are already logged into your GitHub account, navigate to `https://github.com/new` to create a new repository and follow the following steps:

1. Create an appropriate name for your repository. I've chosen to keep the naming convention as section-chapter(n)

2. Select the appropriate visibility. I've chosen it as Private for now.

3. Click Create repository.

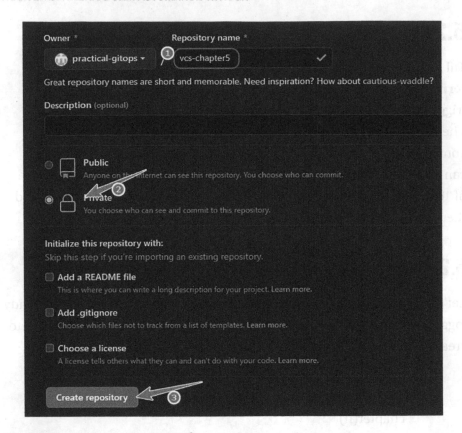

Figure 5-1.   *Creating GitHub repository*

Once your repository has been created, ensure to note down your
repository URL.

If you've configured your SSH keys with GitHub, then you can select
the SSH tab and note down the GitHub SSH URL as shown here.

Figure 5-2. *GitHub SSH URL*

If you've not configured SSH and are going to enter your credentials, then select the HTTPS tab as shown here.

Figure 5-3. *GitHub HTTPS URL*

Note   It is extremely important to know which URL you are using, whether HTTPS or SSH, as depending on that, you'll be authenticated to GitHub when checking in your code.

Now, navigate to the following folder location and let's upload the code to the GitHub repository that we've created.

CLI Output 5-1. Adding code to the GitHub repository

```
cmd> cd chapter5/vcs
cmd> tree -a

.
```

```
├── .gitignore
├── README.md
└── infra
    ├── main.tf
    ├── modules
    │   └── securitygroup
    │       ├── main.tf
    │       ├── output.tf
    │       └── variables.tf
    ├── output.tf
    ├── providers.tf
    ├── scripts
    │   └── user_data.sh
    ├── terraform.auto.tfvars
    └── variables.tf
    ├── README.md

4 directories, 12 files

cmd> git init
cmd> git add .
cmd> git commit -m "first commit"
cmd> git branch -M main

# Enter proper URL here, If you've not configure SSH then enter
HTTPS URL
cmd> git remote add origin <your_https_or_ssh_url_here>
cmd> git push -u origin main
```

Visit the GitHub repository URL to confirm if all files have been uploaded successfully.

5.2.2 Connecting GitHub with Terraform Cloud

Visit the Terraform Cloud application and click on create new workspace as shown here.

practicalgitops
Workspaces
Registry
Settings
HashiCorp Cloud Platform
practicalgitops / Workspaces
Workspaces
All 0
Needs Attention 0
Errored 0
Running 0
On Hold 0
Success 0
Tag
WORKSPACE NAME
RUN STATUS
REPO
You don't have any workspaces yet. Create one now.

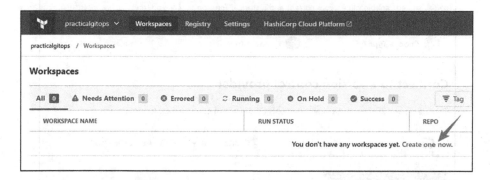

***Figure 5-4.** Creating new Terraform Cloud workspace*

In the new workspace creation screen, select the **Version control workflow** as shown here.

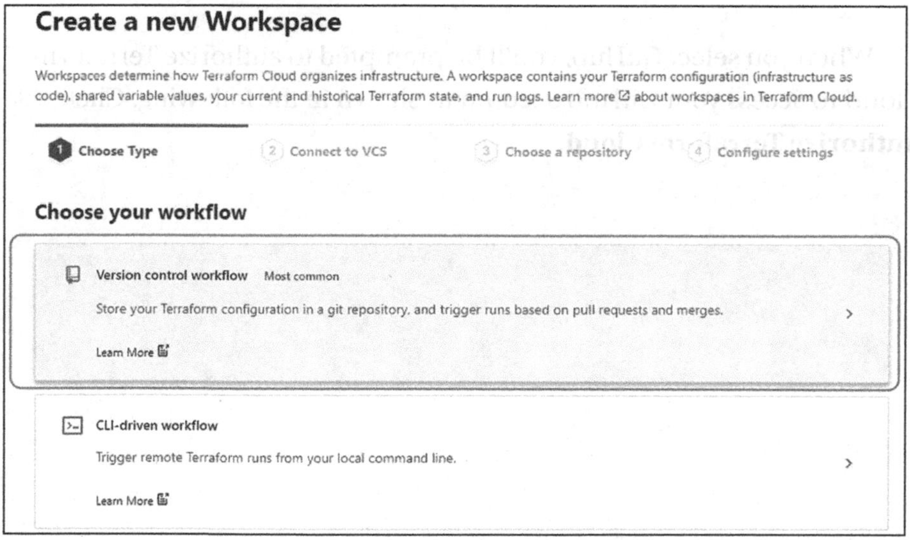

Create a new Workspace
Workspaces determine how Terraform Cloud organizes infrastructure. A workspace contains your Terraform configuration (infrastructure as code), shared variable values, your current and historical Terraform state, and run logs. Learn more about workspaces in Terraform Cloud.
1 Choose Type
2 Connect to VCS
3 Choose a repository
4 Configure settings
Choose your workflow
Version control workflow
Most common
Store your Terraform configuration in a git repository, and trigger runs based on pull requests and merges.
Learn More
CLI-driven workflow
Trigger remote Terraform runs from your local command line.
Learn More

***Figure 5-5.** Selecting Version control workflow*

In the **Connect to VCS** section, select GitHub as shown here.

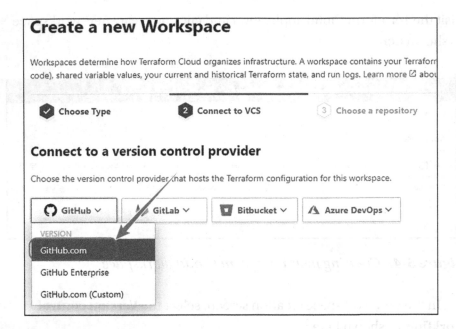

Figure 5-6. *Connecting Terraform Cloud to GitHub.com*

When you select GitHub, you'll be prompted to authorize Terraform Cloud to access your GitHub account as shown in the following. Click **Authorize Terraform Cloud**.

Figure 5-7. Authorizing Terraform Cloud

Note   If you've pop-up blockers installed, then the preceding step will fail. Please allow popups for this particular site.

Next, there will be another popup that will ask your permission to install Terraform Cloud in your GitHub repositories as shown here.

Note   Do not click on Install here as this is an excessive permission and Terraform Cloud will have read access to all your repositories. Please check the next steps.

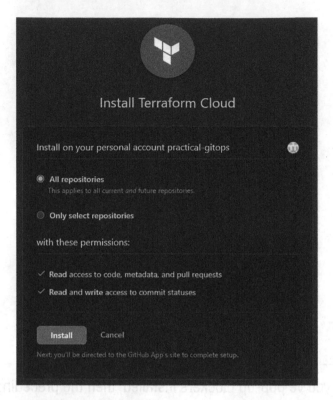

Figure 5-8. Installing Terraform Cloud to the GitHub repository

Since we don't wish to provide access to all our repositories, we'll
follow the following steps:

1. Select radio button **Only select repositories**.

2. Select the repository we just created in the drop-
    down box.

3. Click Install.

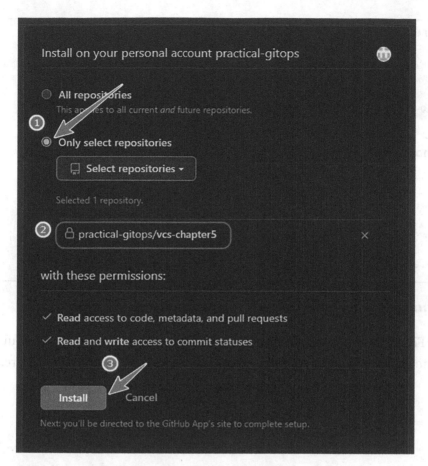

Figure 5-9. *Selecting specific GitHub repository only*

5.2.3 Creating VCS-Driven Workspace

Once the authorization has been completed, you'll be redirected to the Terraform Cloud, and the repository that we had selected will now be shown as follows. Let's click on it to proceed further.

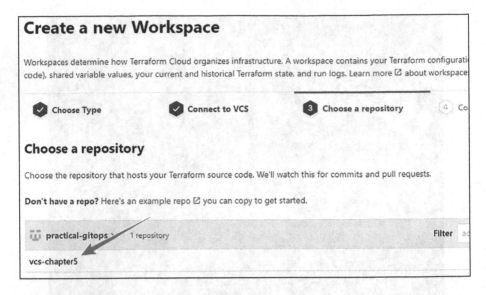

Figure 5-10. *Selecting the GitHub repository connected*

Finally, we'll be on the **Configure Settings** tab where we need to put in some additional configurations. Click **Advanced options** as shown here.

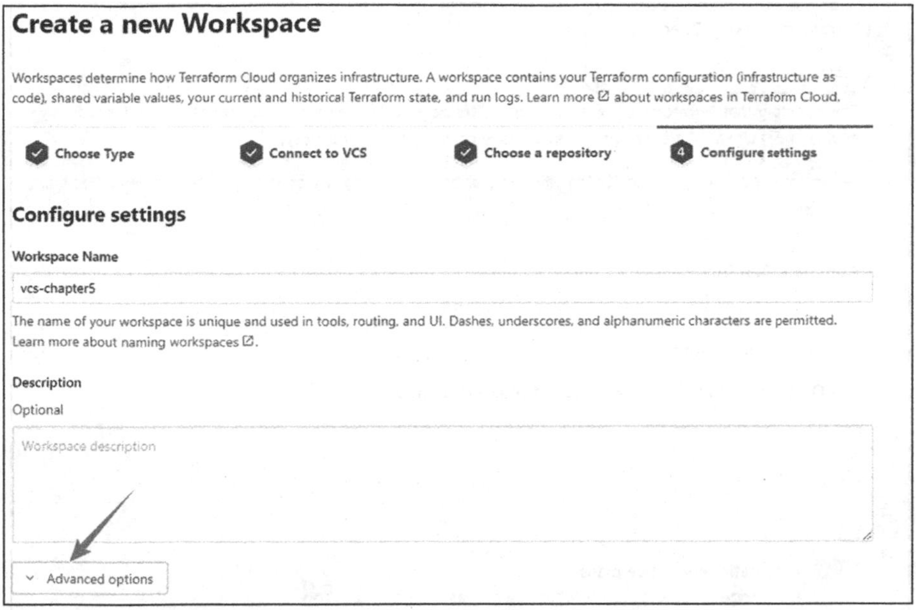

Create a new Workspace

Workspaces determine how Terraform Cloud organizes infrastructure. A workspace contains your Terraform configuration (infrastructure as code), shared variable values, your current and historical Terraform state, and run logs. Learn more ☑ about workspaces in Terraform Cloud.

☑ Choose Type   ☑ Connect to VCS   ☑ Choose a repository   4 Configure settings

Configure settings

Workspace Name

vcs-chapter5

The name of your workspace is unique and used in tools, routing, and UI. Dashes, underscores, and alphanumeric characters are permitted. Learn more about naming workspaces ☑.

Description

Optional

Workspace description

⌄ Advanced options

Figure 5-11. Configuring advanced settings

There is a very important configuration that we need to add, and that is about the working directory as shown here.

1. Enter the name of the **Terraform Working Directory** as **infra**.

2. Click **Create workspace**.

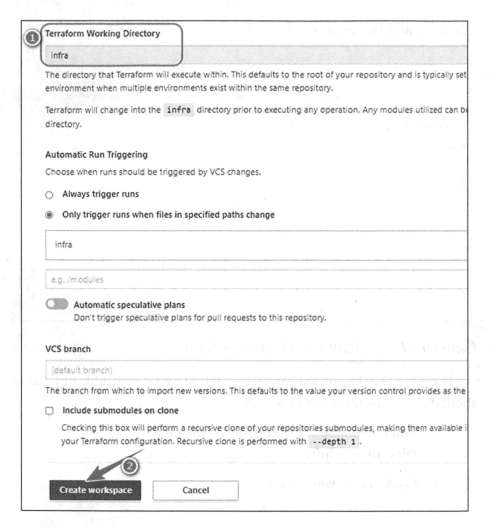

Figure 5-12. *Configuring Terraform Working Directory*

This is a very important configuration because Terraform will be downloading the entire GitHub repository on its own servers. It'll by default run the terraform commands on the root folder, but since there are no ***.tf** files, it'll fail.

Hence, we need to inform Terraform Cloud that all our ***.tf** files are actually in the **infra** folder.

5.2.4 Configuring Environment Variables

Next, we need to configure the variables section as we did in the earlier chapter. The following are the variables that need to be added as shown here:

- Environment variables

  - AWS Access Key ID: *AWS_ACCESS_KEY_ID*

  - AWS Secret Access Key: *AWS_SECRET_ACCESS_KEY*

- Terraform variables

  - Region: *region: us-east-2*

  - Environment: *environment: dev*

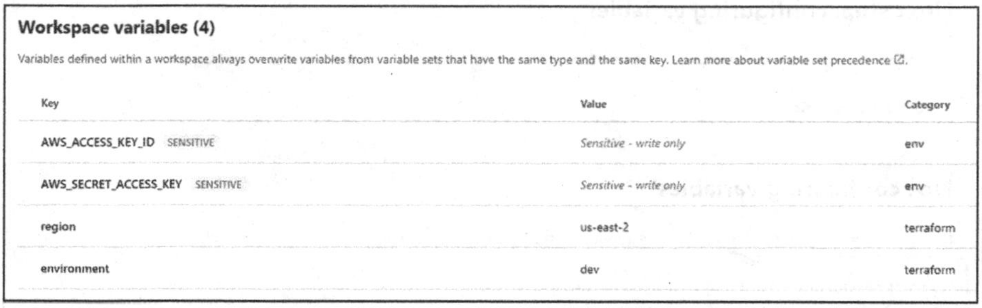

Workspace variables (4)

Variables defined within a workspace always overwrite variables from variable sets that have the same type and the same key. Learn more about variable set precedence ☑.

Key	Value	Category
AWS_ACCESS_KEY_ID SENSITIVE	*Sensitive - write only*	env
AWS_SECRET_ACCESS_KEY SENSITIVE	*Sensitive - write only*	env
region	us-east-2	terraform
environment	dev	terraform

Figure 5-13. *Configuring Terraform and environment variables*

Note   Terraform Cloud UI is constantly changing. The screenshots you'll see are as of Nov 29, 2021.

5.2.5 Executing Plan in Cloud

Now that we've everything configured, let's visit our workspace and start the build. When configuring the VCS with Terraform Cloud for the very first time, we need to trigger the build manually using the **Start new plan** button as shown here.

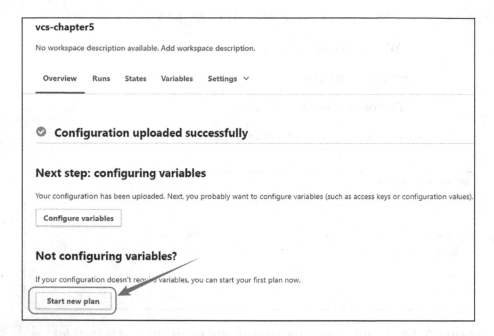

Figure 5-14. *Manually triggering Terraform VCS workflow*

After clicking Start new plan, it'll run ***terraform plan*** and will show what resources are going to be created as shown here.

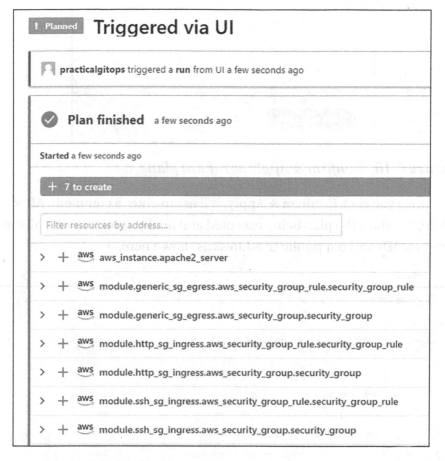

Figure 5-15. *Terraform plan output in Terraform Cloud*

If we scroll down a little, you'll see that the plan is waiting for our confirmation and approval just like how we had in the CLI run. Let's hit **Confirm and Apply**.

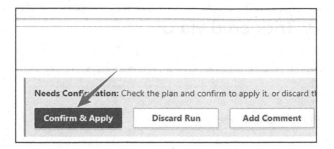

Figure 5-16. *Confirm & Apply terraform plan*

Once you click **Confirm & Apply**, it'll ask to enter a comment. After a while, it'll show the plan being executed and finally complete with all the resource IDs and our public IP address as shown here.

Figure 5-17. *Terraform apply finished*

Accessing the IP publicly lands us on the default Apache2 page as shown here.

Figure 5-18. *Accessing public IP*

5.2.6 Triggering the VCS

What we saw here was a manual trigger that we executed from the Terraform Cloud console. Now let's see how we can trigger it using VCS or GitHub.

So let's say another colleague of yours who has access to this repository wishes to add another EC2 server and wishes to obtain the public IP address of that server. The following are the additions that they have added to our existing code base.

Note   When you access the code under the vcs/infra folder, you'll see that these lines are commented for ease of use. Hence, you just need to uncomment and push the changes to the repository. Uncommented code would look like this as shown here.

Adding a new EC2 named **apache2_server_1**

Code Block 5-2. Adding new EC2

```
File: chapter5/vcs/infra/main.tf

XXXXXXXXXXXXXXX------SNIPPED-------XXXXXXXXXXXXXXXXXXXX

79: }
80:
```

```
81: // Uncomment for Section 5.3.4 - Trigger the VCS
82: resource "aws_instance" "apache2_server_1" {
83:   ami            = data.aws_ami.ubuntu.id
84:   instance_type = var.instance_type
85:   vpc_security_group_ids = [module.http_sg_ingress.sg_id,
86:     module.generic_sg_egress.sg_id,
87:   module.ssh_sg_ingress.sg_id]
88:   key_name  = var.ssh_key_name
89:   user_data = file("./scripts/user_data.sh")
90:   tags = {
91:     env  = var.environment
92:     Name = "ec2-${local.name-suffix}"
93:   }
94:
95:   depends_on = [
96:     module.generic_sg_egress
97:   ]
98: }
```

Adding a new output block as **ip_address_1**

Code Block 5-3. Adding an output block for a new EC2

```
File: chapter5/vcs/infra/output.tf

XXXXXXXXXXXXXXX------SNIPPED-------XXXXXXXXXXXXXXXXXXXXX

6: // Uncomment for Section 5.3.4 - Trigger the VCS
7: output "ip_address_1" {
8:   value = aws_instance.apache2_server_1.public_ip
9: }
```

Let's now push these new changes to our GitHub repository.

CLI Output 5-4. Pushing new EC2 changes to GitHub

```
cmd> git status
On branch main
Your branch is up to date with 'origin/main'.
XXXXXXXXXXXXXXX------SNIPPED-------XXXXXXXXXXXXXXXXXXXXXX

        modified:   infra/main.tf
        modified:   infra/output.tf

no changes added to commit (use "git add" and/or "git
commit -a")

cmd> git add .
cmd> git commit -m "adding a new ec2"
[main c3f37a2] adding a new ec2
 2 files changed, 22 insertions(+)

cmd> git push

XXXXXXXXXXXXXXX------SNIPPED-------XXXXXXXXXXXXXXXXXXXXXX

remote: Resolving deltas: 100% (3/3), completed with 3 local
objects.
To gitops:practical-gitops/vcs-chapter5.git
    3483cdf..c3f37a2  main -> main
```

As soon as our colleague pushed the changes into the GitHub repository, we can see the **terraform plan** getting executed automatically because of the GitHub push trigger.

The name of the trigger is the same as the commit message that we set. We can also observe the name of the new server and the output that we had declared.

Figure 5-19. *New EC2 terraform plan*

Let's confirm and apply the plan, and now we have set up Terraform
in the cloud with state being stored remotely and also leveraging the full
collaboration feature of GitHub. The following screenshot shows that the
new server created by our colleague has been set up and running!

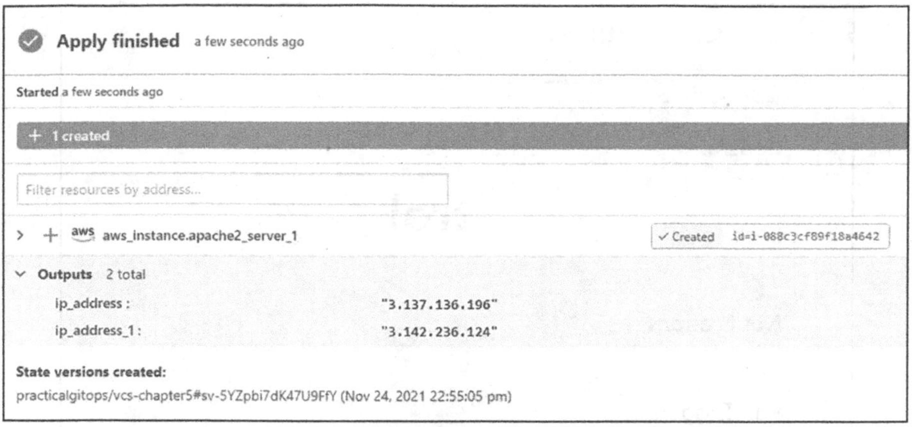

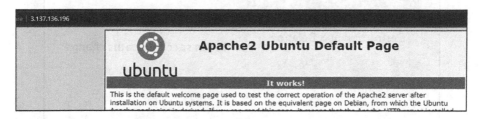

Figure 5-20. *New EC2 terraform apply finished*

The new server is also accessible as the old one!

Figure 5-21. *New EC2 publicly accessible*

We can further fine-tune the collaboration by ensuring that Terraform Cloud triggers deployments only from a specific branch by configuring that branch name as shown here.

1.   Go to Settings.

2.   Click Version Control.

3.   Enter the branch name in the VCS branch field.

Figure 5-22. *Fine-tuning branch settings*

5.2.7 Destroying in Terraform Cloud

The steps to destroy the plan in Terraform Cloud were already discussed in the previous chapter. However, they are repeated in brief here:

1. Click Settings.

2. Click Destruction and Deletion.

3. Click **Queue destroy plan**.

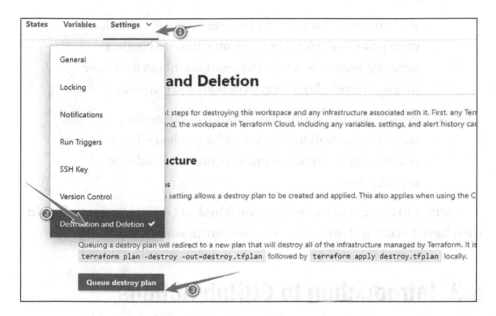

Figure 5-23. *Terraform destroy from Terraform Cloud*

It shall ask for confirmation; please confirm by providing the name of the workspace, and the destroy plan shall be executed.

5.2.8 Drawbacks of Terraform Cloud with VCS

We now have the terraform state stored remotely and also can use Terraform Cloud VCS with GitHub to leverage collaboration with different team members. However, the primary drawback of this approach is that we no longer have control over the entire terraform workflow of init, plan, apply, and destroy. When there is a change in GitHub, it'll trigger the terraform workflow.

Owing to this major limitation

- We cannot perform any linting/testing of the terraform code prior to deployment. We may have to create a separate branch wherein the team members may have to test it locally, but it sort of defeats the purpose.

- We cannot add additional workflows like adding a security guardrail to check if we've not leaked any sensitive information in our commit or introduced a security flaw.

Hence, to overcome these flaws, we'll look at GitHub Actions wherein we'll have full control over the entire Terraform workflow process.

5.3 Introduction to GitHub Actions

5.3.1 CI/CD General Workflow

CI/CD operations are all about workflows that automate a certain set of actions. Tools like Jenkins can help in creating workflows for building, testing, and deploying software artifacts in an automated fashion. A general CI/CD workflow would primarily consist of the following steps:

1. Pull the latest code on a trigger event like a git commit or git push.

2. Build the application or the docker image using whatever build software that application is using.

3. Push the build code to its artifact repository or the docker image to the docker repository.

4. Pull the artifacts or the docker image from their respective repositories and deploy in the staging/ production environment.

5. Run unit tests and security test cases on the deployed environment.

Additional steps would be present depending on the organization and what they wish to automate.

For performing these actions on a CI/CD server like Jenkins, we need to install Jenkins and deploy a Jenkinsfile in our source code. This Jenkinsfile is then read on a trigger event like git commit/push by Jenkins, and it starts the entire workflow like as follows.

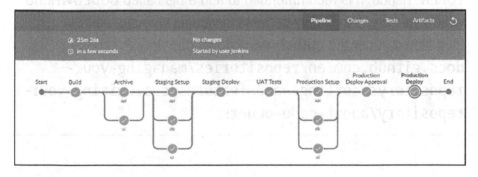

Figure 5-24. *Jenkins stages Reference:* `www.rohitsalecha.com/` `project/practical_devops/img/24.png`

5.3.2 Introduction to GitHub Actions

GitHub Actions is a service provided by GitHub.com to help us achieve a similar workflow as the one created using Jenkins shown previously, without having to install any software or tool. We only need to write a YAML file and keep it in a folder named **.github/workflows.** When an event like commit, push, pull request, etc., is triggered, GitHub would read the YAML file containing all the workflow instructions and start executing those actions, all this without having the headache to install and maintain a full-fledged CI/CD server.

Just like in Jenkins, we have stages and steps that break down the entire process; in GitHub Actions, we have jobs and steps. Each action file must have at least one job, and each job must've at least one step.

Tip   The files under **.github/workflows** will have the potential to execute scripts and even read sensitive information like GITHUB_ TOKEN. Hence, it is recommended to add a file called CODEOWNERS where we can specify only certain individuals who can edit the files stored under the **.github/workflows** directory (`https:// docs.github.com/en/repositories/managing-your- repositorys-settings-and-features/customizing-your- repository/about-code-owners`).

5.3.3 Sample GitHub Actions YAML

Let's look at a sample GitHub workflow YAML file.

Code Block 5-5. Sample GitHub Actions workflow file

File: chapter5/sample_gha.yaml

```
01: name: "Sample GHA Workflow"
02: env:
03:   GLOBAL_VARIABLE: "Can be accessed by all jobs"
04:   API_TOKEN: ${{ secrets.API_TOKEN }}
05:
06: on:
07:   push:
08:     branches:
09:       - main
10:     paths:
11:       - "infra/**"
12:   pull_request:
13:     branches:
14:       - main
15:
16: jobs:
17:   job1:
18:     runs-on: ubuntu-latest
19:     env:
20:       LOCAL_VARIABLE: "This is a Job1 Variable"
21:     defaults:
22:       run:
23:         working-directory: "job1"
24:     steps:
25:       - name: Checkout
26:         uses: actions/checkout@v2
27:
28:       - name: job1_global_variable
29:         run: echo "job1 with $GLOBAL_VARIABLE $API_TOKEN"
30:
31:       - name: job1_local_variable
32:         run: echo "job1 with $LOCAL_VARIABLE"
```

The preceding sample GitHub Actions workflow file can be divided into three main parts.

L1–L4: Declaring the name of the workflow file and environment, secret variables that can be called anywhere throughout the YAML document.

L6–L14: This is the conditions or the triggers under which this workflow will be executed. On a push to the main **branch** *and* on changes of any file in the **infra folder** *or* when a pull request is triggered on the main branch (from any branch), this workflow should be executed.

L16–L32: We are declaring the jobs that need to be executed. Here, we are declaring a job called **job1** for which we are requesting to spin up a temporary Ubuntu (latest) environment. We are declaring an environment variable (LOCAL_VARIABLE) that will be available only to that particular job. We are also declaring a working directory **job1,** which will be the default entry point for executing any scripts.

Each job can have one or more than one step where we specify the commands that we want to execute. The very first step on **L25** is the checkout step where we are fetching the latest code that has been checked in. This code will be stored temporarily in the working directory that has been defined. After that, whatever commands we wish to execute on the latest version of the code, we can specify in the succeeding steps. All steps are executed sequentially by default.

The steps declaration can have either a **run** command or a **uses** attribute.

The checkout step on **L25** is having the **uses** attribute, which is referring to an **action**, which is a predefined reusable template of actions like modules in Terraform.

GitHub Actions has many such predefined actions that can be found in the GitHub Actions Marketplace (`https://github.com/marketplace? type=actions`).

5.3.4 Docker Build Automation with GitHub Actions

Let's take a practical example to better understand GitHub Actions by building and then pushing a Docker image to the DockerHub public repository.

Before we get on with understanding the code, we'll need the following:

– A new repository named **gha-chapter5** or whatever you'd like to name it.

– DockerHub Access Token, which can be generated from the link `https://hub.docker.com/settings/security` once you log into your DockerHub account. Please generate it and store it as a secret in the new GitHub repository as shown here.

– Storing secrets in GitHub:

1. Access Settings of the repository.

2. Click Secrets.

3. Click New repository secret.

   Two secrets need to be stored:

   • DOCKERHUB_USERNAME

   • DOCKERHUB_TOKEN

Figure 5-25. *Configuring GitHub Secrets*

Let's have a look at our GitHub Actions workflow file, which will build and push the docker images to DockerHub.

Code Block 5-6. Workflow file for Docker image deployment

File: chapter5/gha/.github/workflows/app.yaml

```
01: # Github Actions Workflow file that builds and pushes the
    docker images
02: name: practicalgitops.app
03: env:
04:   DOCKERHUB_TAG: "${{ secrets.DOCKERHUB_USERNAME }}/
    practicalgitops"
05:   DOCKERFILE_PATH: app
06:
07: on:
08:   push:
09:     branches:
10:       - main
```

```
11:     paths:
12:       - "app/**"
13:       - "!**/README.md"
14:
15: # Job declaration starts.
16: jobs:
17:   docker:
18:     runs-on: ubuntu-latest
19:     steps:
20:       - name: Check out code
21:         uses: actions/checkout@v2
22:
23:       - name: Set up QEMU
24:         uses: docker/setup-qemu-action@v1
25:
26:       - name: Set up Docker Buildx
27:         uses: docker/setup-buildx-action@v1
28:
29:       - name: Login to DockerHub
30:         uses: docker/login-action@v1
31:         with:
32:           username: ${{ secrets.DOCKERHUB_USERNAME }}
33:           password: ${{ secrets.DOCKERHUB_TOKEN }}
34:
35:       - name: Build and push
36:         id: docker_build
37:         uses: docker/build-push-action@v2
38:         with:
39:           context: "${{ env.DOCKERFILE_PATH }}"
40:           push: true
41:           tags: "${{ env.DOCKERHUB_TAG }}:latest"
```

L1–5: Declaring the workflow name and environment variables that'll be required globally.

L7–16: Trigger this workflow whenever there is a push on the main branch *and* if there are any changes in the **app** folder (the folder containing our source code). Also ignore any changes done to README. md in any of the folders.

L20–27: Check out the latest code and set up the entire docker build environment.

L29–33: Authenticate to DockerHub in order to be able to push the latest images in the next step.

L35–41: Build and push the docker image. Here, we are supplying the context, that is, the folder where Dockerfile is located.

5.3.5 Triggering GitHub Actions

Let's get to action by first pushing our entire code to the new repository, and then we'll trigger the workflow.

CLI Output 5-7. Uploading code to the remote repository for chapter5 gha

```
cmd> cd chapter5/gha
cmd> git init
cmd> git add .
cmd> git commit -m "first commit"
cmd> git branch -m main

# Ensure to add your own repository URL here
cmd> git remote add origin <your_https_or_ssh_url_here>
cmd> git push -u origin main
```

Now that we've committed our code to the repository, let's trigger the workflow by doing a minor edit to one of our HTML template files. Since this file is in the app folder, GitHub will sense a change and trigger the workflow.

Tip You can also manually trigger the workflows from the GitHub GUI by adding the ***workflow_dispatch*** condition as described here: `https://github.blog/changelog/2020-07-06-github-actions-manual-triggers-with-workflow_dispatch/`.

Code Block 5-8. HTML template edit

```
File: chapter5/gha/app/src/main/resources/templates/add-user.html
```

```
13: <body>
14: <div class="container my-5">
15:     <h3> Add Users</h3>
16:     <div class="card">
17:         <div class="card-body">
18:             <div class="col-md-10">
```

Access the file at the **chapter5/gha/app/src/main/resources/templates/add-user.html** location and edit **L15** by changing **Add Users** text to **Add User** or anything you'd like between the <h3> tags as shown previously.

Once this change is done, then simply fire the following commands again to commit the code to trigger the actions.

CLI Output 5-9. Uploading changes of the HTML template to trigger docker workflow

```
cmd> cd chapter5/gha
cmd> git status

On branch main
Your branch is up to date with 'origin/main'.

Changes not staged for commit:
  (use "git add <file>..." to update what will be committed)
  (use "git restore <file>..." to discard changes in working
  directory)
        modified:    app/src/main/resources/templates/add-
        user.html

cmd> git add .
cmd> git commit -m "trigger the workflow"
cmd> git push
```

Once the commit is pushed, visit the Actions tab and observe the workflow being initiated as shown here.

Figure 5-26. *Docker workflow getting triggered*

After a few minutes, you should be able to see our workflow execution being completed as shown here. All our steps are being shown serially.

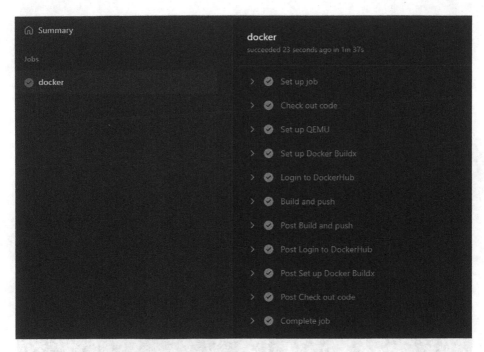

Figure 5-27. *All workflow stages completing execution*

Click on any one step and check out the logs. For example, let's click on the **Build and Push** step to check out the logs.

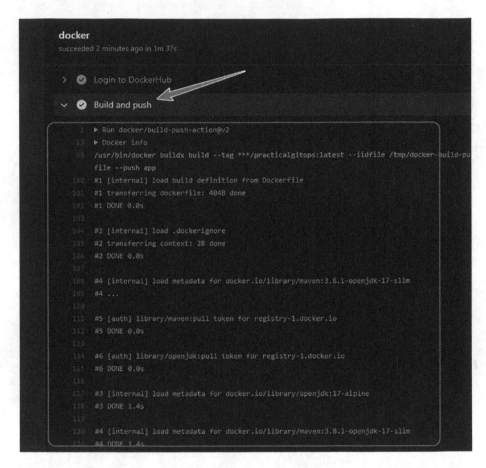

Figure 5-28.   *Logs of the Build and Push step*

By the end of the last step, our docker image is pushed into DockerHub and is accessible to download and run. We'll utilize this image when we deploy our AWS EKS cluster in the upcoming chapters of this book. In my case, the DockerHub image is tagged and accessible as

docker pull salecharohit/practicalgitops

(https://hub.docker.com/r/salecharohit/practicalgitops)

For the purpose of this book, we'll be using the image as default. You are, however, free to use your application image.

5.4 Terraform Automation with GitHub Actions

We saw how we can automate the process of continuously deploying changes to our docker image. In a similar fashion, let's understand how we can facilitate continuous deployment of terraform changes in our **infra** directory.

5.4.1 Code Walkthrough

Let's view the code of the workflow file for terraform automation.

Note   This file will be present in the **chapter5/gha/.github/ workflow** folder but fully commented so as not to disturb the flow of earlier sections. Please uncomment the file for use in this section.

Code Block 5-10. Terraform automation with GitHub Actions

File: chapter5/gha/.github/workflows/infra.yaml

```
01:# Github Actions Workflow file that automates the terraform
    workflow.
02:# UnComment for section 5.4.1 - Terraform Automation with
    Github Actions
03: name: practicalgitops.infra
04:
05: on:
```

```
06:    push:
07:      branches:
08:        - main
09:      paths:
10:        - "infra/**"
11:        - "!**/README.md"
12:
13: jobs:
14:   terraform:
15:     name: "Terraform"
16:     runs-on: ubuntu-latest
17:     defaults:
18:       run:
19:         working-directory: "infra"
20:     steps:
21:       - name: Checkout
22:         uses: actions/checkout@v2
23:
24:       - name: Setup Terraform
25:         uses: hashicorp/setup-terraform@v1
26:         with:
27:           terraform_version: 1.0.0
28:           cli_config_credentials_token: ${{ secrets.TF_API_
                TOKEN }}
29:
30:       - name: Terraform Init
31:         id: init
32:         run: terraform init -backend-config=gha.hcl
33:
34:       - name: Terraform Validate
35:         id: validate
```

```
36:          run: terraform validate -no-color
37:
38:        - name: Terraform Plan
39:          id: plan
40:          run: terraform plan -no-color
41:
42:        - name: Terraform Apply
43:          run: terraform apply
```

L5-11: Is the same as our previous docker automation workflow file other than the folder name. So here, we want to execute this workflow only when there is a change in the terraform code in the infra folder (except README.md files).

L13-19: We are declaring a job called "Terraform" and setting the working directory as **infra**. This means that all the commands/steps will be executed in the **infra** folder where all terraform files are stored.

L21-28: Pulling the latest code and setting up Terraform in the temporary Ubuntu container that we've spun up for the job.

L30-43: Is the general terraform workflow that we are looking to automate by firing all the commands *terraform init* and *terraform validate*

5.4.2 Terraform Login Token

Now that we've understood the code, let's look at how we can deploy this new workflow. For this, there are a couple of changes we need to make and create a new workspace in terraform.

We need to fetch Terraform Token that we'd created in Section 4.4.4. In most cases, the token would be stored in the ~/*.terraform.d/credentials. tfrc.json* file.

Alternatively, you could simply create a new token by visiting https:// app.terraform.io/app/settings/tokens.

We need to store this Terraform Token as a GitHub secret in the gha-chapter5 repository that we'd created as shown here.

TF_API_TOKEN

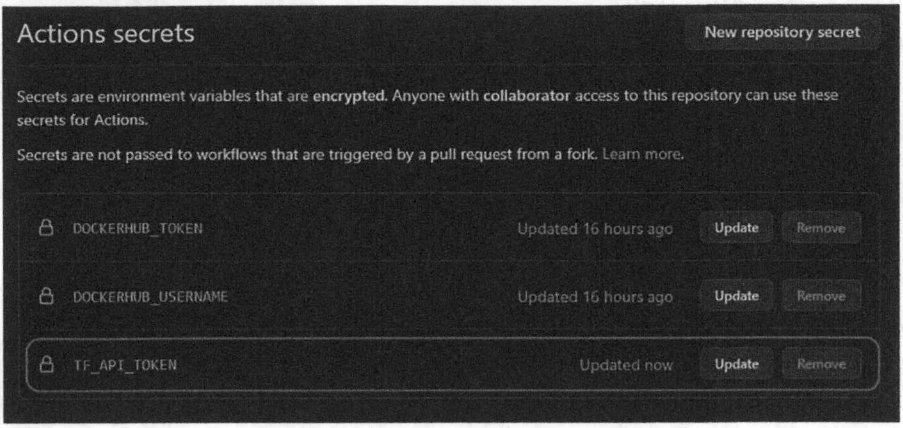

Actions secrets   New repository secret

Secrets are environment variables that are **encrypted**. Anyone with **collaborator** access to this repository can use these secrets for Actions.

Secrets are not passed to workflows that are triggered by a pull request from a fork. Learn more.

🔒 DOCKERHUB_TOKEN   Updated 16 hours ago   Update   Remove

🔒 DOCKERHUB_USERNAME   Updated 16 hours ago   Update   Remove

🔒 TF_API_TOKEN   Updated now   Update   Remove

Figure 5-29. *Configuring Terraform Token as a GitHub secret*

5.4.3 Creating an API-Driven Terraform Workspace

Next, we need to create another terraform workspace but this time, with API-driven workflow as shown here.

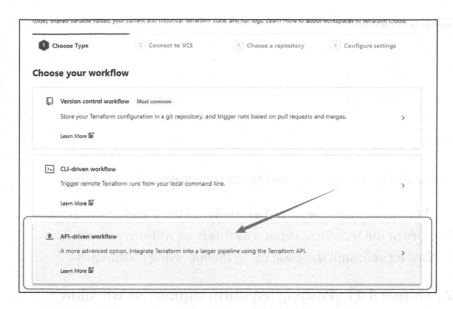

Figure 5-30. *Creating an API-driven terraform workspace*

Next, just like the other workspaces, here too, we need to define the environment terraform variables as shown here:

- – Environment variables

    - – AWS Access Key ID: *AWS_ACCESS_KEY_ID*

    - – AWS Secret Access Key: *AWS_SECRET_ACCESS_KEY*

- – Terraform variables

    - – Region: *region: us-east-2*

    - – Environment: *environment: dev*

Workspace variables (4)		
Variables defined within a workspace always overwrite variables from variable sets that have the same type and the same key. Learn more about variable set precedence ⮺.		
Key	Value	Category
AWS_ACCESS_KEY_ID SENSITIVE	Sensitive - write only	env
AWS_SECRET_ACCESS_KEY SENSITIVE	Sensitive - write only	env
region	us-east-2	terraform
environment	gha	terraform

Figure 5-31. *Terraform workspace environment variables*

That's it! We no longer need to configure the terraform workspace directory or the terraform version as this is an API-driven workflow!

Now let's commit the code using the following commands.

CLI Output 5-11. Pushing terraform automation workflow to remote

```
cmd> cd chapter5/gha
cmd> git status

On branch main
Your branch is up to date with 'origin/main'.

Changes not staged for commit:
  (use "git add <file>..." to update what will be committed)
  (use "git restore <file>..." to discard changes in working
  directory)
        modified:  .github/workflows/infra.yaml

cmd> git add .
cmd> git commit -m "adding infra workflow file"
cmd> git push
```

Once your code is pushed, you won't see any action being executed, but you should be able to see two workflows under the Actions tab as shown here.

Figure 5-32. *Both GitHub Actions workflows showing up on GitHub*

5.4.4 Executing API-Driven Workflow

We now need to provide the name of the workspace that we've created in **gha.hcl** as shown in the following. Ensure to put the complete name as shown here.

Code Block 5-12. Configuring the workspace name

File: chapter5/gha/infra/gha.hcl

```
1: workspaces { name = "gha-chapter5" }
2: hostname     = "app.terraform.io"
3: organization = "practicalgitops"
```

Let's commit and push the code after making the changes to gha.hcl.

CLI Output 5-13. Pushing the workspace configuration file to remote for triggering workflow

```
cmd> cd chapter5/gha
cmd> git status

On branch main
Your branch is up to date with 'origin/main'.

Changes not staged for commit:
  (use "git add <file>..." to update what will be committed)
  (use "git restore <file>..." to discard changes in working
  directory)
        modified:  infra/gha.hcl

cmd> git add .
cmd> git commit -m "adding workspace name"
cmd> git push
```

Once the code is committed, if you navigate to the Actions tab, you should be able to see our new workflow has started as shown here.

Figure 5-33. *Workflow actions triggered*

Click on the workflow, and you should see the execution of all the terraform commands as shown here.

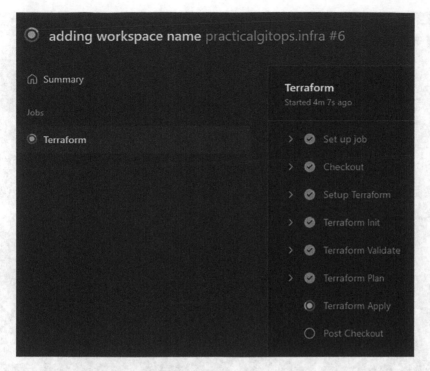

Figure 5-34. *Execution of terraform commands as part of the GitHub workflow*

If you click on the **Terraform Apply** stage, you'll see that the GitHub action execution stage is waiting for our input. However, this input needs to be processed on the Terraform Cloud application.

```
   ∨   ◉   Terraform Apply
227               /
228           + tags_all                = {
228             + "Environment" = "gha"
229           }
230         + vpc_id                   = (known after apply)
231       }
232
233     # module.ssh_sg_ingress.aws_security_group_rule.security_group_rule will be created
234     + resource "aws_security_group_rule" "security_group_rule" {
235         + cidr_blocks              = [
236           + "0.0.0.0/0",
237         ]
238       + from_port                = 22
239       + id                       = (known after apply)
240       + protocol                 = "tcp"
241       + security_group_id        = (known after apply)
242       + self                     = false
243       + source_security_group_id = (known after apply)
244       + to_port                  = 22
245       + type                     = "ingress"
246     }
247
248   Plan: 7 to add, 0 to change, 0 to destroy.
249
250   Changes to Outputs:
251     + ip_address = (known after apply)
252
253   Do you want to perform these actions in workspace "gha-chapter5"?
254     Terraform will perform the actions described above.
255     Only 'yes' will be accepted to approve.
```

Figure 5-35. *Terraform apply stage approval*

We'll need to now visit the app.terraform.io application to confirm the *apply* as shown here.

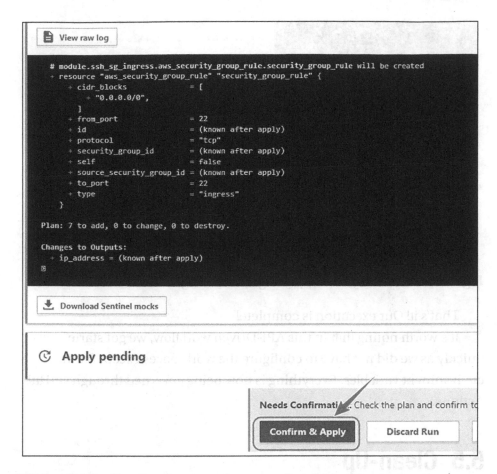

```
View raw log

# module.ssh_sg_ingress.aws_security_group_rule.security_group_rule will be created
+ resource "aws_security_group_rule" "security_group_rule" {
    + cidr_blocks             = [
        + "0.0.0.0/0",
      ]
    + from_port               = 22
    + id                      = (known after apply)
    + protocol                = "tcp"
    + security_group_id       = (known after apply)
    + self                    = false
    + source_security_group_id = (known after apply)
    + to_port                 = 22
    + type                    = "ingress"
  }

Plan: 7 to add, 0 to change, 0 to destroy.

Changes to Outputs:
  + ip_address = (known after apply)
▣
```

```
Download Sentinel mocks
```

🕐 **Apply pending**

Needs Confirmati... Check the plan and confirm t...

Confirm & Apply   **Discard Run**

Figure 5-36. *Confirming terraform apply triggered using Github Actions*

Once **apply** is confirmed, you should be able to see the logs streaming on both ends as shown here.

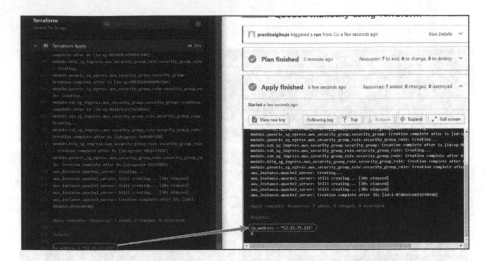

Figure 5-37. *Terraform apply logs streaming on both ends*

That's it! Our execution is complete!

It's worth noting that in this API-Driven workflow, we got started very quickly as we did not have to configure the workspaces except for the environment variables. Everything is now being governed through GitHub Actions.

5.5 Clean-Up

Clean-up for this section should be fairly simple as here we have executed everything from Terraform Cloud. Navigate to **Settings ➤ Destruction and Deletion** of the workspace that we wish to destroy and then click **Queue Destroy Plan.** It'll ask for your confirmation like as follows.

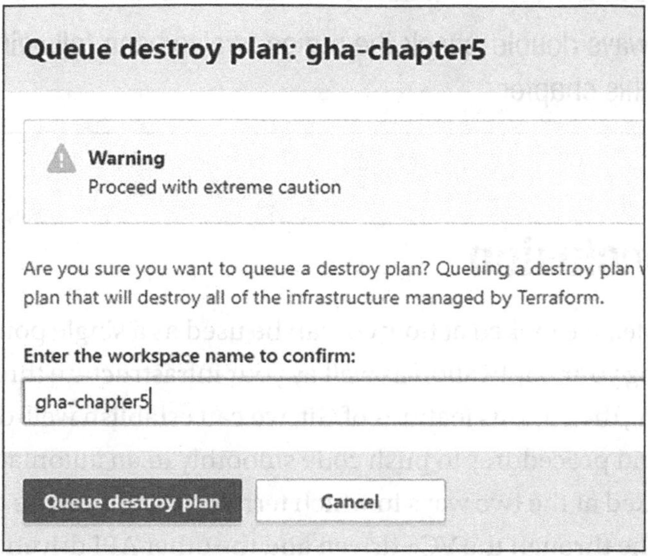

Queue destroy plan: gha-chapter5

⚠️ **Warning**
Proceed with extreme caution

Are you sure you want to queue a destroy plan? Queuing a destroy plan
plan that will destroy all of the infrastructure managed by Terraform.

Enter the workspace name to confirm:

gha-chapter5|

[Queue destroy plan]   [Cancel]

Figure 5-38. *Terraform destroy on cloud confirmation*

Do this for all the workspaces created.

It is also highly recommended that you visit the EC2 console on
the AWS GUI and double-check if everything is deleted. **The Instances
(running) field should show 0.**

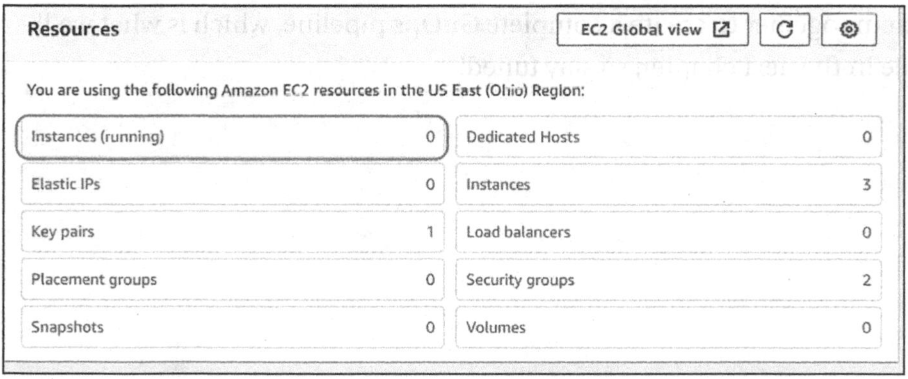

Resources		EC2 Global view 🔗	C	⚙

You are using the following Amazon EC2 resources in the US East (Ohio) Region:

Instances (running)	0	Dedicated Hosts	0
Elastic IPs	0	Instances	3
Key pairs	1	Load balancers	0
Placement groups	0	Security groups	2
Snapshots	0	Volumes	0

Figure 5-39. *EC2 running status*

Note   Always double-check the region; we've been following us-east-2 in this chapter.

5.6 Conclusion

In this chapter, we looked at how Git can be used as a single point of truth for managing your application as well as your infrastructure through code. By leveraging the various features of Git, we can establish well-defined processes and procedures to push code smoothly in an automated fashion. We also looked at the two ways in which terraform code can be deployed using Git: one through the VCS driven and the other API driven. VCS driven is good as long as all the checks and testing are happening at the developers end, which is pretty rare. Hence, API-driven workflow helps in baking in the checks and tests within the GitHub Actions workflow files like *terraform validate, terraform plan,* etc., which gives a greater level of control.

Now that we've learned about Terraform, Terraform Cloud, and GitHub Actions as individual components, it is now time to stitch all of them together to create a complete GitOps pipeline, which is what we'll see in the next chapter, so stay tuned!

CHAPTER 6

Practical GitOps

So far, we looked at Terraform, Terraform Cloud, and GitHub Actions working in tandem. In this chapter, we'll work on establishing a complete workflow involving multiple branches (staging and main) and a peer review process using GitHub Pull Requests. Without this complete workflow, the GitOps process is incomplete as we need to know at every commit what infrastructure changes are happening. We need to review every PR (Pull Request) that clearly describes the ***terraform plan*** to show what changes are being proposed as part of that PR.

We'll be using the same code base as earlier, of creating an EC2 instance on AWS; however, the workflow will be modified a little. We'll be adding some ***if*** conditions within our workflow file to have finer control over the execution of terraform commands.

We'll be first deploying our changes into a staging environment where complete end-to-end testing will be performed. Once the staging environment changes are working as expected, we'll then push the changes into the production environment. This two-stage workflow adds necessary redundancy as infrastructure changes need to be made with caution and speed.

© Rohit Salecha 2023
R. Salecha, *Practical GitOps*, https://doi.org/10.1007/978-1-4842-8673-9_6

6.1 Prerequisites

This chapter requires prerequisites from the previous chapters; however, if you've jumped here directly (assuming you already have a working knowledge of AWS, Terraform, Terraform Cloud, and GitHub Actions), then you'll need the following information handy:

- Git and Terraform installed in your path

- GitHub account

- AWS credentials to set as environment variables in Terraform Cloud workspaces:

  - *AWS_ACCESS_KEY_ID*

  - *AWS_SECRET_ACCESS_KEY*

- Terraform Cloud account and Terraform Cloud Token to be configured as GitHub Secret:

  - TF_API_TOKEN

6.2 Staging Environment Workflow

6.2.1 High-Level Plan

The following diagram will help us in understanding the staging environment workflow.

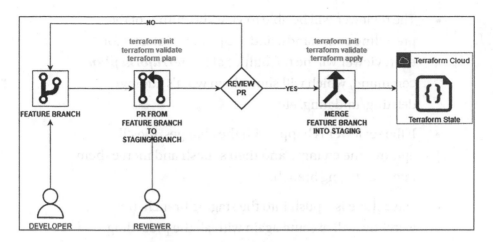

Figure 6-1. *High-level workflow for staging environment*

- The developer forks the existing repository and creates a new branch, let's call it **feature** and then adds some changes to the existing code base.

- After successfully testing the code by running it from their own machine, they check in the changes in the **feature** branch in the remote repository.

- They then create a new Pull Request (PR) to allow merging of the changes into the staging environment and assign a reviewer.

- When they raise the PR, the GitHub Actions workflow will execute three steps:

  - ***terraform init -backend-config=staging.hcl***

  - ***terraform validate***

  - ***terraform plan***

- The reviewer will be able to view the output of the preceding commands, and the primary interest for the reviewer will be the output of the ***terraform plan*** command, which will show them what's adding/deleting/updating, etc.

- If the reviewer is happy with the changes, they'll approve the changes and then squash and merge them into the staging branch.

- Once there is a push into the staging branch, the workflow will execute again with all the preceding three steps but with the addition of one more, that is, ***terraform apply***.

- With this, the changes will then start getting applied in the staging environment in Terraform Cloud.

6.2.2 Code Walkthrough

We'll be reusing the code from the previous chapter with the only difference being in the workflow file and the backend.tf file.

CLI Output 6-1. Directory structure of the workflow folder

```
cmd> cd chapter6/.github/workflows
cmd> tree -a
.
├── app.yaml
├── infra-staging.yaml
└── infra-prod.yaml

0 directories, 3 files
```

In this chapter, we have three workflow files:

- app.yaml – As discussed in the previous chapter, this file orchestrates workflow for application Docker image creation.

- Infra-staging.yaml – This is a modified version of the workflow file that we had created for terraform automation. However, as we'll see later, it's modified specifically for the staging environment.

- Infra-prod.yaml – Same as staging but configured for prod workflow.

Let's look at the *Infra-staging.yaml* file.

Code Block 6-2. L03–27 explanation for infra-staging.yaml

File: code\.github\workflows\infra-staging.yaml

```
01: name: practicalgitops.staging.infra
02:
03: on:
04:    push:
05:       branches:
06:          - staging
07:       paths:
08:          - "infra/**"
09:          - "!**/README.md"
10:    pull_request:
11:       branches:
12:          - staging
13:       paths:
14:          - "infra/**"
15:          - "!**/README.md"
```

```
16:
17: jobs:
18:   terraform:
19:     name: "Terraform"
20:     runs-on: ubuntu-latest
21:     defaults:
22:       run:
23:         working-directory: "infra"
24:     steps:
25:       - name: Checkout
26:         uses: actions/checkout@v2
27:
28:       - name: Uncomment Terraform Cloud Backend
           Configuration file
29:         id: uncomment
30:         run: sed -i 's/^#*//' backend.tf
```

L3-15: The conditions here are scouting for changes in the **infra** directory (except for the README.md file). This file will be triggered by either a push or a pull in the **staging** branch only.

L28-30: The **backend.tf** file, which is used for instructing terraform where to look for the terraform state file, is commented in the source code as shown here.

CLI Output 6-3.   Content of backend.tf commented

```
cmd> cat chapter6/infra/backend.tf

//Donot uncomment this file. This file will be uncommented only
in Github Actions
#terraform {
#   backend "remote" {}
#}
```

Why have I commented this file?

This is required to be commented because as per the high-level plan we discussed earlier, the developer needs to run terraform from their system as well. If we keep the backend.tf configured, then the developer will need to configure their own workspace in Terraform Cloud and maintain the access, which would be an added responsibility on the developers.

Hence, it's best that the developers be provided a separate environment where they can test their terraform code independent of Terraform Cloud.

The following figure depicts the scenario.

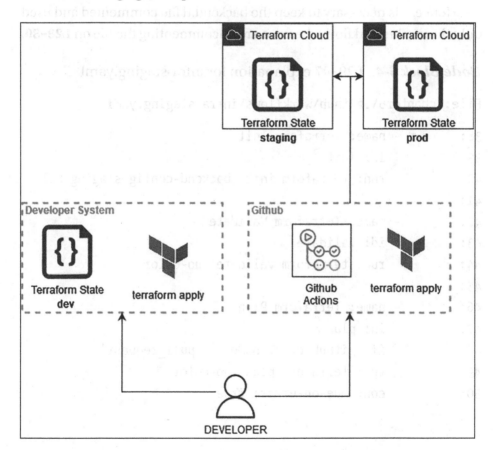

Figure 6-2. *Staging, prod, and dev environments of a developer*

In this scenario, we'll always have the staging and prod environments live, and updates would be continuously pushed between them. The dev environment for the developer will be created and destroyed at will.

There will be a certain level of synergy between the **staging** and **prod** environments with the delta being changes in EC2 configurations (for price sensitivity) and secrets (which we'll learn in a separate chapter in more detail).

As shown earlier in Section 3.7, if we wish to destroy resources in staging and prod environments, we need not run terraform destroy; we can quite simply comment out the code and then run terraform apply.

Hence, it is necessary to keep the backend.tf file commented and used only during the workflow where we are uncommenting the file on **L28–30.**

Code Block 6-4. L29–47 explanation for infra-staging.yaml

File: chapter6\.github\workflows\infra-staging.yaml

```
38:        - name: Terraform Init
39:          id: init
40:          run: terraform init -backend-config=staging.hcl
41:
42:        - name: Terraform Validate
43:          id: validate
44:          run: terraform validate -no-color
45:
46:        - name: Terraform Plan
47:          id: plan
48:          if: github.event_name == 'pull_request'
49:          run: terraform plan -no-color
50:          continue-on-error: true
```

L46–50: We saw previously how *terraform plan* is being executed. However, in this scenario, we wish to run *terraform plan* whenever there is a PR raised for merging code. This is required because the reviewer needs to see what's going to be executed. The entire output is available for the reviewer to understand what are the changes being proposed in this PR.

Code Block 6-5. L49–79 explanation for infra-staging.yaml

File: chapter6\.github\workflows\infra-staging.yaml

```
52:        - name: Terraform Plan Output
53:          uses: actions/github-script@v6
54:          if: github.event_name == 'pull_request'
55:          env:
56:            PLAN: "terraform\n${{ steps.plan.outputs.
                   stdout }}"
57:          with:
58:            github-token: ${{ secrets.GITHUB_TOKEN }}
59:            script: |
60:              const output = `## Terraform Staging
                   Infra Plan
61:
62:              #### Terraform Initialization \`${{ steps.
                   init.outcome }}\`
63:              #### Terraform Validation \`${{ steps.
                   validate.outcome }}\`
64:              #### Terraform Plan \`${{ steps.plan.
                   outcome }}\`
65:
66:              <details><summary>Show Plan</summary>
```

```
67:              ${process.env.PLAN}
68:              </details>
69:
70:              *Pusher: @${{ github.actor }}, Action: \`${{
                 github.event_name }}\`*`;
71:
72:              github.rest.issues.createComment ({
73:                issue_number: context.issue.number,
74:                owner: context.repo.owner,
75:                repo: context.repo.repo,
76:                body: output
77:              })
78:
79:      - name: Terraform Plan Status
80:          if: steps.plan.outcome == 'failure'
81:          run: exit 1
82:
83:      - name: Terraform Apply
84:          if: github.ref == 'refs/heads/staging' && github.
             event_name == 'push'
85:          run: terraform apply
86:
```

L52-77: This is a GitHub Script that we are running wherein we are capturing the output of **Terraform Init**, **Terraform Validate**, and **Terraform Plan**. If you recall, as per our review process, the reviewer needs to be able to see the terraform plan output to get an idea of what is changing in the PR. This script helps in outputting that information in a proper format, which we'll see later. If you still don't understand what's happening, just hold on till we actually see this in action.

L79–81: Since on **L50** we had instructed the workflow to continue execution even in the case our terraform plan is failing, we need to perform a check somewhere.

L83: Here, we are performing terraform apply only when there is a push to the staging branch. This git push could either be through a PR or by directly pushing into the repository. This is where we need to restrict access to the branch/repository so that only approved Pull Requests can be merged into the staging branch. Whenever an approved Pull Request is merged, there'll be a push to the staging branch, and our terraform apply will hence be executed.

The *Infra-prod.yaml* file is an exact replica of the preceding file with the only difference being that all operations are configured to work on the **main** branch rather than the **staging** branch.

6.2.3 Set Up Terraform Staging Workspace

Although we've set up a terraform workspace multiple times by now and you would be quite familiar with it, we'll still repeat the steps one last time.

Visit the Terraform Cloud application and click on New Workspace. Then select API-driven workspace as shown below.

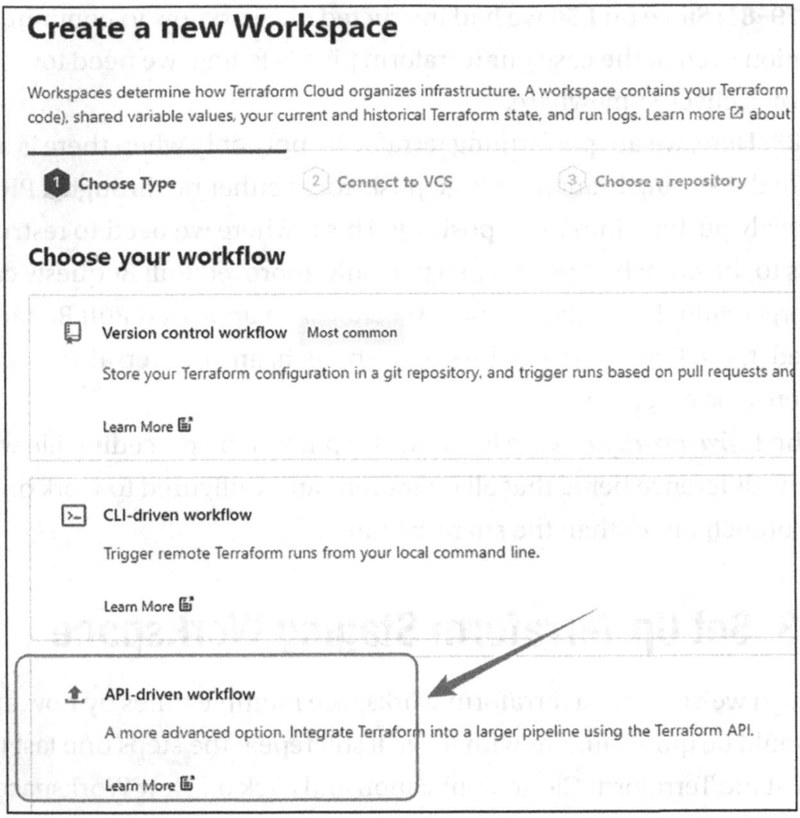

Figure 6-3. *Creating an API-driven workspace*

Configure the name as staging. Once the workspace is created, visit the variables tab and configure the following variables as shown:

- Environment variables

    - AWS Access Key ID: *AWS_ACCESS_KEY_ID*

    - AWS Secret Access Key: *AWS_SECRET_ACCESS_KEY*

- Terraform variables

    - Region: *region: us-east-2*

    - Environment: *environment: staging*

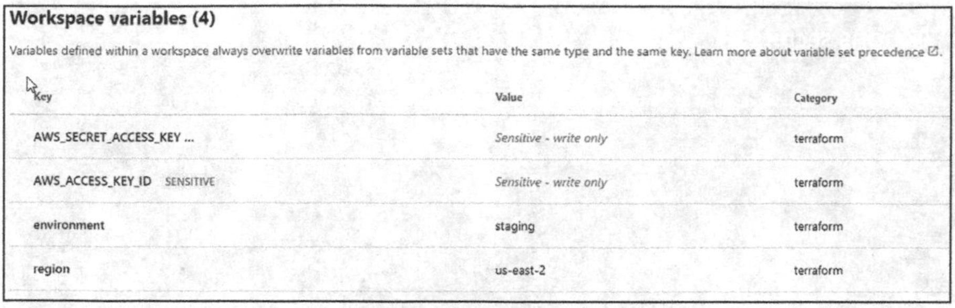

Workspace variables (4)		
Variables defined within a workspace always overwrite variables from variable sets that have the same type and the same key. Learn more about variable set precedence ⬚.		
Key	Value	Category
AWS_SECRET_ACCESS_KEY ...	Sensitive - write only	terraform
AWS_ACCESS_KEY_ID SENSITIVE	Sensitive - write only	terraform
environment	staging	terraform
region	us-east-2	terraform

Figure 6-4. *Configuring workspace variables*

Note   If you ever get a terraform version–related error, you can modify the version in Settings ➤ General and select the appropriate terraform version, preferably 1.0.0 as the code is compatible with this version at the time of writing this book.

6.2.4 Set Up a GitHub Repository

Now that our terraform workspace is configured, let's set up a new GitHub repository where all the GitHub actions will be executed.

Create a new GitHub repository with an appropriate name and configure the following secrets:

– TF_API_TOKEN (mandatory)

– DOCKERHUB_TOKEN (optional)

– DOCKERHUB_USERNAME (optional)

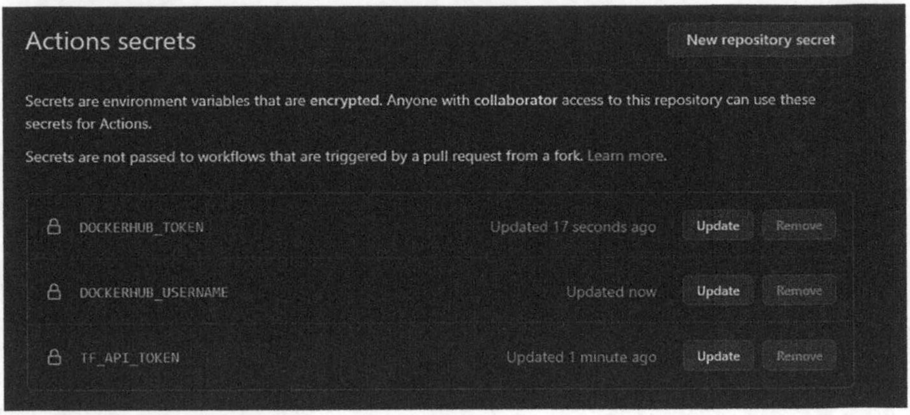

Figure 6-5. *GitHub Secrets configuration*

Note   We at present do not require the DockerHub credentials as we won't be modifying the Docker images any further. Hence, I've kept it optional throughout the book.

Let's upload our code into the main branch of the repository using the following commands.

Ensure you have the correct GitHub repository URL.

CLI Output 6-6. Uploading the code of Chapter 6 to GitHub

```
cmd> git init
cmd> git add .
cmd> git commit -m "first commit"
cmd> git branch -M main
cmd> git remote add origin <github-url>
cmd> git push -u origin main
```

You should be able to see the three actions being configured as part of our repository as shown here.

Figure 6-6. *All actions related to our repository*

6.2.5 Executing Staging Workflow

Let's configure the name of the Terraform Cloud workspace in the staging. hcl file as shown here.

Code Block 6-7. Workspace name configuration

File: chapter6\infra\staging.hcl

```
1: workspaces { name = "staging" }
2: hostname     = "app.terraform.io"
3: organization = "practicalgitops"
```

Now in order to execute our workflow, we'll need to create a **staging** branch and push the changes in that branch. Follow the following commands, which will execute the entire process.

235

CLI Output 6-8. Pushing code into the staging branch

```
cmd> git status
On branch main
Your branch is up to date with 'origin/main'.

Changes not staged for commit:
  (use "git add <file>..." to update what will be committed)
  (use "git restore <file>..." to discard changes in working
  directory)
        modified:   infra/staging.hcl

no changes added to commit (use "git add" and/or "git
commit -a")
cmd> git checkout -b staging
Switched to a new branch 'staging'
cmd(staging)> git add .
cmd(staging)> git commit -m "executing workflow"
[staging 0eec509] executing workflow
 1 file changed, 1 insertion(+), 1 deletion(-)
cmd(staging)> git push origin staging
Enumerating objects: 7, done.

XXXXXXXXXXXXXXX------SNIPPED-------XXXXXXXXXXXXXXXXXXXXX

To github.com:practical-gitops/chapter6.git
 * [new branch]      staging -> staging
```

As soon as we push our changes into the git repository, a new branch called **staging** is created, and the **practicalgitops.staging.infra** workflow is executed as shown here.

Figure 6-7. *Staging branch workflow executing*

The workflow will run through all the stages except **terraform plan,** as we've configured it to run only during Pull Requests as shown here.

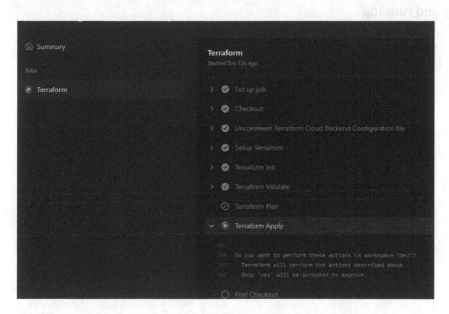

Figure 6-8. *Terraform apply for staging branch workflow*

As can be seen from the preceding screenshot, the workflow has paused its execution and is waiting for our approval on Terraform Cloud as shown here.

Figure 6-9. *Staging branch workflow waiting for approval on Terraform Cloud*

Let's go ahead and approve the plan so that our **staging** environment is up and running.

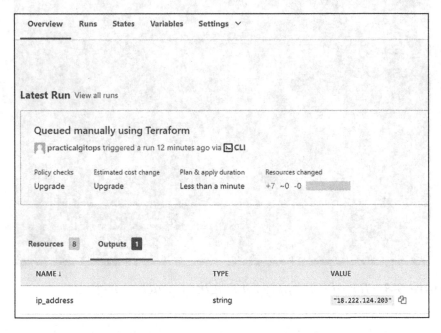

Figure 6-10. *Staging branch workflow after terraform apply*

If you would like to disable the manual approval process in Terraform Cloud and allow the plan to execute once approved in GitHub, then you can visit Settings ➤ General and scroll down to the **Apply Method** section shown in the following where you can select the **Auto apply** check box and save. By default, the **Manual apply** setting is configured.

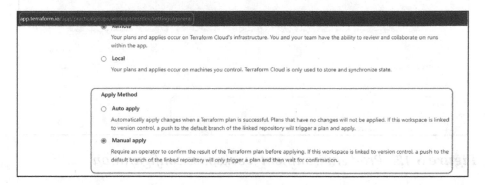

Figure 6-11. *Disabling manual apply in terraform workspace configuration*

6.3 Prod Environment Workflow

Now that our staging environment is up and running and everything looks good, let's go ahead and set up our production environment as well.

We'll need a separate prod terraform workspace, which can be set up using the same instructions as discussed in the previous section. The only difference that will be needed is that we'll need a separate set of keys and a separate region for deployment.

So I've created a new terraform workspace called prod and configured the necessary environment variables as shown in the following. My prod environment will run in the **us-east-1** region.

Figure 6-12. *Prod environment workspace configuration*

6.3.1 SSH Key-Pair Generation

Before we go ahead and execute our prod workflow, there is one tiny step that we need to perform on the AWS Console. We've configured our EC2 instance with a key pair with name **gitops** as discussed in Section 2.3.7. However, that key pair was created in the **us-east-2** region, and here, we are spinning up the server in the **us-east-1** region where this key pair is not available.

Hence, we need to create this one manually using the steps outlined in the following.

Note   Going forward, we may not require to have an SSH key as we'll be spinning up an EKS cluster and not any EC2 machine.

Execute the following commands, which will generate the new AWS key pair and also save it to your disk.

CLI Output 6-9. AWS SSH key-pair generation

```
cmd> export AWS_PROFILE=gitops
cmd> aws --region us-east-1 ec2 create-key-pair \
    --key-name "gitops" \
    --query 'KeyMaterial' > gitops.pem
cmd> ls -al gitops.pem
-rw-r--r-- 1 ubuntu ubuntu 1707 Dec  2 17:55 gitops.pem
```

Now let's go ahead and execute our prod workflow for which we'll need to first edit the prod.hcl as shown in the following with the name of the workspace created for the prod environment.

Code Block 6-10. Prod workspace backend configuration

```
File: chapter6\infra\prod.hcl

1: workspaces { name = "prod" }
2: hostname     = "app.terraform.io"
3: organization = "practicalgitops"
```

CLI Output 6-11. Checking-in prod.hcl for prod workflow trigger

```
cmd(staging)> git checkout main
cmd> git status

On branch main
Your branch is up to date with 'origin/main'.

Changes not staged for commit:
  (use "git add <file>..." to update what will be committed)
  (use "git restore <file>..." to discard changes in working
  directory)
        modified:   infra/prod.hcl
```

```
no changes added to commit (use "git add" and/or "git
commit -a")
```

```
cmd> git add .
cmd> git commit -m "executing prod workflow"
cmd> git push origin main
```

Once the code is checked in, our prod workflow will get kickstarted as shown here.

Figure 6-13. *Prod workflow being triggered*

Just like the staging workflow, here too, the process is awaiting our approval on Terraform Cloud. Let's confirm the execution on Terraform Cloud and allow the ***terraform apply*** to build the prod environment.

So now we have our staging as well as our prod environment up and running with two servers in two different regions (and/or two different AWS accounts).

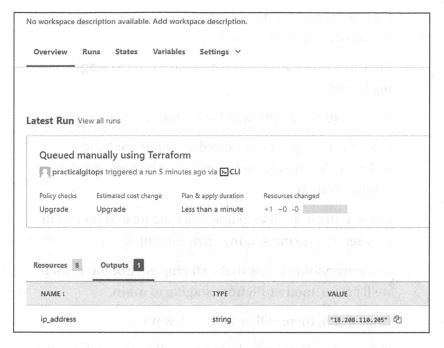

Figure 6-14. Prod workspace apply completed

6.4 Complete Workflow

Now that we are having a server live on the Internet, one of our colleagues wishes to add one more. They'll need to follow the following process:

– Clone the repository and switch to the **staging** branch.

– Make their changes.

– Test the changes by running terraform from their local machine in a **dev** environment that is completely isolated from the **staging** and **prod** environments.

– Create another branch; let's call it **feature1** branch.

– Commit all the changes into the **feature1** branch.

- Push the changes into the remote repository/**feature1** branch.

- Create a Pull Request from the feature1 to the **staging** branch.

- Assign a reviewer and wait for approval.

- Once the changes are reviewed and approved, the reviewer shall merge and squash the changes into the **staging** branch.

- Our **staging** branch workflow will execute and set up our new server into the **staging** environment.

- Once everything is fine in the **staging** environment, then we'll create another PR from **staging** to **main**.

- Once again, there will be a PR review process.

- Once review is approved, changes will be merged into the **main** branch, and our prod execution flow will be triggered.

The following diagram is a depiction of the entire process described previously.

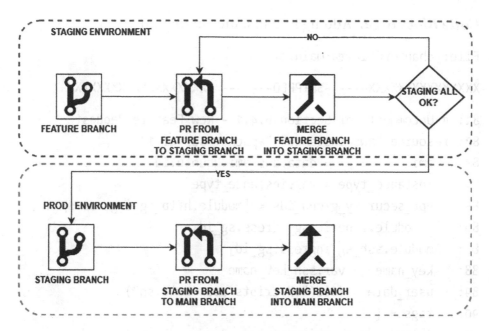

Figure 6-15. *Complete workflow diagram*

6.4.1 New Feature Request

Let's practically experience the workflow described previously. Let's say one of our colleagues wishes to set up another server. They'll first need to add the following code in the main.tf file and the output.tf file as shown in the following.

Note   For simplicity's sake, I've already added that code in both files in a commented format. You've only got to uncomment it. Standard drill :-).

245

Code Block 6-12. Adding EC2 instance in main.tf

File: chapter6\infra\main.tf

XXXXXXXXXXXXXX------SNIPPED-------XXXXXXXXXXXXXXXXXXXXXX

```
81: # Uncomment for Section 6.4.1 - New Feature Request
82: resource "aws_instance" "apache2_server_1" {
83:    ami            = data.aws_ami.ubuntu.id
84:    instance_type = var.instance_type
85:    vpc_security_group_ids = [module.http_sg_ingress.sg_id,
86:      module.generic_sg_egress.sg_id,
87:    module.ssh_sg_ingress.sg_id]
88:    key_name  = var.ssh_key_name
89:    user_data = file("./scripts/user_data.sh")
90:    tags = {
91:      env  = var.environment
92:      Name = "ec2-${local.name-suffix}"
93:    }
94:
95:    depends_on = [
96:      module.generic_sg_egress
97:    ]
98: }
```

Code Block 6-13. Adding output configuration in output.tf

File: chapter6\infra\output.tf

XXXXXXXXXXXXXX------SNIPPED-------XXXXXXXXXXXXXXXXXXXXXX

```
6: # Uncomment for Section 6.4.1 - New Feature Request
7: output "ip_address_1" {
8:   value = aws_instance.apache2_server_1.public_ip
9: }
```

6.4.2 Developer Testing

Now before we check in the code, let's first run it on our system and ensure that the code we are pushing in is running correctly.

One small change that you'll observe when running the terraform commands is that this time, terraform will ask for region and environment as these two variables were hard-coded in our terraform workspace and we've not specified the value of these variables anywhere in our code base. Hence, there are two ways we can provide this information:

1. When we execute *terraform apply*, it'll ask for this information interactively.

2. We can specify it as a CLI argument for *terraform apply*.

I don't prefer interactive interfaces; hence, I'll go ahead with option 2, that is, to specify it as CLI arguments.

Note   Ensure that you are not specifying the same value as staging or prod, else there'll be conflicts. In practice, a new AWS organization should be created for testing purposes to ensure proper isolation.

The following commands will set up a dev environment in the **us-west-1** region. Since we do not have an SSH key in that region, we first need to create one. It is strongly recommended to have a separate key per region/account.

CLI Output 6-14. Testing environment set up for local terraform execution

```
cmd> export AWS_PROFILE=gitops
cmd> aws --region us-west-1 ec2 create-key-pair \
    --key-name "gitops" \
```

```
     --query 'KeyMaterial' > gitops_dev.pem
cmd> terraform init
cmd> terraform plan -var="environment=dev"
-var="region=us-west-1"
cmd> terraform apply --auto-approve \
     -var="environment=dev" -var="region=us-west-1"

aws_instance.apache2_server: Creating...
aws_instance.apache2_server_1: Creating...

XXXXXXXXXXXXXXX------SNIPPED-------XXXXXXXXXXXXXXXXXXXXX
Apply complete! Resources: 2 added, 0 changed, 0 destroyed.

Outputs:

ip_address = "13.57.212.113"
ip_address_1 = "54.183.78.83"

cmd> terraform destroy --auto-approve \
     -var="environment=dev" -var="region=us-west-1"
```

Note   Ensure to execute the destroy command before moving ahead as you'll be billed for two EC2 instances.

6.4.3 Create Pull Request – Dev

Now that our code is running fine and it created two servers as expected, let's go ahead and create another branch **feature1** and check in these changes in it. Then push the changes to the remote repository using the following commands.

CLI Output 6-15. Pushing changes into the feature1 branch

```
cmd> git status
On branch main
Your branch is up to date with 'origin/main'.

Changes not staged for commit:
  (use "git add <file>..." to update what will be committed)
  (use "git restore <file>..." to discard changes in working
  directory)
        modified:    infra/main.tf
        modified:    infra/output.tf

no changes added to commit (use "git add" and/or "git
commit -a")

cmd> git checkout -b feature1
cmd(feature1)> git add .
cmdfeature1> git commit -m "new ec2 added"
cmdfeature1> git push origin feature1
```

Let's visit our GitHub repository online and create a Pull Request by clicking on the tab as shown.

Figure 6-16. *Clicking the Pull requests tab*

Click **New pull request** as shown here.

Figure 6-17. *Clicking New pull request*

Now we need to select the branches that we need to merge as part of this Pull Request as shown here.

1. Select the base branch as **staging**.

2. Select the compare branch as **feature1**.

3. Add an appropriate comment and click **Create pull request**.

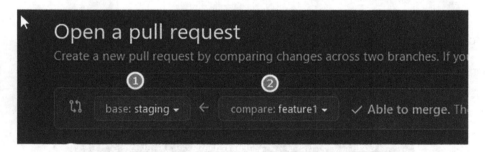

Figure 6-18. *Creating a Pull Request between staging and feature1 branches*

Next is a very important step as we need to inform the team what this Pull Request is all about.

1. Provide a descriptive title.

2. Add comments describing what is changing in this Pull Request.

3. Click **Create pull request**.

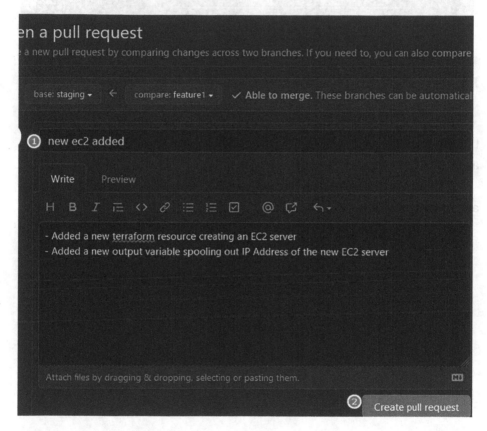

Figure 6-19. Pull Request comments

As soon as the Pull Request is created, our GitHub action gets executed as shown here.

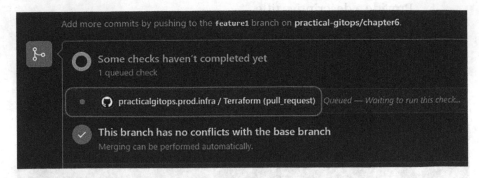

Figure 6-20. *GitHub Actions triggered after Pull Request*

Finally, once the GitHub action execution is complete, you should see the output of the GitHub Script as shown in the following where it shows all our stages.

Terraform Initialization, **Terraform Validation**, and **Terraform Plan** are successfully completed.

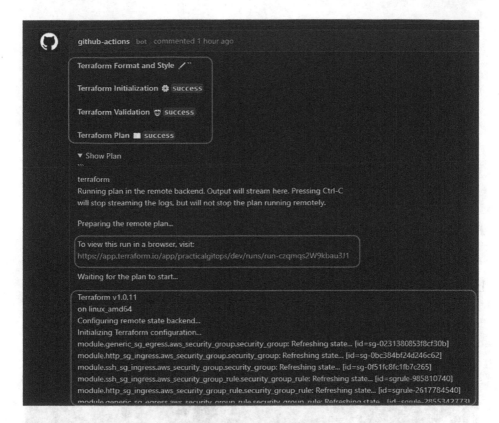

Figure 6-21. Terraform init, validate, and plan review screen

As you scroll down, you should be able to see the entire plan as shown here.

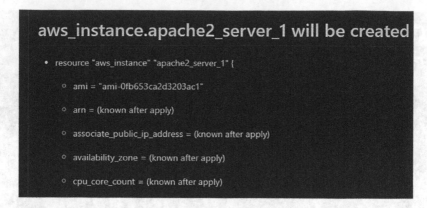

Figure 6-22. Viewing the part of terraform plan

If everything is fine, then we can go ahead and merge the Pull Request by clicking on the **Merge pull request** button as shown here.

Figure 6-23. Clicking Merge pull request

Once the PR is merged, navigate to the Actions tab and you'll see GitHub Actions executing the merge request. This time, the workflow will perform **terraform apply**.

Figure 6-24. *GitHub actions triggered upon merging Pull Requests*

If you navigate to the Terraform Cloud application's staging workspace, you should see that our plan is awaiting our approval.

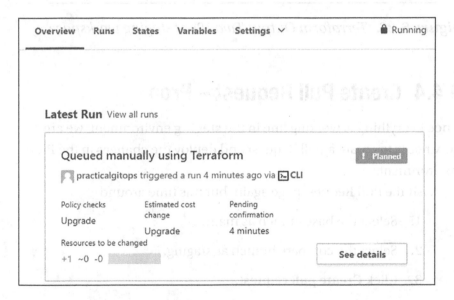

Figure 6-25. *Terraform Cloud staging workspace awaiting approval*

Let's go ahead and apply the plan. After a few minutes, you can see in the output section, it should show two IP addresses.

Latest Run View all runs

Queued manually using Terraform

practicalgitops triggered a run 8 minutes ago via ▶CLI

Policy checks	Estimated cost change	Plan & apply duration	Resources changed
Upgrade	Upgrade	Less than a minute	+1 ~0 -0

Resources 9   Outputs 2   Curr

NAME ↓	TYPE	VALUE
ip_address	string	"18.222.124.203"
ip_address_1	string	"52.14.252.128"

Figure 6-26. *Terraform Output Two IPs of staging workspace*

6.4.4 Create Pull Request – Prod

Once everything is working fine in the **staging** environment, we are
now ready to create a Pull Request and deploy the changes in the Prod
environment.

Visit the Pull Request page again, but this time around

1. Select the base branch as main.

2. Select the compare branch as staging.

3. Click **Create pull request**.

Figure 6-27. *Creating a Pull Request between main and staging
branches*

Exactly the same procedure can be followed while creating the PR, and as shown in the following, our GitHub Actions will be executed again as there is a Pull Request received on the main branch. Hence, our **practicalgitops.prod.infra** workflow is now being executed as shown here.

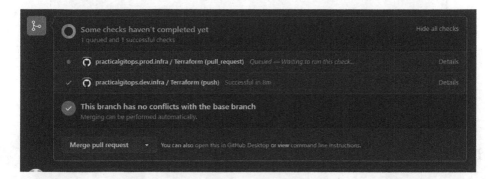

Figure 6-28. *GitHub Action being executed on the prod branch after PR*

Let's confirm and merge the Pull Request after merging our next GitHub action in execution to perform terraform apply just like the previous steps.

If we now navigate to our Terraform Cloud application, we can see our ***terraform apply*** is waiting for approval.

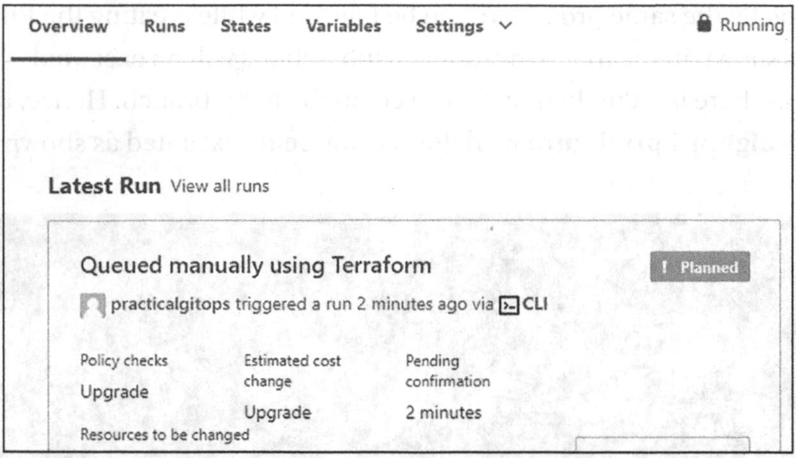

| Overview | Runs | States | Variables | Settings ∨ | 🔒 Running |

Latest Run View all runs

Queued manually using Terraform | Planned

practicalgitops triggered a run 2 minutes ago via >_ CLI

Policy checks	Estimated cost	Pending
Upgrade	change	confirmation
	Upgrade	2 minutes
Resources to be changed		

Figure 6-29. *Prod workspace planned for terraform apply*

Let's go ahead and confirm the **terraform apply**, and in a few minutes, we'll have our changes pushed in the prod environment as shown here.

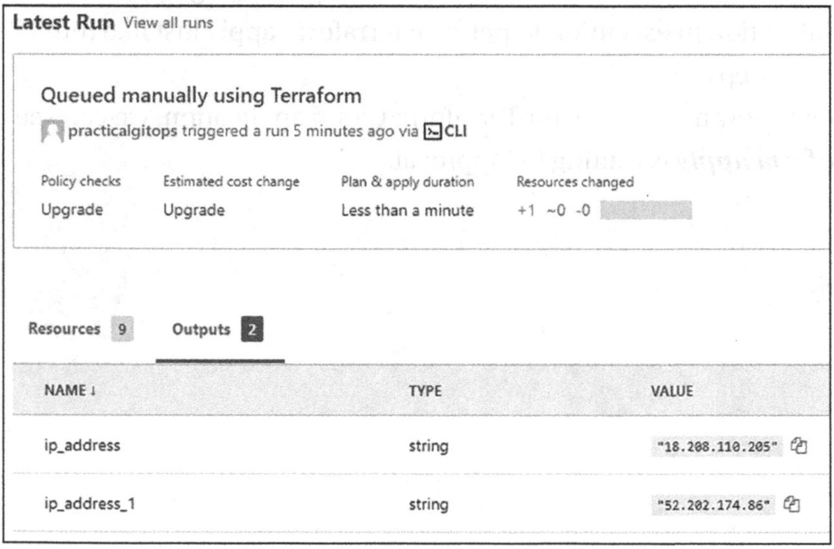

Latest Run View all runs

Queued manually using Terraform

practicalgitops triggered a run 5 minutes ago via >_ CLI

| Policy checks | Estimated cost change | Plan & apply duration | Resources changed |
| Upgrade | Upgrade | Less than a minute | +1 ~0 -0 |

Resources 9   Outputs 2

NAME ↓	TYPE	VALUE
ip_address	string	"18.208.110.205" 📋
ip_address_1	string	"52.202.174.86" 📋

Figure 6-30. *Prod environment up and running*

We now have two EC2 servers deployed in two different regions (and environments) through the GitOps pipeline that we've created!

6.5 Clean-Up

Clean-up for this section should be fairly simple as here we have executed everything from Terraform Cloud. Navigate to **Settings ➤ Destruction and Deletion** of the workspace that we wish to destroy and then click **Queue destroy plan.** It'll ask for your confirmation like as follows.

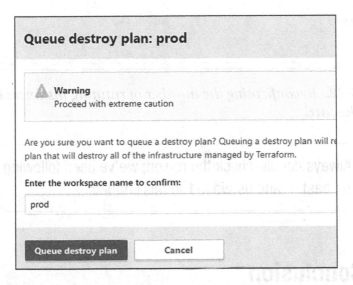

Figure 6-31. *Destroying resources in the prod environment*

Please perform the same for staging as well.

Note   Do not delete the staging and prod workspaces created in this chapter as we'll be reusing them in the upcoming chapters. However, ensure you delete the resources by applying the destroy plan discussed previously.

It is also highly recommended that you visit the EC2 console on the AWS GUI and double-check if everything is deleted. **The Instances (running) field should show 0 for all regions.**

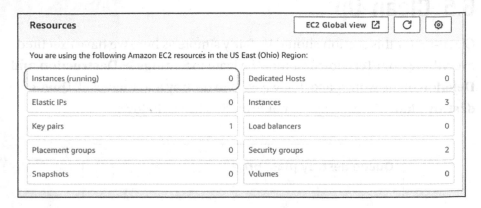

Figure 6-32. *Reconfirming the number of running instances in the EC2 dashboard*

Note   Always double-check the region; we've been following us-east-2, us-east-1, and us-west-1 in this chapter.

6.6 Conclusion

In this chapter, we looked at how an end-to-end GitOps workflow can be orchestrated using GitHub SCM and GitHub Actions with a multi-environment strategy. This workflow makes it easy to audit and control the changes that are being pushed into our AWS infrastructure. This workflow is also quite extensible as we'll see in the later chapters, where we can add various different checks like security and validation checks in an automated fashion.

The customized output of terraform plan provides a good insight for reviewers to be able to make proper decisions.

With this, we've completed the first part (i.e., Part A) of this book where I wanted to practically demonstrate the GitOps process and the different tools and techniques that can be used to facilitate it.

In Part B of this book, we'll use this process and implement it for a practical application built using the Spring Boot technology and run it in an AWS EKS environment, communicate with an AWS RDS Postgres server, and utilize a combination of an AWS Load Balancer and AWS Route53 to expose the application to the outside world. All the AWS technologies, that is, AWS EKS, RDS, Route53, and the Load Balancer, will be created using Terraform, managed in Terraform Cloud, and orchestrated through GitHub Actions. We'll look at different aspects of managing this complex infrastructure like Authentication, Authorization, Secrets Management, Security Tooling, and Operations all in all through our GitOps process that we've completed till now.

CHAPTER 7

Spring Boot App on AWS EKS

In this chapter, we'll look at the architecture and code of the deployment of a working application developed in Spring Boot. We saw the process of building and pushing the docker image of the application using GitHub Actions in the previous chapter. Now we'll use that docker image in a Kubernetes deployment and deploy a complete AWS EKS (Elastic Kubernetes Service) and PostgreSQL RDS using Terraform.

7.1 Prerequisites

From here onward, we'll be utilizing the same setup for all the upcoming chapters; hence, in addition to all the previous requirements, we'll need the following:

- A top-level domain/subdomain name – This is very important as most operations depend on it. I'll be discussing how you can configure the same.

- kubectl utility – kubectl is the default utility to talk with the Kubernetes service that we'll be spinning up using Terraform. Recommended to have version 1.20 or above. As of the writing of the book, my kubectl version is 1.23.6:

    - https://kubernetes.io/docs/tasks/tools/

© Rohit Salecha 2023

R. Salecha, *Practical GitOps*, https://doi.org/10.1007/978-1-4842-8673-9_7

7.1.1 GitHub Repository

From now onward, we'll utilize a single GitHub repository for the rest of the book. Hence, it is important to create a folder in the root directory wherever you've unzipped the repository.

I'll name the folder **pgitops**, and for every chapter, we'll copy the code from the respective folder into this folder and initialize the GitHub repository from here itself. Name of this folder and repository is arbitrary. The following commands will help you in the *nix system; however, feel free to use any GUI software for overwriting the files if CLI doesn't work for you.

CLI Output 7-1. Copying code into a single directory

```
cmd> mkdir pgitops
cmd> cp -a chapter7/. pgitops/
cmd> cd pgitops
# Ensure the copy command worked as expected by executing
tree command
cmd> tree -L 2
.
├── README.md
├── app
│   ├── Dockerfile
│   ├── README.md
│   ├── docker-compose.yaml
│   ├── pom.xml
│   ├── src
│   └── target
└── infra
    ├── README.md
    ├── app.tf
```

```
├── backend.tf
├── dns.tf
├── eks.tf
├── kubernetes.tf
├── modules
├── networking.tf
├── prod.hcl
├── providers.tf
├── rds.tf
├── staging.hcl
├── terraform.auto.tfvars
└── variables.tf
```

5 directories, 18 files

Let's now create a GitHub repository and upload our code in it. I've created a repo called **pgitops**, and using the following commands, I've uploaded the code into the GitHub repository.

CLI Output 7-2. Pushing code into a new repo

```
cmd> git init
cmd> git add .
cmd> git commit -m "first commit"
cmd> git branch -M main
cmd> git remote add origin git@github.com:<username>/
pgitops.git
cmd> git push -u origin main
```

You can verify that the code has been pushed by visiting the GitHub repository on the browser. Also open the Actions tab to view that our actions are now ready for deployment.

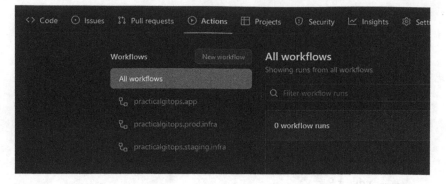

Figure 7-1. *Verifying that code is pushed to GitHub*

Next, we need to add the Terraform Token that was discussed in the previous chapters, which the GitHub Actions utilize to execute the Terraform API in the TF cloud.

The following image highlights the steps that can be utilized to configure TF_API_TOKEN as a secret.

1. Access the Settings page of your repository.

2. Click Secrets ➤ Actions.

3. Add TF_API_TOKEN as the Name and the value of the token.

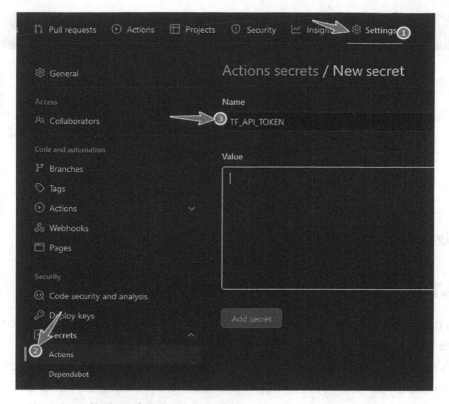

Figure 7-2. Adding TF_API_TOKEN

Terraform Cloud Workspace

We'll be reusing the prod and staging Terraform Cloud workspaces (API driven) created in Chapter 5.

The only small change that we need to make is to remove manual approval required every time Terraform is triggered because now we are controlling everything from our GitHub.

This can be easily configured by visiting **Settings ➤ General Settings ➤ Execution Mode ➤ Auto Apply** as shown here.

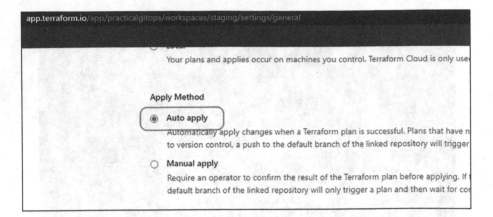

Figure 7-3. *Switching to Auto apply*

7.1.2 DNS Configuration

In order to fully understand the potential or any cloud technology and for the best experience, it's worthwhile to play around with domain names. It's strongly recommended that you get one if you don't have one and put it to use if you have it. I shall hence consider two possibilities, either of which is fine to follow for the remainder of this book. I shall explain both possibilities as follows.

Route53 is a service provided by AWS to help us manage our DNS records. Traditionally, DNS records are managed through a file called "Zone" files, and Route53 makes use of what are called "Hosted Zones," which are a container of DNS records on similar lines of the traditional zone files. Whenever a DNS Hosted Zone is created, AWS provides a set of nameserver records (four records), which need to be configured in your root domain. The way these records will be configured is different depending on your choice of configuring a domain name or a subdomain name, which we'll discuss next.

Note   It doesn't matter from where you've purchased your DNS domain or where you are currently maintaining your DNS records to follow ahead. The only thing that is expected is that you've got the ability to update the DNS records at your current hosting provider in order to follow the following steps. For example, I had purchased my domain rohitsalecha.com from GoDaddy.com; however, I am currently hosting my domain on AWS Route53, which is chargeable and not included in the free tier. In order to do that, I had to update the default nameserver records in GoDaddy with the ones provided by AWS (after configuring my hosted zone in AWS Route53).

As discussed earlier, there are primarily two ways in which we can configure our Route53 Hosted Zones: either as a top-level domain or as a subdomain.

Top-Level Domain

If you wish to configure a top-level domain name for deploying our application, then fire the following command, replacing **rohitsalecha.com** with your domain name.

CLI Output 7-3. AWS Route53 Hosted Zone for TLD

```
cmd> export AWS_PROFILE=gitops
cmd> aws route53 create-hosted-zone --name rohitsalecha.com
--caller-reference 2022-05-15-22:35

{
XXXXXXXXXXXXXXXX------SNIPPED-------XXXXXXXXXXXXXXXXXXXXXX
    "DelegationSet": {
        "NameServers": [
            "ns-849.awsdns-42.net",
```

```
            "ns-290.awsdns-36.com",
            "ns-1129.awsdns-13.org",
            "ns-1713.awsdns-22.co.uk"
        ]
    }
}
```

The command output provides four different nameserver values that need to be configured with your DNS provider by overriding their current values. You'll need to refer to your hosting/DNS provider documentation to be able to do the same.

For example, if you have GoDaddy as your DNS provider, then follow this guide: `https://in.godaddy.com/help/change-nameservers-for-my-domains-664`.

Note If you've done for top-level domain, *do not* repeat this for subdomain.

Subdomain

If you already own a top-level domain and wish to utilize a subdomain only, then you fire the following command and replace your subdomain with **gitops.rohitsalecha.com.**

CLI Output 7-4. AWS Route53 Hosted Zone for subdomain

```
cmd> export AWS_PROFILE=gitops
cmd> aws route53 create-hosted-zone --name gitops.rohitsalecha.
com --caller-reference 2022-05-15-24:35

{
XXXXXXXXXXXXXXX------SNIPPED-------XXXXXXXXXXXXXXXXXXXXXX
```

```
    "DelegationSet": {
    "NameServers": [
        "ns-537.awsdns-03.net",
        "ns-449.awsdns-56.com",
        "ns-1848.awsdns-39.co.uk",
        "ns-1415.awsdns-48.org"
    ]
    }
}
```

The command will output a set of nameservers, which you need to add as a record just like how you would add any other record in your DNS zone. You'll need to refer to the documentation of your DNS service provider on how to perform the same.

For example, in GoDaddy, this is how you can add an NS as a record: https://in.godaddy.com/help/add-an-ns-record-19212.

Note   Both the preceding techniques have different implications; for top-level domain, we are modifying the primary nameserver records, whereas for subdomain, we are only adding a nameserver record against the subdomain. This adding of nameservers as a record in your DNS zone is also called subdomain delegation. Effectively we are delegating the subdomain to another provider. An important point to note here is that not all DNS providers support this.

Delete Route53 Records

While we are doing things manually here, in the next chapter, we are going to use Terraform to create hosted zones for us. If you've configured your subdomain/top-level domain as per your requirement, then you skip the following step.

If in case you'd like to change your mind, that is, if you've created a top-level domain as a hosted zone record and wish to move to a subdomain hosted zone or vice versa, then simply fire the following commands to delete your hosted zone record.

CLI Output 7-5. Listing and deleting Route53 Hosted Zones

```
# List Hosted Zones configured in the account
cmd> export AWS_PROFILE=gitops
cmd> aws route53 list-hosted-zones

{
      "HostedZones": [
          {
            "Id": "/hostedzone/Z0239613358THNF4E3XP9",
            "Name": "gitops.rohitsalecha.com.",
            "CallerReference": "2022-02-20-24:35",
            "Config": {
            "PrivateZone": false
            },
            "ResourceRecordSetCount": 2
          }
      ]
}

# Delete the Hosted Zone record
cmd> aws route53 delete-hosted-zone --id Z0239613358THNF4E3XP9

{
      "ChangeInfo": {
      "Id": "/change/C025940016DSY04M1XJ6W",
      "Status": "PENDING",
      "SubmittedAt": "2022-05-19T17:12:25.570000+00:00"
      }
}
```

Warning   Before moving ahead, ensure that you have your Route53 records configured either as a subdomain or as a top-level domain.

7.2 Solution Architecture

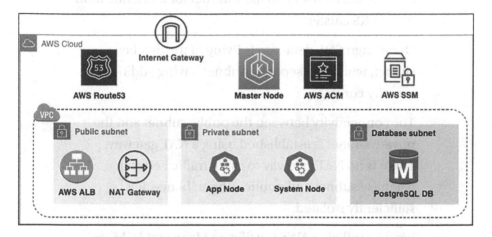

Figure 7-4. *High-level solution architecture*

Note   Only main components are displayed here. Representation of many other small components has been skipped for simplicity.

The preceding diagram shows a high-level architecture of the solution that we'll be building. Other than Route53, rest assured everything will be set up using Terraform in this chapter. A brief description follows:

-   We'll be creating a VPC with three subnets, namely, public, private, and database.

-   Public subnet will have resources that need to be externally facing like the AWS Application Load Balancer, which will be spun up as an ingress controller.

- Our Kubernetes Nodes (managed by us) will be spun up in the private subnet and will not be accessible from the Internet.

- The master node of Kubernetes is completely managed by AWS, and hence, we have no control over its placement. However, the Kubernetes API endpoint will be available over 443 on the Internet for authentication to the EKS cluster.

- Our PostgreSQL database is living in the database subnet, which is a separate subnet having additional security controls.

- The connectivity between the public subnet and the private subnet is established using a NAT gateway. There is no NAT gateway to route traffic between database subnet and public subnet; hence, it is sufficiently isolated.

- We'll be utilizing AWS Certificate Manager (ACM) to generate the public SSL certificates for our application. Our Terraform code will not only generate the certificates but also validate the certificates by creating necessary Route53 name records.

Let's dive into the **infra** folder where all our terraform code resides, and let's try to have an approximate mapping of the different files with the preceding solution architecture that we are building.

CLI Output 7-6. Contents of the infra folder

```
cmd> cd infra
cmd> tree -L 1
.
```

```
├── README.md
├── app.tf
├── backend.tf
├── dns.tf
├── eks.tf
├── kubernetes.tf
├── modules
├── networking.tf
├── prod.hcl
├── providers.tf
├── rds.tf
├── staging.hcl
├── terraform.auto.tfvars
└── variables.tf

1 directory, 13 files
```

- app.tf – Defines Kubernetes deployments, services, and ingresses that are required to be deployed in the EKS environment.

- dns.tf – DNS configurations and Load Balancer mapping required.

- eks.tf – Declaring our master and worker nodes that are needed to set up the entire Kubernetes environment.

- kubernetes.tf – This is a Kubernetes provider file that needs to be maintained separately and provides configuration information on how Terraform can authenticate to Kubernetes to deploy Kubernetes resources like pods, services, etc.

- modules – Consists of reusable components for the infrastructure.

- networking.tf – Defines the creation of VPC and Security Groups necessary for deploying EKS and RDS.

- rds.tf – Creates the PostgreSQL database and the necessary secrets.

7.3 Networking

Let's first run through how the network plumbing is happening using Terraform. The following diagram gives a glimpse of what we are setting up using Terraform from a network perspective.

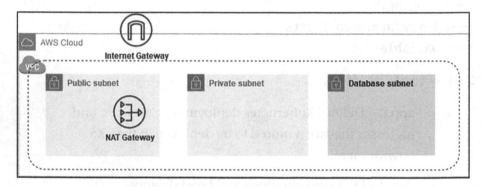

Figure 7-5. *High-level network architecture*

Note   I've captured only the primary components for simplicity. There are many other components like the NACLs (Network Access Control Lists), Route Tables, Security Groups, etc., which are not shown here but are created in our Terraform code.

So the code defined in the *pgitops\infra\networking.tf* creates the following:

- A VPC with a CIDR range of 10.0.0.0/16.

- An Internet gateway to route traffic to the Internet.

- A public subnet with a NAT gateway to route all Internet ingress/egress traffic.

- A private subnet wherein resources can access the Internet through the NAT gateway but not vice versa; that is, nobody can access the resources defined in the private subnet from the Internet.

- A database subnet where we can optionally restrict access to only within the VPC.

All the code related to networking can be found in the *networking.tf* file as follows.

Code Block 7-7. Contents of the networking.tf file

File: pgitops\infra\networking.tf

```
XXXXXXXXXXXXXXX------SNIPPED-------XXXXXXXXXXXXXXXXXXXX
28: module "clustername" {
29:   source = "./modules/clustername"
30:
31:   environment = var.environment
32:   region      = var.region
33:   org_name    = var.org_name
34: }
35:
```

```
36: # Create a VPC with all the associated network plumbing
37: module "networking" {
38:    source = "./modules/vpc"
39:
40:    clustername           = module.clustername.cluster_name
41:    environment          = var.environment
42:    vpc_cidr              = var.vpc_cidr
43:    public_subnets_cidr   = var.public_subnets_cidr
44:    private_subnets_cidr  = var.private_subnets_cidr
45:    database_subnets_cidr = var.database_subnets_cidr
46:    region                = var.region
47:    availability_zones   = data.aws_availability_zones.
                                availability_zones.names
48:
49:    depends_on = [module.clustername]
50: }
```

XXXXXXXXXXXXXXX------SNIPPED-------XXXXXXXXXXXXXXXXXXXXX

L28–34: Here, we are creating a simple string that helps differentiate uniquely the environment, the region, and the name of the organization running this terraform code. For example, if for *gitops* organization we are deploying in us-east-1 in the staging environment, then we can have the clustername as *gitops-us-east-1-staging*. This string can be used to concatenate with various resources for better identification.

L37–50: Defining the entire VPC requirements by providing the environment, CIDR block for the VPC, and public, private, and database subnets. Region and the availability zones in which this VPC should be deployed. The values of the variables being passed are all set in *terraform. auto.tfvars* files. This file holds the values of all variables that can be changed depending on the environment which we wish to deploy.

7.3.1 Network Module

Let's dive into the module/vpc folder and take a look at the implementation of the networking module that was discussed previously.

Code Block 7-8. Contents of the VPC module

File: pgitops\infra\modules\vpc\main.tf

```
01: # Create a VPC
02: module "vpc" {
03:     source  = "terraform-aws-modules/vpc/aws"
04:     version = "3.12.0"
05:
06:     name                        = "${var.clustername}-vpc"
07:     cidr                        = var.vpc_cidr
08:     enable_dns_hostnames        = true
09:     enable_dns_support          = true
10:     enable_nat_gateway          = true
11:     single_nat_gateway          = true
12:     enable_vpn_gateway          = var.enable_vpn_gateway
13:     azs                         = var.availability_zones
14:     private_subnets             = var.private_subnets_cidr
15:     public_subnets              = var.public_subnets_cidr
16:     database_subnets            = var.database_subnets_cidr
17:     create_database_subnet_group = true
```

L3: Terraform maintains a registry of modules developed and maintained by folks at HashiCorp and can be accessed at https:// registry.terraform.io/providers/hashicorp/aws/latest. These modules can be easily integrated into our code by supplying the expected input values and are developed with best practices. We'll be making extensive use of two such modules developed by Terraform internally:

VPC Module – `https://registry.terraform.io/modules/terraform-aws-modules/vpc/aws/latest`

EKS Module – `https://registry.terraform.io/modules/terraform-aws-modules/eks/aws/latest`

RDS Module – `https://registry.terraform.io/modules/terraform-aws-modules/rds/aws/latest`

It's strongly recommended to use these modules as a best practice. As you'll see, I've created quite a lot of modules that are simple to follow and reusable for our current requirements.

Note   Before updating the versions of these modules, ensure to read through the corresponding release notes on GitHub as there can be breaking changes. Hence, for this book, I've frozen the versions of the VPC and EKS modules as can be seen in the code.

7.3.2 Network Tags

AWS EKS internally uses tags attached to resources to perform discovery; hence, it's very important to add the correct tags for operational reasons.

Code Block 7-9. Tags attached to VPC

```
File: pgitops\infra\modules\vpc\main.tf

XXXXXXXXXXXXXXXX------SNIPPED-------XXXXXXXXXXXXXXXXXXXXX

18:
19:    tags = {
20:      "kubernetes.io/cluster/${var.clustername}" = "shared"
21:      "Name"                                      = "${var.
                                                         cluster
                                                         name}-vpc"
```

```
22:     "Environment"                          = var.
        environment
23:     terraform-managed                      = "true"
24:   }
25:
26:   public_subnet_tags = {
27:     "kubernetes.io/cluster/${var.clustername}" = "shared"
28:     "kubernetes.io/role/elb"                   = "1"
29:   }
30:
31:   private_subnet_tags = {
32:     "kubernetes.io/cluster/${var.clustername}" = "shared"
33:     "kubernetes.io/role/internal-elb"          = "1"
34:   }
35: }
```

L19-34: While working with EKS, it is mandatory to add a tag as *kubernetes.io/cluster/$cluster_name* is used for networking discovery and management by AWS internally. Similarly, when creating Load Balancers in addition to this tag, we are required to add *kubernetes.io/role/elb* for external facing and *kubernetes.io/role/internal-elb* for internal Application Load Balancers. We'll understand a bit more about the relation of this tag with load balancers in Section 7.7.

In addition to the preceding tags, I've added a few optional tags like *environment* and *terraform-managed* for better understanding of the resource placement and ownership. Both these tags will appear in all resources that are created through Terraform. This is important as when your infrastructure grows, there may arise situations where you need to manually create/update/delete infrastructure. In such situations, it becomes easier to understand which infrastructure was created manually and which was created through Terraform.

Reference: https://docs.aws.amazon.com/eks/latest/userguide/alb-ingress.html

7.3.3 Security Groups

In addition to the preceding network configuration in the *pgitops\infra\ networking.tf,* we've also specified two security groups as shown here.

Code Block 7-10. Security Groups that need to be attached

File: pgitops\infra\networking.tf

XXXXXXXXXXXXXX------SNIPPED-------XXXXXXXXXXXXXXXXXXXX

```
52: # PGSQL Ingress Security Group Module
53: module "pgsql_sg_ingress" {
54:   source = "./modules/securitygroup"
55:
56:   sg_name        = "pgsql_sg_ingress"
57:   sg_description = "Allow Port 5432 from within the VPC"
58:   environment    = var.environment
59:   vpc_id         = module.networking.vpc_id
60:   type           = "ingress"
61:   from_port      = 5432
62:   to_port        = 5432
63:   protocol       = "tcp"
64:   cidr_blocks    = [var.vpc_cidr]
65:
66:   depends_on = [module.networking]
67: }
68:
69: # Generic Egress Security Group Module
70: module "generic_sg_egress" {
71:   source = "./modules/securitygroup"
72:
73:   sg_name         = "generic_sg_egress"
```

```
74:    sg_description = "Allow servers to connect to outbound
       internet"
75:    environment   = var.environment
76:    vpc_id        = module.networking.vpc_id
77:    type          = "egress"
78:    from_port     = 0
79:    to_port       = 65535
80:    protocol      = "tcp"
81:    cidr_blocks   = ["0.0.0.0/0"]
82:
83:    depends_on = [module.networking]
84: }
```

L53-67: The first security group is created to allow all communication within the VPC with the 5432 database port. This is a very open configuration and can be limited to a specific CIDR, which we'll see in the later chapters.

L70-84: This is a generic security group that allows outbound access to any resource it is attached to.

7.4 Database

Our application needs a database to store the data recorded by the users. In this section, we will learn about how we can set up a PostgreSQL database using the AWS RDS offering.

Reference: https://aws.amazon.com/rds/postgresql/

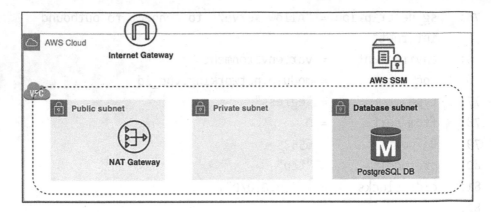

Figure 7-6. *PostgreSQL using AWS RDS*

The preceding diagram shows the implementation of the code defined in the *pgitops\infra\rds.tf,* which is specifying the following:

- A standalone PostgreSQL database with configurable versions, size, family, storage, etc., in the database subnet that was created earlier in the networking section.

- The module generates a 16-digit random password for the database and is stored in the AWS SSM store.

- The database connection URL is also stored in the AWS SSM store.

7.4.1 Database Module

Let's look at the *infra/rds.tf* file to better understand how our database has been set up.

Code Block 7-11. Defining the RDS database in Terraform

File: pgitops\infra\rds.tf

```
XXXXXXXXXXXXXXXX------SNIPPED-------XXXXXXXXXXXXXXXXXXXXXXX
39: module "pgsql" {
40:
41:    source  = "terraform-aws-modules/rds/aws"
42:    version = "4.2.0"
43:
44:    identifier                      = "${module.clustername.
                                           cluster_name}-pgsql"
45:    engine                          = var.db_engine
46:    engine_version                  = var.db_engine_version
47:    family                          = var.db_engine_family
48:    major_engine_version            = var.db_major_
                                           engine_version
52:    storage_encrypted               = true
53:    db_name                         = var.db_name
54:    username                        = var.db_user_name
55:    create_random_password          = true
56:    random_password_length          = 16
61:    vpc_security_group_ids          = [module.pgsql_sg_
                                           ingress.id]
70:    parameters = [
71:      {
72:        name  = "client_encoding"
73:        value = "utf8"
74:      }
75:    ]
84: }
```

Note   I've omitted some fields and focused only on the important ones for brevity.

L41–42: We are informing terraform to load the module from the official terraform registry with a fixed version.

L44: Declaring the identifier with the clustername format as discussed earlier.

L45–48: Specifying the details about the PostgreSQL database, its version, engine, family, etc.

L55–56: Generating the random password with a length of 16 characters.

L61: Referring to the security group we created in the *networking.tf* file for PostgreSQL database connectivity. It is necessary to specify the security group here in order to facilitate database connectivity.

L70–75: Specifying the database configuration parameters.

7.4.2 Database Configuration and Secrets

It is critically important to avoid storage of sensitive information like database passwords, which is what we'll understand next to avoid storing credentials in static files. The following code shows how we can retrieve the password from terraform configuration and store it in an AWS SSM Parameter Store as a SecureString.

Code Block 7-12. Storing DB Creds in AWS SSM

```
File: pgitops\infra\rds.tf

XXXXXXXXXXXXXXXX------SNIPPED-------XXXXXXXXXXXXXXXXXXXXX

086: # Write the DB random password in SSM
087: module "ssmw-db-password" {
```

```
088:    source                  = "./modules/ssmw"
089:    parameter_name          = "db_password"
090:    parameter_path          = "/${var.org_name}/database"
091:    parameter_value         = module.pgsql.db_instance_
                                  password
092:    parameter_description = "DB Password"
093:    clustername             = module.clustername.cluster_name
094:    parameter_type          = "SecureString"
095:    environment             = var.environment
096: }
097:
098: # Write the DB end point URL in SSM
099: module "ssmw-db-endpoint" {
100:    source = "./modules/ssmw"
101:
102:    parameter_name          = "db_endpoint_url"
103:    parameter_path          = "/${var.org_name}/database"
104:    parameter_value         = module.pgsql.db_instance_address
105:    parameter_description = "Endpoint URL of postgresql"
106:    clustername             = module.clustername.cluster_name
107:    parameter_type          = "String"
108:    environment             = var.environment
109: }
```

XXXXXXXXXXXXXXX------SNIPPED-------XXXXXXXXXXXXXXXXXXXXX

L87-96: We are extracting the random password created in the database module referred to as *module.pgsql.db_instance_password* and writing it as a SecureString SSM parameter at the path "$org_name/ database/db_password". SecureString holds the data in an encrypted format using the default AWS KMS key. We can, however, specify our own KMS generated key to store the data, enhancing the security.

> **Note**   Though we are encrypting the string in AWS SSM store, the value of the password is still stored in the Terraform state file in clear-text format. Anyone having access to the state file can derive the password quite easily. Hence, as a defense-in-depth measure, it is necessary to restrict access to state files. We can, however, avoid this by first creating the password manually in the AWS SSM store. In Chapter 9, we shall explore how we can use AWS Secret Manager to store the password.

L99–109: Similar to storing of the password in the AWS SSM store, we are storing the database connection URL in the AWS SSM store as well so that any application wishes to access the database can access it by simply viewing the SSM path "$org_name/database/db_endpoint_url".

7.5 Kubernetes

Kubernetes is one of the most popular Container Orchestration products and is also one of the key components for our GitOps cycle. AWS has an offering called EKS (Elastic Kubernetes Service), which is a managed Kubernetes service wherein AWS is responsible for all the control plane components (etcd, apiserver, scheduler, controller) and the user is responsible for all the data plane components (worker nodes).

References:

AWS EKS

https://aws.amazon.com/eks/

Kubernetes Components

https://kubernetes.io/docs/concepts/overview/components/

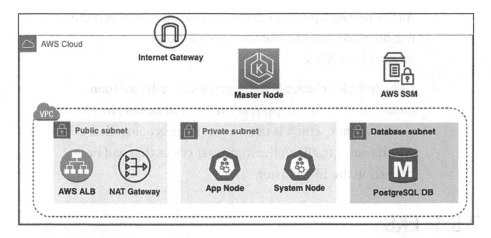

Figure 7-7. *AWS EKS architecture*

We'll be setting up a two-node Kubernetes cluster using the code defined in the *pgitops\infra\eks.tf* file utilizing the following features:

– A master node that is totally abstracted from us and deployed in a separate AWS VPC.

– Two worker nodes, namely, *app* and *system*, both deployed in the private subnet. The worker nodes are nothing but EC2 instances with Kubernetes setup deployed.

– In terms of EKS, there are two types of worker nodes: managed and unmanaged. Managed worker nodes are where AWS takes full control and responsibility to update and scale up the resources and align the worker nodes with the master node. In unmanaged, it is our responsibility to create the nodes, set up Kubernetes dependencies, scale up/down, and authenticate to the master node. This is generally achieved by creating EC2 templates.

- All the network plumbing/communication between the master node and the worker nodes is done internally by AWS.

- Once our EKS cluster is deployed and ready, we then create an AWS ALB (Application Load Balancer) in the public subnet, which is used as an ingress controller, which routes traffic to the ingress services that will be created in the EKS cluster.

7.5.1 EKS

Let's look at the *infra/eks.tf* file to better understand how our EKS cluster has been set up.

Code Block 7-13. EKS server setup in Terraform

File: pgitops\infra\eks.tf

XXXXXXXXXXXXXXX------SNIPPED-------XXXXXXXXXXXXXXXXXXXXX

```
15: # Main module that creates the master plane components
16: module "eks" {
17:     source = "./modules/ekscluster"
18:
19:     clustername     = module.clustername.cluster_name
20:     eks_version     = var.eks_version
21:     private_subnets = module.networking.private_subnets_id
22:     vpc_id          = module.networking.vpc_id
23:     environment     = var.environment
24:     instance_types  = var.instance_types
25:
26: }
```

L15–26: Initiates a module that creates the EKS cluster with master node and two worker nodes. We need to feed in the EKS version, the private subnet where the worker nodes will be spun up.

7.5.2 EKS Module

Let's dig in a bit into the module source to find out what's happening. Detailed implementation can be found here.

Code Block 7-14. EKS Module definition

```
File: pgitops\code\infra\modules\ekscluster\main.tf

02: module "eks" {
03:    source          = "terraform-aws-modules/eks/aws"
04:    version         = "18.7.0"
05:    cluster_name    = var.clustername
06:    cluster_version = var.eks_version
07:    subnet_ids      = var.private_subnets
08:    vpc_id          = var.vpc_id
09:    enable_irsa     = true
10:
11:    cluster_addons = {
12:      coredns = {
13:        resolve_conflicts = "OVERWRITE"
14:      }
15:      vpc-cni = {
16:        resolve_conflicts = "OVERWRITE"
17:      }
18:    }

XXXXXXXXXXXXXXXX------SNIPPED-------XXXXXXXXXXXXXXXXXXXXXX
```

L03: Refers the module in Terraform registry with a specific version number. This module provided by Terraform follows the best practices for setting up a managed/unmanaged EKS cluster and hence is highly recommended to use. However, there are very frequent changes to the minor/major versions, so it is also recommended to keep a tab on the version.

L06–08: Provides input for the specific EKS version, the private subnets, and the VPC where the EKS cluster needs to be placed.

L09: Enables IRSA (IAM Roles for Service Accounts), using which, we can provide granular privileges to Kubernetes PODs by aligning their services accounts to AWS IAM Roles. This is a very important security feature, which we'll explore in more detail in the next chapter.

L11–18: Here, we can specify installation/configuration of Kubernetes add-ons. List of all add-ons supported by AWS EKS off the shelf: `https://docs.aws.amazon.com/eks/latest/userguide/eks-add-ons.html`.

7.5.3 EKS Worker Nodes

One important aspect about EKS is that AWS creates only the master node or the control plane component of Kubernetes. The worker nodes needed to be created by us. The module that we are using allows us to specify the worker node groups that need to be created within which multiple worker nodes can be created as per the scaling configuration.

Let's look at how we are setting up the Managed worker node groups as shown here.

Code Block 7-15. EKS Managed Node groups

File: `pgitops\code\infra\modules\ekscluster\main.tf`

```
XXXXXXXXXXXXXXX------SNIPPED-------XXXXXXXXXXXXXXXXXXXXXX

59:    eks_managed_node_groups = {
60:
```

```
61:    system = {
62:       name             = "system"
63:       use_name_prefix = true
64:
65:       tags = {
66:          Name             = "system"
67:          Environment      = var.environment
68:          terraform-managed = "true"
69:       }
70:    },
71:    app = {
72:       name             = "app"
73:       use_name_prefix = true
74:
75:       tags = {
76:          Name             = "app"
77:          Environment      = var.environment
78:          terraform-managed = "true"
79:       }
80:    }
81:  }
82:
```

XXXXXXXXXXXXXXX------SNIPPED-------XXXXXXXXXXXXXXXXXXXXXX

L61–81: Declaring the nodes with appropriate tags. Using "user_ name_prefix" helps in better identification of the nodes.

Code Block 7-16. EKS Managed Node Groups default settings

File: pgitops\code\infra\modules\ekscluster\main.tf

XXXXXXXXXXXXXXX------SNIPPED-------XXXXXXXXXXXXXXXXXXXXXX

```
44:    eks_managed_node_group_defaults = {
45:      ami_type           = "AL2_x86_64"
46:      disk_size          = 50
47:      ebs_optimized      = true
48:      enable_monitoring  = true
49:      instance_types     = var.instance_types
50:      capacity_type      = "ON_DEMAND"
51:      desired_size       = 1
52:      max_size           = 3
53:      min_size           = 1
54:      update_config = {
55:        max_unavailable_percentage = 50
56:      }
57:    }
```

XXXXXXXXXXXXXXX------SNIPPED-------XXXXXXXXXXXXXXXXXXXXXX

L44–57: We are declaring some common properties of each worker node. Each of these properties can be overridden when we are exclusively defining the node groups on **L59–81**.

We are defining the following:

- **L45** – AMI Type, which is the default AMI for Kubernetes resources

- **L46** – Specifying the EBS Disk Size that will be attached to the EC2 instance to be 50 GB

- **L48** – Enabled monitoring

- **L49** – Specifying the instance type of the EC2

- **L51–53** – Specifying the scaling sizes

- **L54–56** – Specifying at least 50% availability while scaling up/down

7.5.4 EKS Security Groups

The next section of this EKS Module defines the security groups needed for operational purposes.

Code Block 7-17. EKS Security Groups definitions

File: pgitops\code\infra\modules\ekscluster\main.tf

XXXXXXXXXXXXXXX------SNIPPED-------XXXXXXXXXXXXXXXXXXXXXX

```
21:   node_security_group_additional_rules = {
22:
23:     ingress_allow_access_from_control_plane = {
24:       type                          = "ingress"
25:       protocol                      = "tcp"
26:       from_port                     = 9443
27:       to_port                       = 9443
28:       source_cluster_security_group = true
29:       description                   = "Allow access from
                                           control plane to
                                           webhook port of
                                           AWS load balancer
                                           controller"
30:     }
31:
32:     egress_all = {
```

```
33:        description      = "Node all egress"
34:        protocol         = "-1"
35:        from_port        = 0
36:        to_port          = 0
37:        type             = "egress"
38:        cidr_blocks      = ["0.0.0.0/0"]
39:        ipv6_cidr_blocks = ["::/0"]
40:    }
41: }
```

XXXXXXXXXXXXXXX------SNIPPED-------XXXXXXXXXXXXXXXXXXXXX

The EKS Module provided by Terraform as mentioned earlier follows the best practices; hence, in terms of accessibility, it's quite locked down. We need to specify security groups in order to facilitate communication between master node and worker nodes, which is by default limited and locked down to certain ports only like communication between the API server and kubelet over port 10250, etc. These security groups are what we need to define in the preceding section.

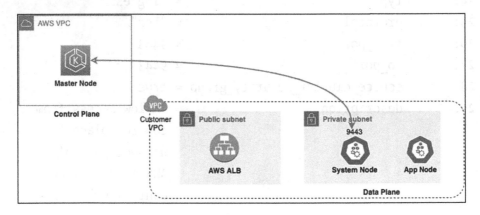

Figure 7-8. *EKS Security Groups visualization*

L23–30: Here, we are defining the security group that allows access from the master node (AWS EKS Control Plane) in an AWS Managed VPC to the worker nodes (EKS Data Plane) on port 9443. What's running on port 9443 is something we'll see in the next subsection.

L32–41: Since the worker nodes are created in the private subnet, they do not have access to the Internet. Hence, it's necessary to set up this default egress group to allow the worker nodes to access the Internet to download docker images or perform DNS lookups. The protocol with a value of "-1" indicates TCP/UDP to facilitate DNS lookups.

7.5.5 EKS Ingress Controller

In Kubernetes, ingress controllers and ingress resources help in shaping up the entire traffic between the client and the individual pods. Ingress controllers are like the load balancers, and ingress resources are the small configuration pieces of that load balancer that help in modularizing the various different configurations that are needed to facilitate the communication to the respective pods. The same has been illustrated in the following diagram.

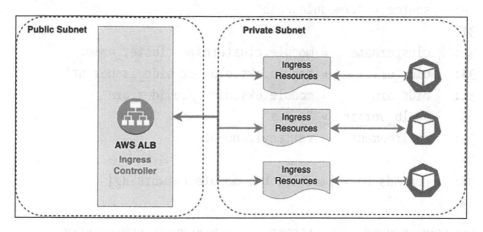

Figure 7-9. *Connectivity between AWS ALB and EKS Ingress Resources*

In order to set up an ingress controller, we need to create a Kubernetes deployment resource of the specific controller that we need to set up. This deployment resource serves as a load balancer controller, which is then used to set up an actual Application Load Balancer in the public subnet using the following code.

This deployment is exposed on port 9443, which is consumed by the Kubernetes API server (master node/control plane) to supervise the creation of the application load balancer. Hence, we need to ensure that a security group exists with port 9443 between the master node and the worker nodes, which was discussed in the earlier section (refer to Figure 7-8).

Code Block 7-18. Setting up AWS ALB ingress controller

File: pgitops\infra\eks.tf

XXXXXXXXXXXXXX------SNIPPED-------XXXXXXXXXXXXXXXXXXXX

```
28: # Module that creates the Application Load Balancer for use
    as an Ingress Controller
29: module "alb_ingress" {
30:   source = "./modules/alb"
31:
32:   clustername  = module.clustername.cluster_name
33:   oidc_url     = module.eks.cluster_oidc_issuer_url
34:   oidc_arn     = module.eks.oidc_provider_arn
35:   awslb_version = "1.4.1"
36:   environment  = var.environment
37:
38:   depends_on = [module.eks, module.networking]
39: }
```

XXXXXXXXXXXXXX------SNIPPED-------XXXXXXXXXXXXXXXXXXXX

L29-39: Sets up an AWS Load balancer controller deployment by providing the OIDC and the Load Balancer controller helm chart version.

Note   We'll be exploring OIDC (OpenID Connect) and IRSA (IAM Roles for Service Accounts) in more detail in Chapter 9.

7.6 DNS

7.6.1 Route53 Record Creation

Once the load balancer controller is created, a separate load balancer for each individual ingress resource with a DNS name taking the format as *<ingress-name>-<account-id>.<region>.elb.amazonaws.com*, for example, *my-ingress-1234567890.us-west-2.elb.amazonaws.com*. We can access our application by following this path; however, it's not something feasible to remember. Hence, we need to map this DNS name to our custom DNS, which is done by the following piece of code.

Code Block 7-19.   Creating the Route53 Record and inserting ALB hostname

File: pgitops\infra\dns.tf

```
XXXXXXXXXXXXXXX------SNIPPED-------XXXXXXXXXXXXXXXXXXXXXX

20: # Fetch the Zone ID of the hosted domains
21: data "aws_route53_zone" "domain" {
22:   name = "${var.domain}."
23:
24: }

XXXXXXXXXXXXXXX------SNIPPED-------XXXXXXXXXXXXXXXXXXXXXX
```

```
38: # Fetching the ZoneID for ELB
39: data "aws_elb_hosted_zone_id" "main" {}
40:
41: # Mapping The Ingress controller hostname with DNS Record
42: resource "aws_route53_record" "app" {
43:    zone_id = data.aws_route53_zone.domain.zone_id
44:    name     = local.url
45:    type     = "A"
46:
47:    alias {
48:      name                       = kubernetes_ingress_
                                       v1.app.status.0.load_
                                       balancer.0.ingress.0.hostname
49:      zone_id                    = data.aws_elb_hosted_zone_
                                       id.main.id
50:      evaluate_target_health = true
51:    }
52:
53:    depends_on = [module.alb_ingress, kubernetes_
       ingress_v1.app]
54:
55: }
```

L20-24: We are fetching the zone ID of the Route53 zone, which we had created in the beginning by executing the aws route53 command. We are querying it using the domain name that we'll be using.

L39: Since every load balancer has a public DNS name as mentioned previously, it also has a specific zone ID where it is deployed, which is managed by AWS. We are simply querying that zone ID.

L43: Creating the DNS record in the Route53 zone that we created earlier.

L47–51: The record that we need to create is an **Alias** record, which is recommended by AWS for setting up DNS records for Load Balancers. On **L48**, we are fetching the hostname of the ingress resource that is created. The value of the variable *local.url* will be used to map the ingress DNS hostname. How the value of *local.url* is derived is explained in the next section.

Tip   This might sound astonishing but yes, AWS Load Balancer Controller deployment will set up a separate AWS Load Balancer. So if we have three ingress resources, we'll see three different AWS Load Balancers. This can be avoided using the ingress group annotation when defining ingress resources that groups different ingress resources as one. This will be discussed in more detail in Chapter 10 where we need to set up two ingress resources.

References:

Kubernetes Ingress Resource Annotations for AWS ALB

```
https://kubernetes-sigs.github.io/aws-load-balancer-
controller/v2.4/guide/ingress/annotations/#ingressgroup
```

7.6.2 Multi-environment DNS

We need to keep our code DRY (Don't Repeat Yourself) and at the same time have it running in multiple environments. While other things can remain the same across different environments, the domain name cannot remain the same; hence, the following code sets up the layout where depending on the environment, the value of the variable *local.url* will change dynamically.

Code Block 7-20. Dynamically configuring App URL as per the environment

File: pgitops\infra\dns.tf

```
01: // Pseudo Code
02: // if(environment==staging){
03: //      url = staging.gitops.rohitsalecha.com
04: // }elseif(environment==prod){
05: //      url = gitops.rohitsalecha.com
06: // }elseif(environment==dev){
07: //      url = dev.gitops.rohitsalecha.com
08: // }
09:
10: locals {
11:
12:    staging_url = var.environment == "staging" ?
       "staging.${var.domain}" : ""
13:    prod_url    = var.environment == "prod" ? "${var.
       domain}" : ""
14:    dev_url     = var.environment == "dev" ? "dev.${var.
       domain}" : ""
15:
16:    url = coalesce(local.staging_url, local.prod_url, local.
       dev_url)
17:
18: }
```

XXXXXXXXXXXXXXX------SNIPPED-------XXXXXXXXXXXXXXXXXXXXX

L01–08: Is the Pseudo Code explanation of the multi-environment problem that we are solving.

L10-18: Since terraform doesn't provide syntaxes like if..else, etc., we make use of the *coalesce* function, which accepts only a non-null value. So if the environment is staging, the variable *staging_url* will be non-null, but the other variables will be null. Hence, the final value of the **url** variables takes the value stored in *staging_url*.

This is a small hackety solution to simulate the if..else statement behavior.

7.6.3 ACM

Now that we've mapped a custom domain for the load balancer hostname (ingress resource hostname), we should also ensure that the application is accessible over an HTTPS communication and not on clear-text HTTP. This can be achieved by utilizing the following code, which generates a public SSL certificate for a given domain specified by the *local. url* variable and the Route53 Zone ID. The Route53 Zone ID is required here because custom. What this essentially does is that it creates an ACM certificate on top of an ELB (Elastic Load Balancer).

Code Block 7-21. Generating an HTTPS certificate using AWS ACM

File: pgitops\infra\dns.tf

```
XXXXXXXXXXXXXXX------SNIPPED-------XXXXXXXXXXXXXXXXXXXXX

26: # Generate Certificate for the particular domain
27: module "acm" {
28:   source = "./modules/acm"
29:
30:   zone_id     = data.aws_route53_zone.domain.zone_id
31:   domain      = local.url
32:   environment = var.environment
33:
```

```
34:    depends_on = [module.alb_ingress]
35:
36: }
```

XXXXXXXXXXXXXXX------SNIPPED-------XXXXXXXXXXXXXXXXXXXXX

7.7 Application

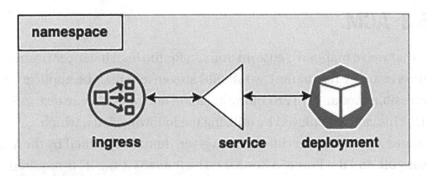

Figure 7-10. *Relationship between Kubernetes ingress, service, and deployment*

Our application is deployed in the EKS and has the following components:

- A specific namespace is created where all the components like the ingress, service, and deployment will be created.

- A deployment resource is created, which holds the Kubernetes pod.

- The Deployment is exposed to the Kubernetes network through a Service configured as "NodePort".

- The Service is exposed to the external (Internet) network through the ingress resource.

- Each ingress resource created creates a unique load balancer.

7.7.1 Namespace

Let's look at how each of the components is described in *pgitops\
infra\app.tf.*

Code Block 7-22.   Creating a Kubernetes namespace using
Terraform

```
File: pgitops\infra\app.tf
03: resource "kubernetes_namespace_v1" "app" {
04:   metadata {
05:     annotations = {
06:       name = var.org_name
07:     }
08:     name = var.org_name
09:   }
10:   depends_on = [module.eks]
11: }
```

XXXXXXXXXXXXXXX------SNIPPED-------XXXXXXXXXXXXXXXXXXXXX

L03–11: We are declaring a Kubernetes namespace using a terraform
declaration syntax. We specify the annotation and the name of the
namespace using a variable *var.org_name,* which is specified in the
terraform.auto.tfvars file.

Just to draw some comparison, the following is the manifest file that
performs the same action in YAML format that would be executed using
the *kubectl* utility provided by Kubernetes.

Code Block 7-23.   Creating a Kubernetes namespace using YAML

```
apiVersion: v1
kind: Namespace
metadata:
```

```
name: "gitops"
labels:
  name: "gitops"
```

7.7.2 Deployment

Before we discuss the Kubernetes deployment resource, there is an important prerequisite without which our deployment would not execute. This important prerequisite is nothing but our PostgreSQL database password that was stored in the AWS SSM store. The same is retrievable using the following code snippet, which reads the value specified at the path.

Code Block 7-24. Reading a database password from AWS SSM

File: pgitops\infra\app.tf

XXXXXXXXXXXXXXX------SNIPPED-------XXXXXXXXXXXXXXXXXXXXX

```
16: module "ssmr-db-password" {
17:   source = "./modules/ssmr"
18:
19:   parameter_name = "db_password"
20:   parameter_path = "/${var.org_name}/database"
21:
22:   depends_on = [module.ssmw-db-password]
23: }
```

XXXXXXXXXXXXXXX------SNIPPED-------XXXXXXXXXXXXXXXXXXXXX

The value for the AWS SSM can be retrieved using the following syntax: "**module.ssmr-db-password.ssm-value**", as we'll see being used in the Kubernetes deployment specification next.

Code Block 7-25. Kubernetes deployment

File: pgitops\infra\app.tf

```
25: resource "kubernetes_deployment_v1" "app" {
26:    metadata {
27:       name      = var.org_name
28:       namespace = kubernetes_namespace_v1.app.metadata.0.name
29:       labels = {
30:          app = var.org_name
31:       }
32:    }
XXXXXXXXXXXXXXX------SNIPPED-------XXXXXXXXXXXXXXXXXXXXX
50:       spec {
051:          container {
052:             image = "salecharohit/practicalgitops"
053:             name  = var.org_name
054:             env {
055:                name  = "DB_PORT"
056:                value = "5432"
057:             }
058:             env {
059:                name  = "DB_HOST"
060:                value = module.pgsql.db_instance_address
061:             }
062:             env {
063:                name  = "DB_NAME"
064:                value = var.db_name
065:             }
066:             env {
067:                name  = "DB_USERNAME"
068:                value = var.db_user_name
069:             }
```

```
070:            env {
071:                name  = "DB_PASSWORD"
072:                value = module.ssmr-db-password.ssm-value
073:            }
074:
75:             port {
76:                container_port = "8080"
77:                protocol       = "TCP"
78:             }
```

XXXXXXXXXXXXXXXX------SNIPPED-------XXXXXXXXXXXXXXXXXXXXXX

L28: Here, we are explicitly referencing the namespace that we created earlier using the terraform reference syntax. This ensures an implicit dependency in a way that first the namespace will be created and then the deployment. Hence, it is extremely important to add this line as we want this dependency to be maintained.

L52: Specifying the container image for the deployment pod specification. This image is currently stored in DockerHub; however, you can store it in any container registry accessible by your EKS Node.

Note   For the purpose of this book, I've used DockerHub, but yes using an ECR would be highly recommended especially when working in a complete AWS environment as you get much lesser latency while downloading the images and also capability to scan the docker images for security vulnerabilities.

L54–73: Specifying the database environment variables like the database port, hostname, name, username, and finally the password. The password field is being populated dynamically from the AWS SSM read module as specified earlier. Hence, no manual intervention of entering password is now required.

L75–78: We are specifying the container port on which our pod will be exposed, that is, port 8080.

7.7.3 NodePort Service

In Kubernetes, it is a best practice to expose a Deployment/Pod through a service to the internal network. Hence, we've created a Kubernetes service as shown in the following within the same namespace as the Deployment and exposed it over port 8080.

Code Block 7-26. Kubernetes service

```
File: pgitops\infra\app.tf

XXXXXXXXXXXXXXXX------SNIPPED-------XXXXXXXXXXXXXXXXXXXXX
106: resource "kubernetes_service" "app" {
107:   metadata {
108:     name      = var.org_name
109:     namespace = kubernetes_namespace_v1.app.
           metadata.0.name
110:   }
111:   spec {
112:     port {
113:       port        = 8080
114:       target_port = 8080
115:     }
116:     selector = {
117:       app = var.org_name
118:     }
119:     type = "NodePort"
120:   }
```

```
121:    depends_on = [kubernetes_deployment_v1.app]
122: }
```

XXXXXXXXXXXXXXX------SNIPPED-------XXXXXXXXXXXXXXXXXXXXXX

L116-118: The service connects the Deployment pods over port 8080 using the selector label app.

7.7.4 Ingress

The following code is used to create a Kubernetes ingress resource with all the specific annotations described here.

Code Block 7-27. Creating a Kubernetes ingress resource

File: pgitops\infra\app.tf

XXXXXXXXXXXXXXX------SNIPPED-------XXXXXXXXXXXXXXXXXXXXXX

```
124: resource "kubernetes_ingress_v1" "app" {
125:    wait_for_load_balancer = true
126:    metadata {
127:      name       = var.org_name
128:      namespace = kubernetes_namespace_v1.app.
         metadata.0.name
129:      annotations = {
130:        "kubernetes.io/ingress.class"              = "alb"
131:        "alb.ingress.kubernetes.io/scheme"         =
           "internet-facing"
132:        "alb.ingress.kubernetes.io/target-type"    = "ip"
133:        "alb.ingress.kubernetes.io/certificate-arn" =
           module.acm.acm_arn
134:        "alb.ingress.kubernetes.io/listen-ports"   =
           "[{\"HTTP\": 80}, {\"HTTPS\":443}]"
135:      }
```

```
136:    }
137:    spec {
138:      rule {
139:        host = local.url
140:         http {
141:           path {
142:             backend {
143:               service {
144:                 name = var.org_name
145:                 port {
146:                   number = 8080
147:                 }
148:               }
149:             }
150:             path = "/*"
151:           }
152:
153:        }
154:      }
155:    depends_on = [module.alb_ingress, kubernetes_
ingress_v1.app]
156: }
```

XXXXXXXXXXXXXXX------SNIPPED-------XXXXXXXXXXXXXXXXXXXXX

L129-134: We are defining the annotations that govern the complete operation of the ingress resource.

– **L130:** We are defining the ingress class as "alb" since we are using the AWS ALB as the ingress controller deployed earlier in the EKS section. Each ingress resource will hence communicate with the ingress controller deployment in EKS to spin up a fresh new Load Balancer.

– **L131:** There are two schemes: Internet facing and internal. By configuring our ingress resource as Internet facing, it automatically gets added in the public subnet by querying for the particular tag. These are the same tags we configured in Section 7.3 if you recall.

– **L132:** The target type we are defining as IP based as we are configuring the service as NodePort type.

– **L133:** We are configuring the SSL certificate in the ingress resource generated by the AWS ACM module. Since the ingress resource is spinning up a unique ALB, it is important to configure the SSL certificate here as SSL offloading will happen at this point.

– **L134:** Configuring the ports on which the AWS ALB will be listening on to the external Internet. If we are specifying 443 as a port, it is mandatory to have an AWS ACM ARN, which we are providing on L133.

– **L155:** Here, we are explicitly declaring the dependency on the AWS ALB ingress controller deployment module as it needs to be created prior to the ingress resource. As stated earlier, this dependency is critical because the ingress resource communicates with the ingress controller deployment to spin up an AWS Application Load Balancer.

– **L125:** This line is of critical importance as our Route53 record creation as discussed in the DNS module depends on the Application Load Balancer hostname, which in turn depends on the ingress resource. However, the ALB will take time to start up and have a hostname assigned to it. Hence, this line performs regular checks on whether the load balancer has been set up or not and will wait before moving the execution to other modules.

7.7.5 Kubernetes Provider

I discussed terraform providers in Section 3.2 where these providers are nothing but plugins for different cloud and cloud-native environments. Similar to how we've got for AWS, we are declaring a provider for Kubernetes and Helm in *pgitops/infra/kubernetes.tf* as shown here.

Code Block 7-28. Defining a Kubernetes provider

```
File: pgitops\infra\kubernetes.tf

03: provider "kubernetes" {
04:   host                   = module.eks.cluster_endpoint
05:   cluster_ca_certificate = base64decode(module.eks.cluster_
                               certificate_authority_data)
06:   exec {
07:     api_version = "client.authentication.k8s.io/v1alpha1"
08:     command     = "aws"
09:     args = [
10:       "eks",
11:       "get-token",
12:       "--cluster-name",
13:       module.eks.cluster_id
14:     ]
15:   }
16: }

XXXXXXXXXXXXXXXX------SNIPPED-------XXXXXXXXXXXXXXXXXXXXX
```

Reference: Kubernetes Provider for Terraform Documentation
(`https://registry.terraform.io/providers/hashicorp/kubernetes/
latest/docs`)

L04-05: Every provider needs authentication information in order
to perform the requested operations. For AWS, we are supplying the
AWS Access Key and ID using environment variables. However, for the
Kubernetes provider, we need the hostname of the Kubernetes cluster
and the CA certificate that is used for generating the authentication token
for the Kubernetes API. These details are obtained from the EKS Module
defined in the *pgitops/infra/eks.tf* file and are fetched once the EKS
Module has been set up.

L06-13: This Kubernetes provider directly interacts with the
Kubernetes API over HTTPS.

Once we have the hostname and the Cluster CA certificate, Terraform
needs to obtain the Kubernetes API token in order to authenticate to
the Kubernetes API. This authentication is performed using the aws
command, that is, *aws eks get-token –cluster-name $cluster-id*, where
$cluster-id is nothing but the cluster name created using the EKS Module.

This provider (Kubernetes and Helm) will be kicked into action
whenever we need to deploy any resource within Kubernetes. If we do not
define this provider, we won't be able to deploy/create any Kubernetes
resource, not even a simple namespace. Hence, this provider is needed
purely for all Kubernetes operations.

7.7.6 Variables

Last, but one of the most important configurations, is setting the variable
values defined in *pgitops/infra/terraform.auto.tfvars*. We can keep all the
variable values as is except for the following two.

Code Block 7-29. Defining Kubernetes variables

File: pgitops\infra\kubernetes.tf

```
XXXXXXXXXXXXXXX------SNIPPED-------XXXXXXXXXXXXXXXXXXXXXX
40: org_name = "gitops"
41: domain   = "change.me.please"
```

L40–41: Kindly replace the following values before attempting to execute the code. Your domain should be the one which you've set as per the DNS configurations in Section 7.1.

Note   The value that I've set for myself is *gitops.rohitsalecha.com*, which is what you'll see throughout this book.

7.7.7 Default Environment

By default, the environment that has been configured is the *dev* environment and the region as *us-east-1* as is evident from the following file. This is done because the developers need to independently test their code from their local systems before pushing the changes into staging. Hence, they can see their changes live and test it out.

While for the prod and staging environments, we need to configure these two variables in Terraform Cloud as explained in the previous chapter.

Code Block 7-30. Defining the default environment for Kubernetes

File: pgitops\infra\kubernetes.tf

```
04: variable "environment" {
05:    description = "The Deployment environment"
```

```
06:    type        = string
07:    default     = "dev"
08: }

XXXXXXXXXXXXXXX------SNIPPED-------XXXXXXXXXXXXXXXXXXXXX

15: variable "region" {
16:    description = "AWS region"
17:    type        = string
18:    default     = "us-east-1"
19: }
```

7.8 Execution

Now that we've a good understanding of the different infrastructure items that we are going to spin up, let's go ahead and start the entire infrastructure.

Note   Prior to running Terraform, it's necessary to set up the Route53 Hosted Zone as discussed in DNS configuration in the Prerequisites section of this chapter. I currently have my Route53 Hosted Zone set up with the domain name as *dev.gitops. rohitsalecha.com.*

7.8.1 Setting Up the EKS Cluster

Fire the following commands to get started; ensure you've got your AWS credentials configured in the CLI as well.

CLI Output 7-31. Executing new infra

```
export AWS_PROFILE=gitops
cd pgitops/infra
terraform init
terraform apply -auto-approve
```

Terraform apply should take about close to ~15 minutes to complete. Once done, simply browse to the development domain name as by default for developers, application is hosted on dev.$domain_name as configured in the *pgitops/infra/dns.tf.*

The following screenshot shows that our application is now up and running.

Figure 7-11. *Development environment up and running*

Viewing all the users.

Let's add a test user to check if everything is working fine.

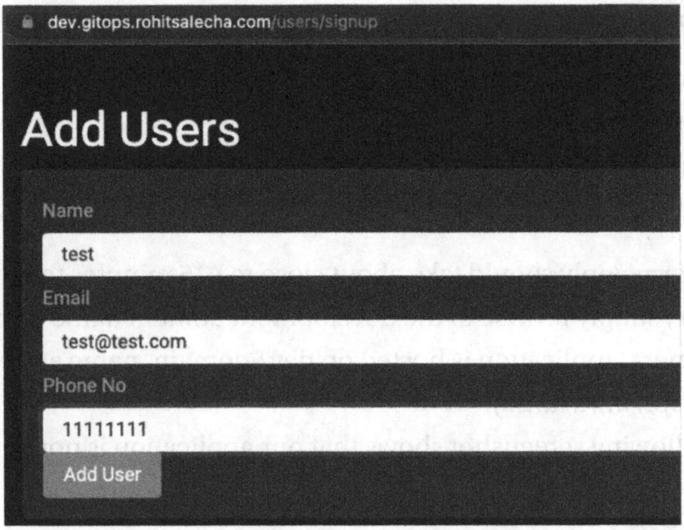

Figure 7-12. *User Adding screen*

Figure 7-13. *List of users added*

7.8.2 Accessing the EKS Cluster

Now that our application is up and running let's check how our Kubernetes environment has been configured by accessing it using the *kubectl* utility.

AWS CLI has a very useful command to setup the Kubeconfig file which the kubectl utility needs in order to authenticate to the Kubernetes cluster. The command is

aws eks --region $REGION update-kubeconfig --name $CLUSTER

So, let's execute this command and then explore the Kubernetes cluster.

CLI Output 7-32. Accessing the Kubernetes development environment

```
cmd> EXPORT AWS_PROFILE=gitops
cmd> aws eks --region us-east-1 update-kubeconfig --name
gitops-us-east-1-dev
Added new context arn:aws:eks:us-east-1:147611229030:cluster/
gitops-us-east-1-dev to /Users/rohitsalecha/.kube/config

cmd> kubectl get nodes
NAME                          STATUS   ROLES    AGE
    VERSION
ip-10-0-11-206.ec2.internal   Ready    <none>   6m
    v1.20.11-eks-f17b81
ip-10-0-11-63.ec2.internal    Ready    <none>   6m11s
    v1.20.11-eks-f17b81

cmd> kubectl get all -n gitops

NAME                          READY    STATUS    RESTARTS   AGE
pod/gitops-795f75dd58-zmkv2   1/1      Running   0          3m1s

NAME             TYPE       CLUSTER-IP      EXTERNAL-IP
    PORT(S)          AGE
service/gitops   NodePort   172.20.192.96   <none>
    8080:30307/TCP   2m50s
```

NAME	READY	UP-TO-DATE	AVAILABLE	AGE
deployment.apps/gitops	1/1	1	1	3m4s

NAME	DESIRED	CURRENT	READY	AGE
replicaset.apps/gitops-795f75dd58	1	1	1	3m4s

7.9 Clean-Up

Since our use case is done, let's destroy the environment using the following commands. It should take approximately ten minutes to destroy the entire environment.

CLI Output 7-33. Destroying the Kubernetes environment

```
cmd> export AWS_PROFILE=gitops
cmd> terraform destroy --auto-approve
```

Note   At any point, if Terraform is unable to destroy, please check Annexure A where steps have been presented to delete the resources manually.

7.10 Conclusion

In this chapter, we saw the different components we are spinning up using Terraform and that other than setting the Route53 Zone manually, everything else was completely automated.

However, we did not explore the GitOps workflow here; we did not deploy this code in the staging and then in the production environment, which this book is all about. The major reason to do that is that we haven't yet created separate AWS accounts for staging/production/development, which is what we'll explore in the next chapter. We'll be creating separate accounts and also creating users with different privileges and authorization roles not just for accessing AWS but also for Kubernetes!

From the next chapter onward, we'll start improving this code, and as a first step, we'll work on implementing a proper authentication and authorization in the entire infrastructure including AWS + Kubernetes in the next chapter.

CHAPTER 8

Authentication and Authorization

In this chapter, we'll look at how to create AWS accounts using AWS organizations for different environments and use cases using Terraform. We'll create four different AWS accounts, which will be aligned with three different organization units or OUs. Each account is being created for specific use cases, which will be discussed in this chapter. We'll also look at how we can create Route53 Zones for each of the operational accounts for better segregation of DNS records. However, this time around, we'll be doing completely through Terraform, and no manual intervention will be required. Lastly, we'll create IAM Users and IAM Roles with set permissions to interact with different AWS accounts and also do mapping of AWS IAM Roles with Kubernetes Groups to provide a seamless authentication and authorization through code!

8.1 Prerequisites

In addition to all the previous requirements, we'll need the following:

- GNU PG Utility to generate public/private keys.
    - Please download and install for your respective OS using the following link: `https://gnupg.org/download/index.html`

- AWS account that we'll be using here should not have AWS organization setup previously, that is, the Root AWS organization account should not be created.

Ensure that you have the following before getting started:

- The pgitops directory created in Chapter 7

- Access to the DNS console of your top-level domain or sub-domain as we'll be adding a few more NS records

- Terraform Cloud configured with prod and staging workspaces

8.1.1 Code Update

Before diving into the code, let's first ensure that we've updated the pgitops directory with the code from Chapter 8 folder. To do this, follow the following steps:

- First, copy contents of Chapter 8 folder into the pgitops folder.

- Get inside the pgitops directory and then check which files/folders are changing.

- Commit changes into the repository; however, while committing, ensure to have the *"[skip ci]"* added in the commit as shown in the following as I don't intend to execute the actions yet as the code is still incomplete:

Tip   Github Actions execute whenever there is a new commit in the branch. If we wish to skip the execution for a specific commit, we can simply add [skip ci] verbatim in the commit message.

```
cmd> cp -a chapter8/. pgitops/
cmd> cd pgitops
cmd> git status
On branch main
Your branch is up to date with 'origin/main'.

Changes not staged for commit:
  (use "git add <file>..." to update what will be committed)
  (use "git restore <file>..." to discard changes in working
  directory)
        modified:   README.md
        modified:   infra/README.md
        modified:   infra/app.tf
        modified:   infra/dns.tf
        modified:   infra/kubernetes.tf
        modified:   infra/providers.tf
        modified:   infra/terraform.auto.tfvars
        modified:   infra/variables.tf

Untracked files:
  (use "git add <file>..." to include in what will be
  committed)
        .github/workflows/global.yaml
        global/
        infra/rolebindings.tf

no changes added to commit (use "git add" and/or "git
commit -a")

cmd> git add .
# Please ensure to add [skip ci] in the commit message.
cmd> git commit -m "chapter 8 commit [skip ci]"
cmd> git push
```

The changes can be summarized as follows:

- Added a new folder called "global," which contains all the code related to creating AWS organizations, Route53 Zones, and IAM User/Roles. So basically, we'll be having terraform files in two folders (i.e., infra and global).

- Added a new workflow file called global.yaml to have a proper Git workflow just like staging/production changes

- Added a new file called rolebindings.tf under the infra folder, which does mapping of Kubernetes groups with IAM roles in the AWS ConfigMap.

- Rest all files under the infra folder have been modified as per the changes done with the global folder.

Each change/addition will be discussed in detail in this chapter.

8.2 AWS Organizations

AWS organizations is a service provided by AWS where we can create and centrally administer/manage multiple different accounts that are created for a specific purpose. There are two primary concepts that need to be understood in AWS organizations, and they are root account/management account and member accounts with OUs or organization units. Let's understand in more detail.

8.2.1 Root Account

Root account as the name suggests is the main account that we signed up with. It is also called the management account as it has full control over the billing and cloud deployments. As of now, I am accessing everything through the Root account, and our current authentication framework is extremely risky from a security and scalability perspective. Let's understand our current design and call out the drawbacks/limitations of it.

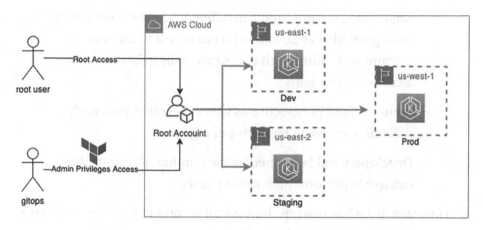

The previous diagram provides a glimpse into the operating model that we have currently:

- Using the root user, I created an AWS account, which is also known as the "root account" or the "Management account."

- I then created another user called "gitops" and provided Administrator privileges.

- I then accessed the AWS Console using the "gitops" user credentials to download the AWS Access Keys and AWS Access ID.

- This set of AWS Access Keys and Access ID was then used to configure the Terraform environment to spin up the Dev/staging and prod environments.

Limitations/drawbacks of the previous architecture are as follows:

- Currently if we need to create new users, then everyone will need to access the root account with certain pre-defined privileges.

- Segregating environments in different regions is definitely not a good idea as anyone who has access to the root account with Admin privileges can easily gain access to all the environments.

- From a billing perspective as well, it becomes extremely difficult to create bill reports per region.

- Developers will be limited by the number of regions they can use to perform their checks/tests.

These are just a few reasons; however, if we attempt to align with AWS Best Practices, then it would almost fill two pages or maybe more.

8.2.2 Member Accounts and OUs

Member accounts and Organizational Units are created to have a proper segregation of duties and responsibilities for the various different accounts an Organization may have. These accounts can inherit the organizational structure (but not limited to it) that a typical organization has like having segregated departments like Finance, Marketing, Engineering, etc. Since all these departments function separately, it's best that their operations are very well segregated. This is where AWS organizations can be utilized to its fullest extent by helping to design and implement the operational aspects of running an entire organization while at the same time having full control over every small aspect of it.

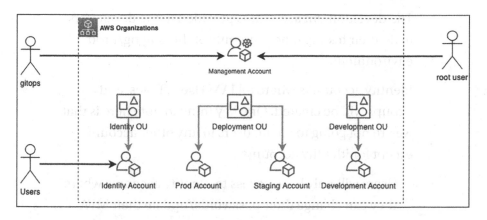

Figure 8-1. *AWS organization high-level view*

In the preceding diagram we are using AWS organizations to create multiple OUs or Organizational Units and member accounts associated with each OU. Let's understand better:

- The management account or the root account is now accessible only by the gitops user that I created and also the root user credentials. Other than these two, no one else has access and no one will ever need it as well with exception for billing purposes.

- I've created OUs with specific purposes like Identity OU, Deployment OU, and Development OU. OUs are created to group similar member accounts where their functionality is aligned. We can then apply Service Control Policies or SCPs at OU level, which makes it easier to govern. We'll be exploring SCPs in greater depth in the next chapter.

- Each member account is serving a specific purpose.

- The prod and staging accounts are for deploying the application and are LIVE environments.

- The development account is provided to the developers to do their testing independently of the staging/prod environment.

- Identity account is where all IAM Users, Roles, and Groups will be created. One key thing to note here is that we are not going to create users in any other account except for identity accounts.

  - Users will only have access to identity accounts where they can change their passwords/update their MFA and perform only IAM-related activities.

  - They will not be allowed to create an EC2 instance or any other functions in the identity account.

  - They will be allowed to perform all other operations only in dev environments, which are accessible by Assuming IAM Roles created in the dev account. We'll be covering more details on the User and Role Management later in this chapter.

Let's now look into how the AWS organizations and the member accounts have been created in Terraform.

All the magic is happening in the *pgitops/global/organisations.tf* file as shown in the following.

Code Block 8-1. Creating the AWS organization using Terraform

File: pgitops/global/organisations.tf

```
01: # Initializing Root Organization
02: resource "aws_organizations_organization" "root" {
03: }
04:
```

```
05: # Create an OU for Identity management
06: resource "aws_organizations_organizational_unit"
    "identity" {
07:   name     = "Identity Management Account"
08:   parent_id = aws_organizations_organization.root.
    roots[0].id
09: }
10:
11: # Create an OU for deployment accounts
12: resource "aws_organizations_organizational_unit"
    "deployment" {
13:   name     = "Deployment Accounts"
14:   parent_id = aws_organizations_organization.root.
    roots[0].id
15: }
16:
17: # Create an OU for development/sandbox accounts
18: resource "aws_organizations_organizational_unit"
    "development" {
19:   name     = "Development Accounts"
20:   parent_id = aws_organizations_organization.root.
    roots[0].id
21: }
```

XXXXXXXXXXXXXXXX------SNIPPED-------XXXXXXXXXXXXXXXXXXXXXX

L02–03: This is where it all starts by first creating a root organization. This line is not actually creating anything; it's just setting up the AWS organization service and assigning the current account where you've logged in as a root account or a management account.

L06–20: Creating the Organizational Units as discussed earlier and assigning the root account as the parent account.

Let's look at how I am creating the member accounts in the same file *gitops/global/organisations.tf.*

Code Block 8-2. Creating member accounts

File: pgitos/global/organisations.tf

```
XXXXXXXXXXXXXXX------SNIPPED-------XXXXXXXXXXXXXXXXXXXXX
25: module "identity_account" {
26:    source = "./modules/awsaccounts"
27:
28:    name      = var.accounts["identity"].name
29:    email     = var.accounts["identity"].email
30:    parent_id = aws_organizations_organizational_unit.
       identity.id
31:
32: }
33:
34: # Org hosting Production infrastructure
35: module "prod_account" {
36:    source = "./modules/awsaccounts"
37:
38:    name      = var.accounts["prod"].name
39:    email     = var.accounts["prod"].email
40:    parent_id = aws_organizations_organizational_unit.
       deployment.id
41:
42: }

XXXXXXXXXXXXXXX------SNIPPED-------XXXXXXXXXXXXXXXXXXXXX
```

L25–42: AWS account creation has been modularized as in general it requires three primary information for a unique setup (i.e., account name, email address, and parent account ID).

The parent account ID is nothing but the Organizational Unit IDs, whereas the name and the email addresses are retrieved from the *pgitops/global/terraform.auto.tfvars*, which is shown as follows.

Code Block 8-3. Member account email and names' configurations

```
File: pgitops/global/terraform.auto.tfvars

02: accounts = {
03:   dev = {
04:     name  = "dev"
05:     email = "email+dev@changeme.please"
06:   },
07:   identity = {
08:     name  = "identity"
09:     email = "email+identity@changeme.please"
10:   },
11:   prod = {
12:     name  = "prod"
13:     email = "email+prod@changeme.please"
14:   },
15:   staging = {
16:     name  = "staging"
17:     email = "email+staging@changeme.please"
18:   }
19: }
```

XXXXXXXXXXXXXXX------SNIPPED-------XXXXXXXXXXXXXXXXXXXXX

L02-19: The accounts variable here is a "map of maps" type. The first-level map is the accounts that we need to create, and the second-level map is the details of those accounts.

Each account creation requires a specific email address, and since I don't wish to manage multiple emails, I recommend to use the '+' identifier as shown previously that maps all the different accounts (i.e., prod, identity, staging, and dev) to a single email inbox. This gives the flexibility to create multiple emails with a single inbox.

It is not necessary to login using any of those accounts that are generally used for "break-the-glass" emergency moments when the management account/admin account is locked out and you need to access any of these accounts. You would, however, receive email notifications on these emails informing that your account has been created and, in some scenarios, also be asked for verification without which you won't be able to perform any operations.

We'll see the email notifications in action when we execute the terraform files in the "Global" folder.

8.2.3 AWS Provider

An important question to answer is, what access will be needed to create these accounts?

The answer is pretty simple; we'll need the existing Admin account keys that we've been using so far. All operations for AWS organizations must be done through the admin user credentials.

An interesting observation to keep a note on is AWS organizations cannot be created using your root account access. Hence, you need to create a user account and provide administrator access to that user and then only you'll be able to operate AWS organizations.

A top-up question would be, how will Terraform administer the other AWS accounts since the current credentials that we have can only access the Management Account?

To answer this question, let's look at the code in the awsaccounts Module located at *pgitops/global/modules/awsaccounts/main.tf*.

Code Block 8-4. AWS accounts module

File: pgitops/global/modules/awsaccounts/main.tf

```
03: resource "aws_organizations_account" "default" {
04:    name      = var.name
05:    email     = var.email
06:    parent_id = var.parent_id
07:    role_name = "Administrator"
08:    lifecycle {
09:       ignore_changes = [role_name]
10:    }
11: }
```

L07: While other lines are self-explanatory, it's important to understand what's happening at this line. Whenever an AWS account is created using AWS organizations, a default IAM Role with Administrator privileges is created in the target account with a corresponding AssumeRole created in the management account. This is also called an Organization Administrator Role, which is then used to access and create resources in the target account through the management account credentials.

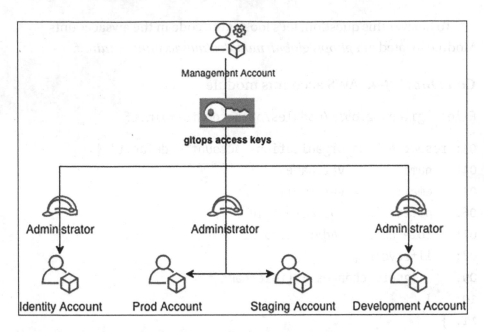

Figure 8-2. *High-level view of all AWS accounts*

This operation is facilitated by declaring the following code in the *pgitops/global/providers.tf* as shown as follows.

Code Block 8-5. Declaring AWS Providers for different accounts using Assume Role

File: pgitops/global/providers.tf

```
17: provider "aws" {
18:   # Any region can be set here as IAM is a global service
19:   region = var.region
20: }
21:
22: # Provider configuration for Assuming Administrator Role in
    Identity account.
23: provider "aws" {
```

```
24:    assume_role {
25:      role_arn = "arn:aws:iam::${module.identity_account.
         id}:role/Administrator"
26:    }
27:
28:    alias  = "identity"
29:    region = var.region
30: }
```

L17–20: This is the primary provider that will utilize the provided access keys of the management account (gitops in our case) and perform all the magic.

L23–30: This is where we are declaring a different provider with an alias as "identity." This provider has an assume role configured at **L25**, which will assume the "Administrator" IAM role created in the identity account and perform all the requested operations.

Similarly, different providers are configured for prod, staging and development accounts as well as shown in the following code.

Code Block 8-6. Declaring AWS Providers in code

File: pgitops/global/main.tf

```
02: module "staging" {
03:    source = "./staging"
04:
05:    account               = "staging"
06:    identity_account_id = module.identity_account.id
07:    domain                = "staging.${var.domain}"
08:
09:    providers = {
10:      aws = aws.staging
11:    }
```

```
12:
13: }
14:
16: module "prod" {
17:   source = "./prod"
18:
19:   account             = "prod"
20:   identity_account_id = module.identity_account.id
21:   domain              = var.domain
22:
23:   providers = {
24:     aws = aws.prod
25:   }
26:
27: }
```

8.3 AWS IAM

Now that we've seen how AWS organizations is being used to create accounts, let's do a deep dive to understand how we can go about creating user accounts and provide them with the necessary privileges to perform the requisite set of actions.

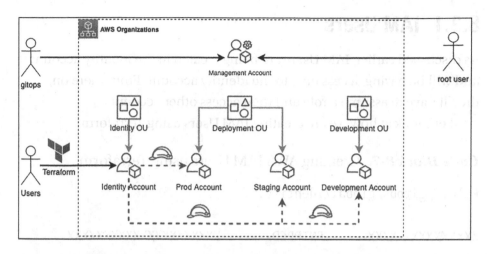

Figure 8-3. *AWS organizations and user access*

The preceding diagram depicts what we are ultimately trying to accomplish:

- All users will be created in the identity account only.

- Privileges assigned to the users in the identity account will be limited and defined by the groups that will be created. However, no user will be able to perform any non-IAM operation in the identity account.

- IAM Roles with predefined permissions will be created in each of the non-identity accounts.

- Each IAM User will be required to Assume the IAM Roles created in the non-identity accounts. This is also called Cross-Account IAM Roles Access.

- Terraform also will have access only to the identity account and will be required to Assume roles into differ-ent accounts to perform the required operations.

8.3.1 IAM Users

As discussed earlier, IAM Users are being created in the identity account and will be having access only to the identity account. From there on, they'll have to assume a role and then access other accounts.

Let's look at how we are creating IAM Users using Terraform.

Code Block 8-7. Creating AWS IAM Users using Terraform

File: pgitops/global/identity.tf

```
XXXXXXXXXXXXXXX------SNIPPED-------XXXXXXXXXXXXXXXXXXXXX

62: module "users" {
63:   for_each = var.users
64:
65:   source = "./modules/awsusers"
66:
67:   user_name = var.users[each.key].username
68:   pgp_key   = file("data/${var.users[each.key].pgp_key}")
69:
70:   groups = var.users[each.key].role == "admin" ? [aws_iam_
      group.iam_admin.name] : [aws_iam_group.self_manage.name]
71:
72:   providers = {
73:     aws = aws.identity
74:   }
75: }

XXXXXXXXXXXXXXX------SNIPPED-------XXXXXXXXXXXXXXXXXXXXX
```

L63: Iterating through a map of users that we need to create. I'll show the map of users shortly.

L68: When creating IAM Users using terraform, we'll need a Public GPG Key that is used by Terraform to encrypt the passwords for each user. The encrypted password is then shown on the console and decrypted only by the private GPG Key, which only the user has access to. All Public PGP keys need to be stored under the *pgitops/global/data* folder only.

L70: Within the identity account, I've created two groups, and depending on the role, that is, admin/non-admin, the user is dynamically assigned to that particular group in the identity account.

L72–74: In the "AWS Provider" section, we saw how Terraform will assume the Administrator IAM Role in the identity account. Hence, here we are specifying the provider to inform Terraform to execute all the code written in this module in the identity account only. If the provider is not specified, it will execute the code in the context of the current account, which is nothing but the management account.

Let's look at the *users* variable, which is a map of user-related information as shown in the following.

Code Block 8-8. Configuring the Users variable

File: pgitops/global/terraform.*auto*.tfvars

```
XXXXXXXXXXXXXXX------SNIPPED-------XXXXXXXXXXXXXXXXXXXXX

21: users = {
22:   raadha = {
23:     username = "raadha"
24:     pgp_key  = "raadha.pub"
25:     role     = "developer"
26:   },
27:   sita = {
28:     username = "sita"
29:     pgp_key  = "sita.pub"
```

```
30:     role     = "admin"
31:     },
32:     padma = {
33:       username = "padma"
34:       pgp_key  = "padma.pub"
35:       role     = "readonly"
36:     }
37: }
```

XXXXXXXXXXXXXX------SNIPPED-------XXXXXXXXXXXXXXXXXXXXX

The first-level map is the username, and the second-level map is the username with the role and the name of the GPG Key assigned for that particular user.

I've currently defined three different organization roles, that is, developer, admin, and readonly. IAM Roles with requisite permissions will be created in different environments implementing access for the respective roles as we'll see in the "IAM Roles" section a little later.

Let's understand what's going behind the scenes in the */modules/awsusers*; the code for the main.tf file is shown in the following.

Code Block 8-9. AWS Users module implementation

File: pgitops/global/modules/awsusers/main.tf

```
01: # Create an AWS Human user with provided username
02: resource "aws_iam_user" "default" {
03:   name = var.user_name
04:   tags = {
05:     terraform-managed = "true"
06:   }
07: }
08:
```

```
09: # Create a login profile to generate a temporary password
      encrypted with the provided GPG Key
10: # Mandatory Reset of password
11: resource "aws_iam_user_login_profile" "default" {
12:   user                    = aws_iam_user.default.name
13:   pgp_key                 = var.pgp_key
14:   password_reset_required = true
15:   lifecycle {
16:     ignore_changes = [
17:       password_reset_required
18:     ]
19:   }
20: }
21:
22: # Add User to the Groups provided
23: resource "aws_iam_user_group_membership" "default" {
24:   user   = aws_iam_user.default.name
25:   groups = var.groups
26: }
```

XXXXXXXXXXXXXXX------SNIPPED-------XXXXXXXXXXXXXXXXXXXXX

L02-07: Creating an AWS IAM User with a specific username.

L11-20: Every user's login profile needs to be created with a temporary encrypted password, which mandatorily needs to change on first access. Once the user accesses the console and changes the password, the *password_reset_required* attribute in the user's metadata flips to *false*.

However, whenever there is an update to the Terraform code, the *password_reset_required* attribute flips to true and the user's password is resetted. To avoid the *ignore_changes* lifecycle attribute on **L16** is required, which states that ignore the changes to the *password_reset_required* attribute.

If the user forgets the password, then the admin user will log into the console and generate a new set of passwords for that user. It's neither feasible nor advisable to run the entire terraform code just to change a user's password.

L22-26: Lastly, every user in the identity account must be mapped to at least one group, which is what we'll explore next.

Lastly, we are enforcing the password policy as well for all Users configured in the identity account using the following code.

Code Block 8-10. Setting Password policy on identity account

File: pgitops/global/identity.tf

```
01: # Create a Password Policy in the Identity Account as users
      will be created in this account only
02: resource "aws_iam_account_password_policy" "strict" {
03:    minimum_password_length        = 10
04:    require_lowercase_characters   = true
05:    require_numbers                = true
06:    require_uppercase_characters   = true
07:    require_symbols                = true
08:    allow_users_to_change_password = true
09:
10:    provider = aws.identity
11:
12: }
```

XXXXXXXXXXXXXXX------SNIPPED-------XXXXXXXXXXXXXXXXXXXXX

8.3.2 IAM Groups

The identity account serves as the landing zone for all the users. Hence, basic permissions need to be provided to each user so that they can access their own account. Hence, I've created two sets of IAM Groups, and depending on the role provided to the user, she is added to that particular group.

Let's look at the IAM Administrator Group.

Code Block 8-11. Creating IAMAdmin Role for identity account

File: pgitops/global/identity.tf

```
XXXXXXXXXXXXXXXX------SNIPPED-------XXXXXXXXXXXXXXXXXXXXX

38: resource "aws_iam_policy" "iam_admin" {
39:    name    = "IAM Administrator"
40:    policy = file("data/iamadmin.json")
41:
42:    provider = aws.identity
43: }
44:
45: # Create an IAM Administrator Group
46: resource "aws_iam_group" "iam_admin" {
47:    name = "IAM Administrator"
48:
49:    provider = aws.identity
50: }
51:
52: # Attach the IAM Administrator Policy with Group
53: resource "aws_iam_group_policy_attachment" "iam_admin" {
54:    group      = aws_iam_group.iam_admin.name
55:    policy_arn = aws_iam_policy.iam_admin.arn
```

```
56:
57:    provider = aws.identity
58: }
```

L45–50: Create an IAM group called IAM Administrator.

L38–43: Assign an IAM Policy with the permissions specified in the file located at *pgitops/global/data/iamadmin.json* as shown in the following. This Policy states that it provides all IAM-related permissions on all IAM resources.

Code Block 8-12. IAM Administrator Permissions Policy

File: global/*data*/iamadmin.json

```
01: {
02:    "Version": "2012-10-17",
03:    "Statement": [
04:        {
05:            "Sid": "IAMAdmin",
06:            "Effect": "Allow",
07:            "Action": [
08:                "iam:*"
09:            ],
10:            "Resource": "*"
11:        }
12:    ]
13: }
```

L52–58: Attach the IAM Policy to the IAM Group.

The Self-Managed group allows users to be able to access the identity account using the username/password provided by the administrator, change her password, and download her access keys. All other actions are prohibited.

The Terraform code for the Self-Managed group remains the same as that of IAM Administrator with the exception of the policy that is too verbose to mention here. Hence, a snippet of the policy can be seen in the following.

Code Block 8-13. Self-Manage IAM Permissions Policy

File: global/*data*/self_manage.json

```
XXXXXXXXXXXXXXX------SNIPPED-------XXXXXXXXXXXXXXXXXXXX
13:          {
14:              "Sid": "AllowManageOwnPasswords",
15:              "Effect": "Allow",
16:              "Action": [
17:                  "iam:ChangePassword",
18:                  "iam:GetUser"
19:              ],
20:              "Resource": "arn:aws:iam::*:user/${aws:u
                 sername}"
21:          },
22:          {
23:              "Sid": "AllowManageOwnAccessKeys",
24:              "Effect": "Allow",
25:              "Action": [
26:                  "iam:CreateAccessKey",
27:                  "iam:DeleteAccessKey",
28:                  "iam:ListAccessKeys",
29:                  "iam:UpdateAccessKey"
30:              ],
31:              "Resource": "arn:aws:iam::*:user/${aws:u
                 sername}"

XXXXXXXXXXXXXXX------SNIPPED-------XXXXXXXXXXXXXXXXXXXX
```

L14–19: Policy allows users to manage their own passwords. **L20** provides an explicit declaration of the username that also enforces authentication.

L23–30: Policy allows users to manage their AWS Access Keys.

8.3.3 IAM Roles

Before we begin the discussion of how I am creating the role, let's discuss a little bit about how Cross-Account Roles function.

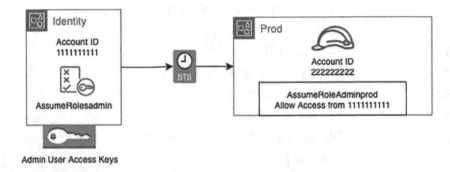

Figure 8-4. *Cross-Account IAM Roles Access*

Let's take an example of an Admin user in the identity account who needs to login and operate in the prod account. How will this operation happen?

In the prod account, we first need to create an IAM Role called "AssumeRoleAdminprod" and attach the existing policy of "arn:aws:iam::aws:policy/AdministratorAccess". In addition to this, we also need to add an Assume Role Policy where we are specifying the identity account ID as a Trusted Entity. In Terraform, this can be achieved through the following code.

Code Block 8-14. AWS IAM Cross-Account Role

```
01: # Create an IAM Role with an AssumeRole Policy for a
    trusted entity
02: resource "aws_iam_role" "default" {
03:   name = "AssumeRoleAdminprod"
04:   assume_role_policy = jsonencode({
05:     Version = "2012-10-17",
06:     Statement = [
07:       {
08:         Effect = "Allow",
09:         Action = "sts:AssumeRole",
10:         Principal = {
11:           "AWS" : "arn:aws:iam::1111111111:root"
12:         }
13:     }]
14:   })
15:   tags = {
16:     terraform-managed = "true"
17:     account           = var.account
18:   }
19: }
20:
21: # Attach the Policies provided to the IAM role
    created above
22: resource "aws_iam_role_policy_attachment" "default" {
23:
24:   policy_arn = ["arn:aws:iam::aws:policy/
    AdministratorAccess "]
25:   role       = aws_iam_role.default.name
26: }
```

L02–19: In the prod account, we first need to create an IAM Role called "AssumeRoleAdminprod" and attach an assume role policy specifying the identity account ID as a Trusted Entity as shown on **L11**.

L21–26: We then attach the predefined policy of arn "*arn:aws:iam::aws:policy/AdministratorAccess*" to the IAM Role created previously.

Next, in the identity account, we create an IAM Policy called "AssumeRolesadmin" and attach it to the IAM User "admin," thereby granting only the admin user to access the Administrator role in the prod account. A sample terraform code to do this is as shown in the following.

Code Block 8-15. AWS IAM Cross-Account Role Contd

```
02: resource "aws_iam_policy" "default" {
03:    name         = "AssumeRolesadmin"
04:    description = "Allow IAM User to Assume the IAM Roles"
05:    policy = jsonencode({
06:       Version = "2012-10-17",
07:       Statement = [
08:          {
09:             Effect   = "Allow",
10:             Action   = "sts:AssumeRole",
11:             Resource = ["arn:aws:iam::2222222222:role/
                AssumeRoleAdminprod"]
12:       }]
13:    })
14: }
15:
16: resource "aws_iam_user_policy_attachment" "default" {
17:    user        = "admin"
18:    policy_arn = aws_iam_policy.default.arn
19: }
```

L02-14: We are defining the AWS IAM Policy, which will allow the user/group to whom this policy would be attached to, to assume the specific role in the specific account mentioned on **L11**.

L16-19: Attaching the Policy created previously to the specific user.

Tip   Many terraform developers and AWS IAM architects would advise to attach these policies to a group rather than a user for better/broader access management. I've attached the policy to a user in this book to keep things simple.

The following code snippet shows how we are creating the AWS IAM Roles in the **prod** account and supplying the identity account id to add as a trusted entity.

Code Block 8-16. Creating AWS IAM Roles in prod account

File: pgitops/global/prod/main.tf

```
XXXXXXXXXXXXXXX------SNIPPED-------XXXXXXXXXXXXXXXXXXXXXX
12: # Create an AWS ReadOnly Role with a Managed
    ReadOnlyAccess Policy
13: module "assume_readonly_role" {
14:   source = "./modules/assumerolepolicytrust"
15:
16:   role_name     = "AssumeRoleReadOnly${var.account}"
17:   trusted_entity = "arn:aws:iam::${var.identity_account_
                       id}:root"
18:   policy_arn    = ["arn:aws:iam::aws:policy/
      ReadOnlyAccess"]
19:   account       = var.account
20:
```

```
21: }
22:
23: # Create an Admin Role with Administrator Access Policy
24: module "assume_admin_role" {
25:    source = "./modules/assumerolepolicytrust"
26:
27:    role_name       = "AssumeRoleAdmin${var.account}"
28:    trusted_entity = "arn:aws:iam::${var.identity_account_
       id}:root"
29:    policy_arn      = ["arn:aws:iam::aws:policy/
       AdministratorAccess"]
30:    account         = var.account
31:
32: }
```
XXXXXXXXXXXXXXX------SNIPPED-------XXXXXXXXXXXXXXXXXXXXX

For performing the IAM Roles Mapping, we are using the local variable called *user_role_mapping* as shown in the following.

Code Block 8-17. user_role_mapping variable

File: pgitops/global/identity.tf

XXXXXXXXXXXXXXX------SNIPPED-------XXXXXXXXXXXXXXXXXXXXX

```
80: locals {
81:    user_role_mapping = {
82:       developer = [
83:          module.staging.assume_dev_role_arn,
84:          module.prod.assume_dev_role_arn,
85:          module.dev.assume_admin_role_arn
86:       ],
87:       admin = [
88:          module.staging.assume_admin_role_arn,
```

```
89:        module.prod.assume_admin_role_arn,
90:        module.dev.assume_admin_role_arn
91:      ],
92:      readonly = [
93:        module.staging.assume_readonly_role_arn,
94:        module.prod.assume_readonly_role_arn,
95:        module.dev.assume_readonly_role_arn
96:      ]
97:    }
98: }
```

XXXXXXXXXXXXXXX------SNIPPED-------XXXXXXXXXXXXXXXXXXXXX

Here I am simply declaring which IAM Role should be assigned to the role that I've defined in the users variable. For example, A developer role will get access to the dev IAM Roles in the staging and the prod environment and admin role in the dev environment. Any user who takes up the developer role will automatically get access to the staging and prod environment as a developer and the dev environment as an admin.

The following code performs this mapping between the users and their respective roles by iterating over the *user_role_mapping* local variable we saw previously.

Code Block 8-18. Looping through user_role_mapping variable

File: pgitops/global/identity.tf

XXXXXXXXXXXXXXX------SNIPPED-------XXXXXXXXXXXXXXXXXXXXX

```
103: module "user_role_mapping" {
104:   source = "./modules/useriamrolepolicyattachment"
105:
106:   for_each = var.users
107:
```

```
108:    roles      = local.user_role_mapping[each.value["role"]]
109:    user_name = each.key
110:
111:    providers = {
112:       aws = aws.identity
113:    }
114:
115:    depends_on = [module.users]
116: }
```

XXXXXXXXXXXXXXX------SNIPPED-------XXXXXXXXXXXXXXXXXXXXX

Table 8-1 should help summarize how I've configured the IAM Roles access for different users.

Table 8-1. *Permissions Table*

User	Org Role	IAM Role
Sita	admin	AssumeRoleAdminprod
		AssumeRoleAdminstaging
		AssumeRoleAdmindev
Padma	readonly	AssumeRoleReadOnlyprod
		AssumeRoleReadOnlystaging
		AssumeRoleReadOnlydev
Raadha	developer	AssumeRoleDeveloperprod
		AssumeRoleDeveloperstaging
		AssumeRoleAdmindev

8.4 AWS Route53

In the last chapter, we created a Route53 Zone record in the root account through the AWS CLI. However, in this chapter, we'll look at how we can create the same using Terraform and one each for every deployment account for better segregation as depicted in the following.

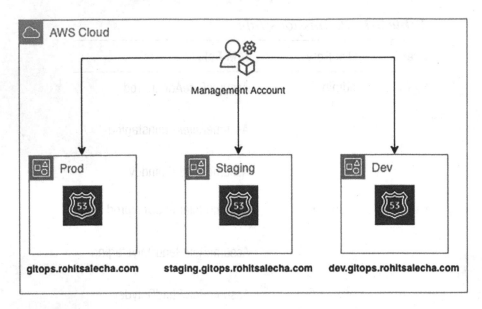

Figure 8-5. *AWS Route53 Hosted Zone for each account*

The following code shows how AWS Route53 zone can be created for the staging account.

Code Block 8-19. Creating Route53 Hosted Zone for Staging

File: pgitops/global/main.tf

```
02: module "staging" {
03:    source = "./staging"
04:
05:    account             = "staging"
06:    identity_account_id = module.identity_account.id
07:    domain              = "staging.${var.domain}"
08:
09:    providers = {
10:      aws = aws.staging
```

```
11:   }
12:
13: }
```

XXXXXXXXXXXXXXX------SNIPPED-------XXXXXXXXXXXXXXXXXXXXX

L07: This is how I am passing the value of the domain name that is needed for each environment. Similarly for every environment, I am passing the respective domain value.

Under the hood in the individual module folder, this is how I am creating the Route53 Zones by passing the value of the domain at **L37** as shown in the following.

Code Block 8-20. Creating Route53 Hosted Zone for Staging Contd

File: pgitoos/global/staging/main.tf

XXXXXXXXXXXXXXX------SNIPPED-------XXXXXXXXXXXXXXXXXXXXX

```
36: resource "aws_route53_zone" "default" {
37:   name = var.domain
38:
39:   tags = {
40:     Account           = var.account
41:     terraform-managed = "true"
42:   }
43: }
```

8.5 Executing Global

Under the global folder, I've added only those resources that need to be created only once and are required for operation of the staging/production and development environments. Resources like IAM Users and their Roles, Route53 Records, and AWS accounts need to be created only once; hence, they all have been grouped together. It would not be possible to create these resources along with the application infrastructure that we've set up in the last chapter as things like User's Access Keys, Route53 records, and IAM Roles would be needed to create the entire infrastructure for the application in different environments.

Hence, we'll first need to ensure that all the terraform code in the global folder is executed first and then execute each environment. Also, one crucial information that will be needed while creating the environments is the account IDs of the environments that we need to operate in.

For example, when spinning up the dev environment, we'll need to pass the account ID of the dev environment in terraform code of the infra folder and same for each of the other accounts. We'll see why we need the account ID when I will be executing the infra folder.

8.5.1 Generate GNU PG Keys

Every user who needs access to the AWS Console needs to generate a pair of GPG keys. The private key is configured in her system, and the public key is to be shared to the administrator along with an approved level of access required in the different environments. Once the Terraform is executed, the administrator shall share the encrypted password string with every user, which needs to be changed on first login. Once the user logs in, she can download her access keys to operate on the AWS environment.

Let's walk through the entire process for user "sita" who is having administrator access to all environments.

Ensure that GNU PG has been installed as mentioned in the "Prerequisites" section before going ahead. Once you fire the command to generate the key as shown in the following, you'll be asked to enter your real name and email address and then confirm with an O(kay).

After that, you'll be prompted to enter your passphrase twice.

Note   Ensure you don't lose the passphrase as without that you won't be able to decrypt your key back.

CLI Output 8-21. Generating GPG Keys

cmd> gpg --generate-*key*
prompt> Real name: sita
prompt> Email address: test@test.com
prompt> Change (N)ame, (E)mail, or (O)kay/(Q)uit?: O
prompt> Enter passphrase
prompt> Re-enter passphrase

Let's now save the public key so that terraform can utilize it to encrypt your console password. To save the key, first we'll need to list the keys to understand the Key ID as highlighted in blue in the following. Once we have the Key ID, we can export it into the data folder as shown in the following.

CLI Output 8-22. Listing and Exporting GPG Public Key

cmd> cd pgitops
cmd> gpg --*list*-keys

gpg: checking the trustdb
gpg: marginals needed: 3 completes needed: 1 trust model: pgp
gpg: depth: 0 valid: 1 signed: 0 trust: 0-, 0q, 0n,
0m, 0f, 1u
gpg: *next* trustdb check due at 2024-06-21
/Users/rohitsalecha/.gnupg/pubring.kbx
----
pub   ed25519 2022-06-22 [SC] [expires: 2024-06-21]
      27B6CF62B1352FC30F3F14C6D3B5FCD325AAEC25

```
uid              [ultimate] sita
sub      cv25519 2022-06-22 [E] [expires: 2024-06-21]

cmd> gpg --export 27B6CF62B1352FC30F3F14C6D3B5FCD325AAEC25 |
base64 > global/data/sita.pub

cmd> ls global/data/sita.pub
global/data/sita.pub
```

Note   Similarly, we need to perform the same operations for other users defined (i.e., padma and radha and have their public keys saved in the global/data directory). It is extremely important to have their public keys generated and saved as well because I need to demonstrate the Role-Based Access control that has been configured.

8.5.2 Configure Variables

Next, an important task that we need to do is ensure the *pgitops/global/terraform.auto.tfvars* file is properly configured with all the values.

The emails for the various environments must be configured properly and must be unique and valid as an example shown in the following, which I'll be using for showing the rest of the demonstrations through the book. Please ensure to change these before moving ahead; else you'll get an error stating that this account already exists.

Warning   These email addresses need to be unique and never used for creating AWS accounts; if any existing email addresses are used, you'll get an error stating the email address already exists.

Code Block 8-23. Configuring emails for the AWS accounts

File: pgitops/global/terraform.*auto*.tfvars

```
02: accounts = {
03:   dev = {
04:     name  = "dev"
05:     email = "i+dev@rohitsalecha.com"
06:   },
07:   identity = {
08:     name  = "identity"
09:     email = "i+identity@rohitsalecha.com"
10:   },
11:   prod = {
12:     name  = "prod"
13:     email = "i+prod@rohitsalecha.com"
14:   },
15:   staging = {
16:     name  = "staging"
17:     email = "i+staging@rohitsalecha.com"
18:   }
19: }
```

XXXXXXXXXXXXXXX------SNIPPED-------XXXXXXXXXXXXXXXXXXXXX

Configure the Users with the exact username and the exact name of the public key as stored under the data folder as shown in the following.

Code Block 8-24. Configure users and their GPG keys

File: global/terraform.*auto*.tfvars

XXXXXXXXXXXXXXX------SNIPPED-------XXXXXXXXXXXXXXXXXXXXX

```
21: users = {
22:   raadha = {
23:     username = "raadha"
24:     pgp_key  = "raadha.pub"
25:     role     = "developer"
26:   },
27:   sita = {
28:     username = "sita"
29:     pgp_key  = "sita.pub"
30:     role     = "admin"
31:   },
32:   padma = {
33:     username = "padma"
34:     pgp_key  = "padma.pub"
35:     role     = "readonly"
36:   }
37: }
```

XXXXXXXXXXXXXXX------SNIPPED-------XXXXXXXXXXXXXXXXXXXXX

And finally, the org name and the main domain name, which should be either your subdomain or your top level whichever you've chosen in the previous chapter.

Code Block 8-25. Adding Domain and Org values

File: pgitops/global/terraform.*auto*.tfvars

XXXXXXXXXXXXXXX------SNIPPED-------XXXXXXXXXXXXXXXXXXXXX

```
39: org_name = "gitops"
40: domain   = "gitops.rohitsalecha.com"
```

XXXXXXXXXXXXXXX------SNIPPED-------XXXXXXXXXXXXXXXXXXXXX

8.5.3 Terraform Cloud Workspace

Next, one very important step is to configure Terraform Cloud workspace for the global folder. All the information about the state of the infrastructure setup in the global folder will now be available in terraform cloud.

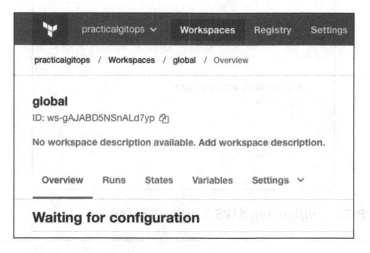

Figure 8-6. *Terraform Cloud Global workspace*

Ensure the name you choose for the Global workspace is also recorded here.

Code Block 8-26. Global workspace configuration

File: pgitops/global/global.hcl

```
1: workspaces { name = "global" }
2: hostname     = "app.terraform.io"
3: organization = "practicalgitops"
```

L1: Need to update the name of the global folder

Next, ensure your AWS Keys have been configured as environment variables. For the Global workspace, we only need the AWS Keys configured in the variables section; nothing else is needed. These keys are of the administrator user "gitops" that we created initially.

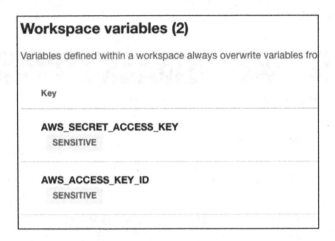

Figure 8-7. *Configuring AWS Keys in Workspace*

Note   The account that you'll be using here should not have an existing AWS organization root account. It should be a fresh account.

8.5.4 Terraform Apply

Now that we are all set to perform our **terraform apply,** let's follow the process of first pushing our changes in a branch, creating a PR, reviewing the PR, and then merging the branch into master.

CLI Output 8-27.   Pushing Code for Global

```
cmd> git status
On branch main
```

```
Your branch is up to date with 'origin/main'.

Changes not staged for commit:
  (use "git add <file>..." to update what will be committed)
  (use "git restore <file>..." to discard changes in working
  directory)
        modified:    global/data/padma.pub
        modified:    global/data/raadha.pub
        modified:    global/data/sita.pub
        modified:    global/terraform.auto.tfvars

no changes added to commit (use "git add" and/or "git
commit -a")
cmd> git checkout -b global1
Switched to a new branch 'global1'

cmd(global1)> git add .
cmd(global1)> git commit -m "first commit"
cmd(global1)> git push --set-upstream origin global1
```

As soon as the changes are pushed, you should be able to see the message on github.com.

Let's Compare and Pull Request and start the process.

Once the PR is created, you should see the following screen.

Figure 8-8. *PR Screen request to merge*

After a while, it will start the Terraform Plan and show us the following in our Github Comments and we can review the full plan.

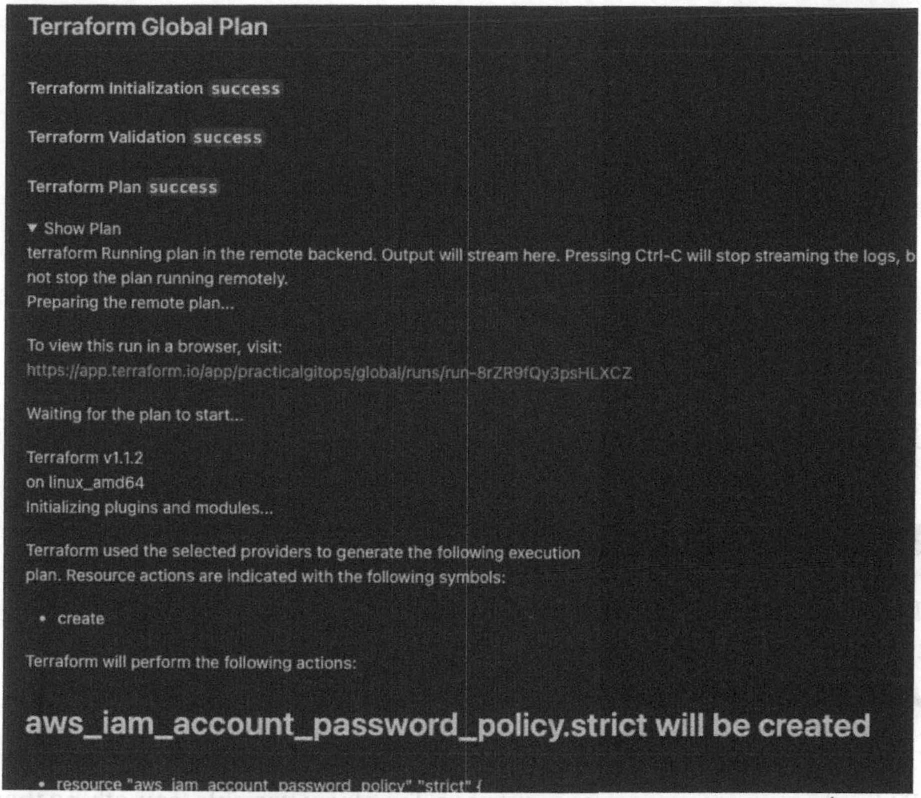

```
Terraform Global Plan

Terraform Initialization success

Terraform Validation success

Terraform Plan success

▼ Show Plan
terraform Running plan in the remote backend. Output will stream here. Pressing Ctrl-C will stop streaming the logs, b
not stop the plan running remotely.
Preparing the remote plan...

To view this run in a browser, visit:
https://app.terraform.io/app/practicalgitops/global/runs/run-8rZR9fQy3psHLXCZ

Waiting for the plan to start...

Terraform v1.1.2
on linux_amd64
Initializing plugins and modules...

Terraform used the selected providers to generate the following execution
plan. Resource actions are indicated with the following symbols:

  • create

Terraform will perform the following actions:

aws_iam_account_password_policy.strict will be created

  • resource "aws_iam_account_password_policy" "strict" {
```

Figure 8-9. *Review Terraform Plan in PR*

Once the PR is merged, terraform apply shall start and finally
Terraform output would look something like the following once apply is
finished.

Resources 49 Outputs 4		Current as of the most recent state versic
NAME ↓	**TYPE**	**VALUE**
account_ids	object	{"dev":"9▪▪ ▌▐ 37","identity":"4.▪▪▪ ▐0","prod":"▪▪6 03▪ ▪2","staging":"1.▪ ▐ ▪▪9"}
links	object	{"aws_console_sign_identity_account":"https://▪▪▌ ▪▪ 80.signin.aws.amazon.com/console/","aws_console_sign_prod _accoun…
name_servers	object	{"dev":{"domain":"dev.gitops.rohitsalecha.com","name_ser vers":"ns-1337.awsdns-39.org.\nns-1988.awsdns-56.co.uk.\n ns-42.a…
users	object	{"padma":{"role_arns_assigned":["arn:aws:iam::1▪,▪▪▌▐ 49:role/AssumeRoleReadOnlystaging","arn:aws:iam::▪▪▌▐34 ▪▐:ro…

Figure 8-10. *Terraform output*

8.5.5 Terraform Output

Let's understand each of the terraform output.

Account IDs

The account IDs need to be noted as we'll need to configure each account ID for the respective environments as a Terraform variable, something that we'll discuss later while executing the infra folder.

Also, as soon as you see this output, you would also receive a Welcome email from Amazon on each of the email addresses specified for the account creation.

Links

The links provided here are just for bookmarking the identity account ID URL for sign-in and the respective Roles that need to be assumed into different accounts.

Name Servers

The Name Servers provided here need to be updated in your DNS records for each of the account as shown in the following.

Code Block 8-28. DNS nameservers

```
{
  "dev": {
    "domain": "dev.gitops.rohitsalecha.com",
    "name_servers": "ns-1337.awsdns-39.org.\nns-1988.awsdns-56.
    co.uk.\nns-42.awsdns-05.com.\nns-654.awsdns-17.net."
  },
  "prod": {
    "domain": "gitops.rohitsalecha.com",
    "name_servers": "ns-1046.awsdns-02.org.\nns-1921.awsdns-48.
    co.uk.\nns-214.awsdns-26.com.\nns-706.awsdns-24.net."
  },
  "staging": {
    "domain": "staging.gitops.rohitsalecha.com",
    "name_servers": "ns-1040.awsdns-02.org.\nns-1595.awsdns-07.
    co.uk.\nns-303.awsdns-37.com.\nns-807.awsdns-36.net."
  }
}
```

So as an example, to update the prod account DNS Servers, I need to add the following as NS Records against gitops.rohitsalecha.com:

ns-1046.awsdns-02.org.

ns-1921.awsdns-48.co.uk.

ns-214.awsdns-26.com.

ns-706.awsdns-24.net.

☐	gitops.rohitsalecha.com	NS	Simple	-	ns-1046.awsdns-02.org. ns-1921.awsdns-48.co.uk. ns-214.awsdns-26.com. ns-706.awsdns-24.net.
☐	dev.gitops.rohitsalecha.com	NS	Simple	-	s-1337.awsdns-39.org. ns-1988.awsdns-56.co.uk. ns-42.awsdns-05.com. ns-654.awsdns-17.net.
☐	staging.gitops.rohitsalecha.com	NS	Simple	-	ns-1040.awsdns-02.org. ns-1595.awsdns-07.co.uk. ns-303.awsdns-37.com. ns-807.awsdns-36.net.

Figure 8-11. *Configuring nameservers*

Users

Next, output of the users block consists of the users encrypted temporary passwords and their assumable roles. As an example, let's view the details of the administrator Sita.

Code Block 8-29. Sample Users Output

```
"sita":{
  "role_arns_assigned": [
    "arn:aws:iam::1xxxxxxxx9:role/AssumeRoleAdminstaging",
    "arn:aws:iam::2xxxxxxxx2:role/AssumeRoleAdminprod",
    "arn:aws:iam::9xxxxxxxx97:role/AssumeRoleAdmindev"
  ],
  "temp_password": "wV4Dg8bNTGnmb5USAQdA8+383VwQHuVL3HJ4YXF4
tlnRAYgOVSmJU9fHHV7R1UUwzKJgvFoJi7y+4784x4muIYeO+kialt/
6QfgB8iHPCxedgXovISPJzhYgw8ArlOoJ1FABBwEMkLPQrwCqZE+d3Z
KuwtOBsP7j4xAPYepnY6IBOxj55DiWO4VdRLGzaaosLwthHkT5CSPX
crpfhHxpyfFeb2a7Oi8pXOn5SnJEw8pCA=="
}
```

Let's decrypt the passwords encrypted using the GPG key generated earlier.

CLI Output 8-30. Decrypting the password

```
cmd> export GPG_TTY=$(tty)
cmd> echo "<temp_password string>" | base64 -d | gpg --decrypt
```

Using the password output on the console and the Identity URL link provided in the links' section, you can now log into the AWS Console using the temporary password. At first, you'll be prompted to change your password, which must be done immediately. Once authenticated, download the keys and configure an AWS Profile on the CLI using the following commands.

CLI Output 8-31. Configuring Sita's AWS Profile

```
cmd> aws configure --profile sita
prompt> AWS Access Key ID : AKIAXXXXXXXXXXXXXXXXXXXX
prompt> AWS Secret Access Key : o9PxxxxxxxxxxxxxxxxxxxxxxxxxxUc
prompt> Default region name : us-east-2
prompt> Default output format : json
```

Note   You'll need to repeat all the previous steps for all the other users in order to see Access Control in action.

8.5.6 Possible Issues

This is a tidy bit of a complicated setup as there are many variables involved here and in most scenarios executing terraform more than once may be required, hence just highlighting some possible issues that you may run into.

Email Already Exists

CLI Output 8-32. Email already exists error

```
| Error: error waiting for AWS Organizations Account (identity)
create: unexpected state 'FAILED', wanted target 'SUCCEEDED'.
last error: EMAIL_ALREADY_EXISTS
|
|   with module.identity_account.aws_organizations_account.
    default,
|   on modules/awsaccounts/main.tf line 3, in resource "aws_
    organizations_account" "default":
|    3: resource "aws_organizations_account" "default" {
```

This is a typical error if you are using an email address that is already tied to an AWS account. Every AWS account needs an email; hence any duplication globally can result in this error.

Hence, the solution here would be to change the email address in the pgitops/global/terraform.auto.tfvars file and push the changes.

AWS Subscription Not Found

CLI Output 8-33. AWS subscription not found error

```
| Error: error creating Route53 Hosted Zone: OptInRequired: The
  AWS Access Key Id needs a subscription for the service
|    status code: 403, request id: 671818a6-464f-4815-b56a-
     da2c74b3555c
|
|   with module.staging.aws_route53_zone.default,
|   on staging/main.tf line 36, in resource "aws_route53_zone"
    "default":
|   36: resource "aws_route53_zone" "default" {
```

If you encounter this error, follow the following solution.

The solution to this problem is ridiculously simple: Just login into your AWS account using the root email address and password of the management account and rerun the terraform code.

You can quite simply just select *Actions*▶*Start new run* from the Terraform Workspace as shown here.

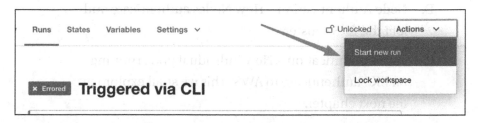

Figure 8-12. *Terraform Cloud running apply from cloud*

If at all you get any error other than the preceding scenarios, the best solution is to just search on Google as it's impossible to cater into all different scenarios.

8.6 EKS Authz

Services like RDS using MySQL/PostgreSQL or EKS using the Kubernetes specifications have their own set of authentication when deployed independently of AWS. However, once AWS provides these services, the authentication and authorization (authz) to these services are then managed or sometimes even overridden by AWS IAM for the sole purpose of uniformity.

Having a uniform/standard approach toward authentication is very important and strongly emphasized by AWS.

In AWS EKS as well, the authentication to the Kubernetes cluster is through AWS IAM and not utilizing the existing methods for authenticating to Kubernetes. We'll be exploring the following different authentication mechanisms employed by EKS:

A.   Client Authentication – Authentication of kubectl to AWS EKS.

B.   Node Authentication – How Nodes authenticate and join the EKS Cluster.

C.   Pod Authentication – How individual pods running on EKS authenticate to AWS. This we shall explore in the next chapter.

8.6.1 EKS Client Authentication

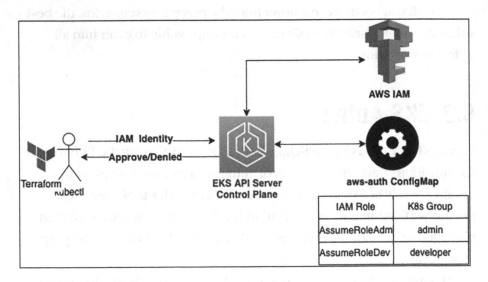

Figure 8-13. *EKS Client Authentication*

The preceding diagram shows a very high-level overview of how AWS IAM Authentication is used for authenticating a user and Kubernetes RBAC

(Role-Based Access Control) is used for implementing authorization. The following are the highlights of the authentication and authorization process:

- AWS IAM recognizes an IAM User or an IAM Role as an identifier as an AWS Identity. Hence, while authenticating using kubectl, the identifier information is first passed to the API Server along with the authentication token generated by the *"aws eks get-token."* If you can recall, this is the same command that is configured in the *kubernetes.tf* file where we've declared the Kubernetes provider.

- EKS API Server relays this information to AWS IAM and performs the verification. This verification is nothing but authentication.

- Once the authentication is successful, then the EKS API Server checks the aws-auth ConfigMap that stores the information about IAM Role Mapping against the Kubernetes Groups. Based on this information, it authorizes the AWS Identity to access the cluster.

This is how any client, be it kubectl or terraform, needs to perform to access the Kubernetes cluster. In our case, we've implemented the AWS Identity as an IAM Role and not an IAM User.

The following is the same AWS-Auth ConfigMap that shows the mapping between the IAM Role that we created in the global folder for the dev account.

Code Block 8-34. AWS ConfigMap (sample)

```
apiVersion: v1
data:
  mapRoles: |
XXXXXXXXXXXXXXX------SNIPPED-------XXXXXXXXXXXXXXXXXXXXXX
```

```
    - rolearn: arn:aws:iam::XXXXXXXXXX:role/AssumeRoleEKSAdmindev
      username: admin
      groups:
        - admin
    - rolearn: arn:aws:iam::XXXXXXXXXX:role/
      AssumeRoleEKSDeveloperdev
      username: developer
      groups:
        - developer
    - rolearn: arn:aws:iam::XXXXXXXXXX:role/
      AssumeRoleEKSReadOnlydev
      username: readonly
      groups:
        - readonly
kind: ConfigMap
metadata:
  name: aws-auth
  namespace: kube-system
```

The following code is the template that is used to generate the preceding ConfigMap.

Code Block 8-35. AWS ConfigMap creation in Terraform

```
File: pgitops/infra/rolebindings.tf

2: data "aws_caller_identity" "current" {}
3:
4: locals {
5:
6:   # Creating the AWS-AUTH
07:   aws_auth_configmap_yaml = <<-EOT
08:   ${chomp(module.eks.aws_auth_configmap_yaml)}
```

```
09:          - rolearn: arn:aws:iam::${data.aws_caller_identity.
             current.id}:role/AssumeRoleAdmin${var.environment}
10:          username: admin
11:          groups:
12:            - system:masters
13:          - rolearn: arn:aws:iam::${data.aws_caller_identity.
             current.id}:role/AssumeRoleDeveloper${var.
             environment}
14:          username: developer
15:          groups:
16:            - developer
17:          - rolearn: arn:aws:iam::${data.aws_caller_identity.
             current.id}:role/AssumeRoleReadOnly${var.
             environment}
18:          username: readonly
19:          groups:
20:            - readonly
21:    EOT
22:
23: }
```

XXXXXXXXXXXXXXX------SNIPPED-------XXXXXXXXXXXXXXXXXXXXXX

L09-12: We are first fetching the ID of the current account where Terraform is executing, which is also the same environment configured. We've templated the name of the IAM Role to match the environment. Here, we are mapping the Admin IAM Role with the system-masters, which is a default administrator group in Kubernetes. So any user assuming this role will access the Kubernetes cluster with admin privileges.

L13-16: Here we are associating the Developer IAM Role with the developer group created in Kubernetes. So any user who would be assuming this role will access the Kubernetes cluster with developer privileges. Same is implemented for the readonly group as well.

The following code shows how using Terraform we are creating the developer Role and RoleBinding and assigning it to the "developer" group.

Code Block 8-36. Kubernetes RoleBindings

File: infra/rolebindings.tf

```
XXXXXXXXXXXXXXX------SNIPPED-------XXXXXXXXXXXXXXXXXXXXX

27: resource "kubernetes_role_v1" "developer" {
28:   metadata {
29:     name      = "developer"
30:     namespace = kubernetes_namespace_v1.app.metadata.0.name
31:   }
32:
33:   rule {
34:     api_groups = ["*"]
35:     resources  = ["pods", "deployments", "services",
         "ingresses", "namespaces", "jobs", "daemonset"]
36:     verbs      = ["*"]
37:   }
38: }
39:
40: resource "kubernetes_role_binding_v1" "developer" {
41:   metadata {
42:     name      = "developer"
43:     namespace = kubernetes_namespace_v1.app.metadata.0.name
44:   }
45:   role_ref {
46:     api_group = "rbac.authorization.k8s.io"
47:     kind      = "Role"
48:     name      = "developer"
49:   }
```

```
50:    subject {
51:      kind      = "Group"
52:      name      = "developer"
53:      api_group = "rbac.authorization.k8s.io"
54:    }
55: }
```

XXXXXXXXXXXXXXXX------SNIPPED-------XXXXXXXXXXXXXXXXXXXXXX

L27-31: Here I am creating the developer role and assigning it specific privileges that a developer may need while accessing the Kubernetes cluster.

L40-55: Here we are binding the developer role to a group called "developers," which is what is mapped in the aws-auth ConfigMap as well.

Similarly, I've created the readonly group as well in the same file.

8.6.2 EKS Node Authentication

Node authentication is happening with the kubelet utility installed on the node servers. However, it still needs a specific AWS Identity as all authentication is with AWS IAM only and not with any X509 certificates that are traditionally used for Node authentication.

Let's look at the sample aws-auth ConfigMap again to better understand how node authentication works as shown in the following.

Code Block 8-37. AWS ConfigMap post apply

```
apiVersion: v1
data:
  mapRoles: |
    - rolearn: arn:aws:iam::XXXXXXXXXXX:role/app-eks-node-gro
      up-2022020812202410610000003
      username: system:node:{{EC2PrivateDNSName}}
```

```
      groups:
        - system:bootstrappers
        - system:nodes
    - rolearn: arn:aws:iam::XXXXXXXXXXX:role/system-eks-node-gr
      oup-20220208122024106000000002
      username: system:node:{{EC2PrivateDNSName}}
      groups:
        - system:bootstrappers
        - system:nodes
XXXXXXXXXXXXXXXX------SNIPPED-------XXXXXXXXXXXXXXXXXXXXXX
kind: ConfigMap
metadata:
  name: aws-auth
  namespace: kube-system
```

Here we can see that the mapping is between a specific IAM Role and the groups as Kubernetes default groups of "system:bootstrappers" and "system:nodes" that have the capabilities to join and manage worker nodes.

This IAM Role is created by the EKS Module and has very specific permissions that allow joining to the master node.

Hence, when kubelet needs to authenticate to the AWS IAM, it'll make use of this specific IAM Role as the AWS Identity to AWS IAM for authentication.

Previously, it can be understood that aws_auth ConfigMap is an extremely critical resource and hence I've created it separately as shown in the following.

Code Block 8-38. Implementing AWS-Auth ConfigMap

```
File: pgitops/infra/rolebindings.tf
XXXXXXXXXXXXXXXX------SNIPPED-------XXXXXXXXXXXXXXXXXXXXXX
```

```
091: resource "kubectl_manifest" "aws_auth" {
092:   yaml_body = <<YAML
093: apiVersion: v1
094: kind: ConfigMap
095: metadata:
096:   labels:
097:     app.kubernetes.io/managed-by: Terraform
098:   name: aws-auth
099:   namespace: kube-system
100: ${local.aws_auth_configmap_yaml}
101: YAML
102:
103:   depends_on = [module.eks]
104:
105: }
```

It is important to study the terraform plan generated during apply as well as destroy as it indicates the approximate order in which the resources will be created/destroyed. In both cases, the order is extremely important and depends_on meta-attribute plays a pivotal role.

For example, if we don't add "resource.kubectl_manifest.aws_auth" as a depending resource for the namespace creation/destruction as shown on **L10**, then terraform will happily destroy the aws_auth ConfigMap prior to destroying the namespace, which will lead to errors and the namespace will need to be manually destroyed.

Code Block 8-39. AWS-AUTH ConfigMap and Namespace dependency

File: pgitops/infra/app.tf

```
03: resource "kubernetes_namespace_v1" "app" {
04:   metadata {
```

```
05:     annotations = {
06:       name = var.org_name
07:     }
08:     name = var.org_name
09:   }
10:   depends_on = [module.eks, resource.kubectl_manifest.
      aws_auth]
11: }
```
XXXXXXXXXXXXXXX------SNIPPED-------XXXXXXXXXXXXXXXXXXXXXX

L10: Explicitly defining the dependency of aws_auth ConfigMap before creating the namespace.

Note   It's also worth noting that the way I am creating the aws-auth ConfigMap is not a standard Terraform format. I'm using a third-party provider called *kubectl_manifest* whose detailed documentation can be found here `https://registry.terraform.io/providers/ gavinbunney/kubectl/latest/docs/resources/kubectl_ manifest`.

This provider is used when it's required to execute yaml files directly as we do using the kubectl utility such as *kubectl apply -f k8s.yaml*.

8.6.3 Provider Configuration

In the previous chapter, we were passing the identity as an AWS User by simply configuring the AWS provider with ACCESS KEY ID and SECRET ACCESS KEY. This worked well as I was creating resources within the same account.

However, here I have all our users created in the identity account, and all resources need to be created in the accounts of their respective environments. Hence, if we need to access the other accounts using the identity account, then we need to perform Cross-Account IAM Role access, and hence, the IAM Role ARN has been specified in the assume_role section on **L51-52** as shown in the following.

Code Block 8-40. Cross-Account Provider configuration

```
File: pgitops/infra/providers.tf
XXXXXXXXXXXXXXX------SNIPPED-------XXXXXXXXXXXXXXXXXXXXX

47: locals {
48:   assume_role_arn = "arn:aws:iam::${var.assume_role_
      account_id}:role/AssumeRoleAdmin${var.environment}"
49: }
50: provider "aws" {
51:   assume_role {
52:     role_arn = local.assume_role_arn
53:   }
54:   region = var.region
55: }
```

The role that is being accessed is the Administrator IAM role that has been created for each environment. So only a user who has access to this IAM Role will be able to execute these Terraform files. In our case, it is the user Sita whose access keys need to be configured in Terraform Cloud staging and prod workspaces. However, in most scenarios, a Terraform user can also be created and assigned the IAM Administrator role or any specific high privilege role.

The variable *var.assume_role_account_id* is a new variable that has been added that holds the value of the account id where the role needs to be accessed. So, when we are running in prod, we need to populate this value with the prod account ID and so on.

However, the default value for this would be the development environment value and needs to be added in the terraform.auto.tfvars file as shown in the following.

Code Block 8-41. Adding the development environment Account ID

File: pgitops/infra/terraform.auto.tfvars

```
42: assume_role_account_id = "5XXXXXXXXXXXX5"
```

For prod and staging environments, this value needs to be added in the respective Terraform Cloud workspaces in the variables section, which we'll see when we are ready to execute our infra changes.

In the *pgitops/infra/kubernetes.tf* file, we also need to update our *aws eks get-token* command to pass in the role arn to be able to assume the role as shown on **L12-13**.

Code Block 8-42. Adding Assume Role configuration in the Kubernetes provider

File: infra/kubernetes.tf

```
03: provider "kubernetes" {
04:   host                    = module.eks.cluster_endpoint
05:   cluster_ca_certificate = base64decode(module.eks.cluster_
      certificate_authority_data)
06:   exec {
07:     api_version = "client.authentication.k8s.io/v1alpha1"
08:     command     = "aws"
09:     args = [
10:       "eks",
11:       "get-token",
12:       "--role-arn",
13:       local.assume_role_arn,
```

```
14:        "--cluster-name",
15:        module.eks.cluster_id
16:    ]
17:  }
```

8.7 Executing Infra

Let us now go ahead and start deployment of the application and its related infrastructure in different environments. We shall first start with the deployment into the development environment on the local system, and then the changes will be migrated to the staging and prod environments, which will be executed from the Terraform Cloud workspace.

8.7.1 AWS Profiles

Before we move ahead, we need to ensure that we've configured the AWS Profiles of all the users that have been created (i.e., Sita, Padma and Raadha). The following is the sample AWS Credentials file that I've configured for Sita, which includes the ability to be able to assume roles into different accounts. The same needs to be configured for Padma and Raadha as well.

Code Block 8-43. AWS Credential file for Sita

```
[sita]
aws_access_key_id = AKIAxxxxxxxxxxxWMX
aws_secret_access_key = o9PRxxxxxxxxxxxxxxxxxxxxxxxxxxxxWfUc
[sita-dev]
role_arn = arn:aws:iam::9xxxxxxxxx97:role/AssumeRoleAdmindev
source_profile = sita
[sita-prod]
role_arn = arn:aws:iam::2xxxxxxxxx42:role/AssumeRoleAdminprod
```

```
source_profile = sita
[sita-staging]
role_arn = arn:aws:iam::1xxxxxxxxx9:role/AssumeRoleAdminstaging
source_profile = sita
```

You'll need to update your account numbers as per the output shown in your Terraform Cloud Global workspace. Let's test the profiles if they have been properly configured using the following commands.

Note   Everywhere for infrastructure provisioning we'll be using Sita's access key as she has the administrator rights. We can always create a terraform user and assign it those rights.

Code Block 8-44. Accessing all AWS Profiles configured

```
cmd> export AWS_PROIFLE=sita
cmd> aws sts get-caller-identity
{
    "UserId": "AIDAWG4C7562DXE4Y3C3Q",
    "Account": "4xxxxxxxxxx0",
    "Arn": "arn:aws:iam::4xxxxxxxxxx0:user/sita"
}

cmd> export AWS_PROFILE=sita-prod
cmd> aws sts get-caller-identity
{
    "UserId": "AROATOK7P4B7EGWNWTDXN:botocore-
    session-1656261720",
    "Account": "2xxxxxxxxxx2",
    "Arn": "arn:aws:sts::2xxxxxxxxxx2:assumed-role/
    AssumeRoleAdminprod/botocore-session-1656261720"
}
```

8.7.2 Development

Let's first start our development environment but prior to doing that ensure that the value of *assume_role_account_id* in the pgitops/infra/terraform.auto.tfvars file is populated with the development account id.

Code Block 8-45. Set up the development environment

```
cmd> cd pgitops/infra
cmd> export AWS_PROFILE=sita-dev
cmd> terraform init
cmd> terraform validate
cmd> terraform apply --auto-approve
```

Terraform apply would take about ~15 minutes, and DNS propagation would take another 5 minutes after terraform apply is completed. The following is the post that we can see our application up and running.

Figure 8-14. *Development environment up and running*

8.7.3 Staging

Open up your terraform cloud staging workspace and ensure that the following variables are properly configured.

AWS_ACCESS_KEY_ID and *AWS_SECRET_ACCESS_KEY* should be of the sita user as she has the rights to assume administrator roles into all accounts.

assume_role_account_id variable must be populated with the staging account id.

Key	Value	Category
AWS_ACCESS_KEY_ID SENSITIVE	Sensitive - write only	env
AWS_SECRET_ACCESS_KEY SENSITIVE	Sensitive - write only	env
region	us-east-2	terraform
environment	staging	terraform
assume_role_account_id SENSITIVE	Sensitive - write only	terraform

Figure 8-15. *Adding an Assume Role Account ID variable in staging workspace*

Next, let's create a new branch called staging and then check in the code. Since this is the first time we are creating the staging branch and since we've tested everything is working in development, terraform apply would run directly as per the workflow rules setup in *.github/workflows/infra-staging.yaml*:

```
cmd> git status
On branch main
Your branch is up to date with 'origin/main'.

Changes not staged for commit:
  (use "git add <file>..." to update what will be committed)
```

```
(use "git restore <file>..." to discard changes in working
directory)
    modified:   infra/terraform.auto.tfvars
```

no changes added to commit (use "git add" and/or "git
commit -a")

```
cmd> git checkout -b staging
cmd(staging)> git add .
cmd(staging)> git commit -m "deploying to staging"
cmd(staging)> git push --set-upstream origin staging
```

Staging environment live !

Figure 8-16. *Staging environment is up*

8.7.4 Prod

Let's now create and merge the PR and deploy the changes into the prod
environment!

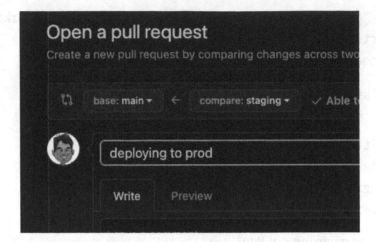

Figure 8-17. PR for prod deployment

Prod environment is live !

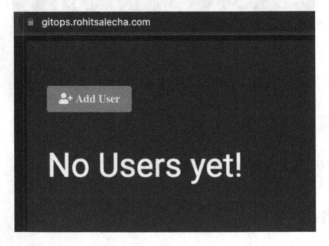

Figure 8-18. Prod environment is up

8.8 EKS Access Control

Now that all three environments are live, let's see how access control has
been implemented in the prod EKS environment.

Before we move ahead, let's have a summary of the Users and their Roles for better understanding.

Table 8-2. *AWS User Kubernetes Permissions*

User	Role	K8s Permissions
Sita	Admin	Perform any actions on all resources
Raadha	Developer	Perform any action on pods, deployments, services, ingresses, namespaces, jobs, daemonsets
Padma	Readonly	Perform only read action on pods, deployments, services, ingresses, namespaces, jobs, daemonsets

Let's understand the access control for Sita by executing the commands as shown in the following. Since she is the administrator, she has full access.

CLI Output 8-46. Testing Kubernetes Auth for Sita in Prod

```
cmd> export AWS_PROFILE=sita-prod
cmd> aws eks --region us-west-1 update-kubeconfig --name
gitops-us-west-1-prod

cmd> kubectl auth can-i get nodes
yes

cmd> kubectl auth can-i create pod
yes

cmd> kubectl auth can-i get secrets -n gitops
yes
```

Let's switch profile to that of Raadha and observe that she being a developer has only read/write access to limited resources in *gitops* namespace only.

CLI Output 8-47. Testing Kubernetes Auth for Radha in Pro

```
cmd> export AWS_PROFILE=radha-prod
cmd> aws eks --region us-west-1 update-kubeconfig --name
gitops-us-west-1-prod

cmd> kubectl auth can-i get nodes
no

cmd> kubectl auth can-i create pod
no

cmd> kubectl auth can-i create pod -n gitops
yes

cmd> kubectl auth can-i get secrets -n gitops
no
```

Let's now switch profile and see the access that Padma has, which is readonly and that too limited to *gitops* namespace only.

CLI Output 8-48. Testing Kubernetes Auth for Padma in Prod

```
cmd> export AWS_PROFILE=padma-prod
cmd> aws eks --region us-west-1 update-kubeconfig --name
gitops-us-west-1-prod
cmd> kubectl auth can-i get nodes
no

cmd> kubectl auth can-i create pod -n gitops
no
```

```
cmd> kubectl auth can-i get pod -n gitops
yes
cmd> kubectl auth can-i get pod
no
```

8.9 Clean-Up

It's best that we do a proper clean-up for this chapter as we are using 3X resources. We won't be needing staging and prod environments in the next chapters as we'll be focusing on different aspects like security and observability. Hence, it's best to destroy all environments, and we'll spin them up again in next chapters.

8.9.1 Dev

Dev environment was created from the local machine; hence, we only need to execute the following commands to destroy it.

CLI Output 8-49. Destroying Dev Environment

```
cmd> export AWS_PROFILE=sita-dev
cmd> cd pgitops/infra
cmd> terraform destroy --auto-approve
```

Note   At any point if Terraform is unable to destroy, please check Annexure A where steps have been presented to delete the resources manually.

8.9.2 Staging/Prod

Staging and prod environments need to be destroyed from the Terraform Cloud workspace as shown in the following by navigating to *Settings➤Destruction and Deletion.* Similar steps need to be followed for the prod environment as well.

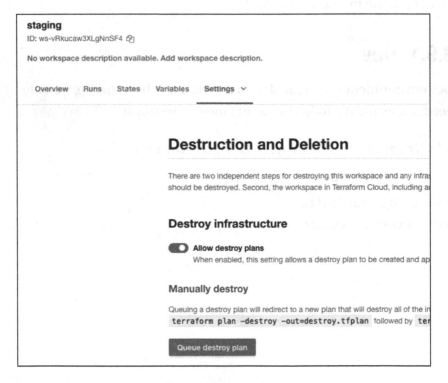

Figure 8-19. *Destroying the staging environment*

Note   At any point if Terraform Cloud is erroring to destroy, please check Annexure B where steps have been presented to delete the resources manually. If this doesn't work, then follow Annexure A.

The global environment can also be destroyed in the same manner; however, hold on for now as we'll be needing it for the next two chapters ahead. Hence, please keep the Global workspace as it is.

8.10 Conclusion

In this long chapter, we saw how Access Control can be implemented using AWS IAM on the AWS environment in general as well as on the AWS EKS environment completely through Terraform and that too in a completely automated Git-controlled manner.

In the next chapter, we'll explore a few other security measures that are necessary for cloud environments like Secret encryption, HTTPS redirection, Network Segregation, Service Control Policies, implementing security scanning for IaC, and how pods running on EKS can access AWS services securely!

CHAPTER 9

Security and Secrets Management

In this chapter, we'll look into various different areas pertaining to the security of our application and infrastructure. We'll discuss how to manage the database using AWS Secrets Manager and how it can directly be injected into the pods. Then we'll look at a few small aspects of securing our ALB and restricting the network for the RDS. After that, we'll look at how pods can authenticate to AWS and access different resources. Then we'll look at how the disk of the EKS nodes can be encrypted using AWS KMS and how we can enforce Service Control Policies or SCPs on different OUs such that developers cannot spin up expensive EC2 resources. Finally, we'll end by adding a tool called Checkov in the GitHub Actions pipeline, which will continuously spill out security issues on every PR.

9.1 Code Update

Before diving into the code, let's first ensure that we've updated the pgitops directory with the code from the Chapter 9 folder. To do this, follow these steps:

- First copy the contents of the Chapter 9 folder into the pgitops folder.

- Get inside the pgitops directory and then check which files/folders are changing.

R. Salecha, *Practical GitOps*, https://doi.org/10.1007/978-1-4842-8673-9_9

- We shall commit only the global and .github directories as we need the changes to be reflected in the global environment.

- Changes done in the infra folder can be committed, and the CI can be skipped as we'll be testing the changes only in the development environment for this chapter.

CLI Output 9-1. Updating Chapter 9 code

```
cmd> cp -a chapter9/. pgitops/
cmd> cd pgitops
cmd> git status
On branch main
Your branch is up to date with 'origin/main'.

Changes not staged for commit:
  (use "git add <file>..." to update what will be committed)
  (use "git restore <file>..." to discard changes in working
  directory)
      modified:   .github/workflows/global.yaml
      modified:   .github/workflows/infra-prod.yaml
      modified:   .github/workflows/infra-staging.yaml
      modified:   README.md
      modified:   global/README.md
      modified:   global/organisations.tf
      modified:   infra/README.md
      modified:   infra/app.tf
      modified:   infra/eks.tf
      modified:   infra/modules/alb/iam_policy.json
      modified:   infra/modules/alb/main.tf
      modified:   infra/modules/alb/variables.tf
      modified:   infra/modules/ekscluster/main.tf
```

```
modified:    infra/modules/ekscluster/variables.tf
modified:    infra/networking.tf
modified:    infra/rds.tf
modified:    infra/variables.tf

Untracked files:
  (use "git add <file>..." to include in what will be committed)
    global/data/deny_creating_users.json
    global/data/ebs_rds_encryption_check.json
    global/data/instance_type_limit.json
    global/data/padma.pub.old
    global/data/raadha.pub.old
    global/data/region_lock.json
    global/data/sita.pub.old
    global/modules/awsorgpolicy/
    global/scp.tf
    global/terraform.auto.tfvars.old
    infra/data/
    infra/modules/awskms/
    infra/modules/awssm/
    infra/modules/csisecretsdriver/
    infra/modules/irsa/
    infra/terraform.auto.tfvars.old

no changes added to commit (use "git add" and/or "git commit -a")
```

The changes can summarized as follows:

- Enhancing security of EKS by encrypting the EBS using the default AWS KMS key

- Encrypting secrets stored in EKS using the custom AWS KMS key.

- Enhancing AWS ALB security using mandatory HTTPS redirection and dropping invalid headers.

- Restricting RDS to private subnet and not VPC.

- Installing Secrets Store CSI (Container Storage Interface) Driver that fetches secrets directly from AWS Secrets Manager reducing exposure of secrets in K8s files.

- Implementing and understanding IRSA (IAM Roles for Service Accounts) that fetches secrets from AWS Secrets Manager.

- In the workflow files, we've added a new step that introduces a security scanning tool called "Checkov" (`www.checkov.io/`). This tool scans terraform files for known bad security practices.

- We've added multiple Service Control Policies (SCPs):

  - To lock the regions of deployment

  - Ensuring that only encrypted EBS and RDS are deployed in staging/production

  - Disabling user creation in all accounts except identity

  - Restricting the instance types that can be created in Development OU

9.1.1 Committing only Global

For the sake of simplicity and for ensuring that the global folder is committed, let's execute the following commands.

Note   - - (double hyphens) after the commit message indicates that we wish to commit only the specific directories, which is exactly the use case here.

CLI Output 9-2. Comitting only changes in the Global folder

```
cmd> git add .
cmd> git commit -m 'committing only global and .github' --
global .github
cmd> git push
```

Once we fire *git push*, it can be observed that only global changes have gone live as shown here.

Figure 9-1. *Global folder Comit triggering action*

With this, the following items have been created:

- All the SCPs described previously have been created and now operational.

- Our new GitHub workflow with Checkov is now operational.

9.1.2 Committing Infra

The other changes, that is, infra, etc., are still in staging in our local system as shown in the following. Let's push these changes as well but without triggering the GitHub Actions, that is, by adding [skip ci] in our commit message.

CLI Output 9-3. Skipping comitting changes in the infra folder

```
cmd> git status
On branch main
Your branch is up to date with 'origin/main'.

Changes to be committed:
  (use "git restore --staged <file>..." to unstage)
      modified:   README.md
XXXXXXXXXXXXXXXX------SNIPPED-------XXXXXXXXXXXXXXXXXXXXX
      modified:   infra/rds.tf
      new file:   infra/terraform.auto.tfvars.old
      modified:   infra/variables.tf

cmd> git commit -m '[skip ci] committing infra'
cmd> git push
```

9.2 Enhancing EKS Security

As stated earlier, the master node or the control plane of Kubernetes in AWS EKS is managed completely by AWS. Hence, AWS takes full responsibility of keeping it highly available and secure. However, security of the data plane components like Kubernetes Secrets and of the worker nodes (which are nothing but EC2 instances) like EBS encryption, implementing IMDSv2 metadata, etc., needs to be done by us. In this section, we'll see how that can be done completely through terraform.

9.2.1 Encrypting K8s Secrets

One of the best practices of Kubernetes security is to encrypt the secrets. We need encryption keys that'll be used to encrypt the secrets. AWS KMS (Key Management Services) is a popular service that has two types of keys:

- Managed by AWS – These keys are generated and managed by AWS internally and are not chargeable.

- Managed by User – These keys are also generated by AWS but managed by us and are chargeable.

If you recall, we set up our RDS database using the code as shown in the following in *pgitops/infra/rds.tf*.

Code Block 9-4. Encrypting PostgreSQL

File: pgitops/infra/rds.tf

```
39: module "pgsql" {
XXXXXXXXXXXXXXX------SNIPPED-------XXXXXXXXXXXXXXXXXXXXX
52:    storage_encrypted                  = true
53:    db_name                            = var.db_name
54:    username                           = var.db_user_name
XXXXXXXXXXXXXXX------SNIPPED-------XXXXXXXXXXXXXXXXXXXXX
84: }
85:
```

L52: By having the storage_encrypted=true, the module internally is using the default AWS KMS keys and encrypting the entire database.

However, for storing secrets in Kubernetes, let's make use of a custom AWS KMS key, which is generated using the following module.

Code Block 9-5. Creating a KMS key

File: pgitops/infra/eks.tf

```
15: module "eks_kms" {
16:   source = "./modules/awskms"
17:
18:   environment              = var.environment
19:   description              = "KMS Key to encrypt secrets in
                                  the Cluster"
20:   kms_alias                = "eks2"
21:   deletion_window_in_days  = 7
22:
23: }
```

L20: This value should be unique for the account as it helps as an identifier to the key.

L21: KMS keys are not deleted immediately; hence, we can configure the time uptil which we can retrieve the keys back, which is generally between 7 and 30 days.

We are then using the ARN (Amazon Resource Name) of the key generated from the preceding module and then pass it into the EKS module as shown here.

Code Block 9-6. Attaching the KMS key to EKS

File: pgitops/infra/eks.tf

```
25: module "eks" {
26:   source = "./modules/ekscluster"
27:
28:   clustername    = module.clustername.cluster_name
29:   eks_version    = var.eks_version
```

```
30:    private_subnets = module.networking.private_subnets_id
31:    vpc_id          = module.networking.vpc_id
32:    environment     = var.environment
33:    kms_key_arn     = module.eks_kms.key_arn
34:    instance_types  = var.instance_types
35:
36: }
```

L33: Reference to the KMS Key ARN from the KMS module.

Let's dive inside the module and see how exactly the value is being passed.

Code Block 9-7. Encrypting all Kubernetes Secrets with the AWS KMS key

```
File: pgitops/infra/modules/ekscluster/main.tf

XXXXXXXXXXXXXXX------SNIPPED-------XXXXXXXXXXXXXXXXXXXXX
19:
20:    cluster_encryption_config = [{
21:      provide    r_key_arn = var.kms_key_arn
22:      resources         = ["secrets"]
23:    }]
24:
XXXXXXXXXXXXXXX------SNIPPED-------XXXXXXXXXXXXXXXXXXXXX
```

L21: Providing reference of the KMS Key ARN, which must be used to encrypt the data.

L22: Configuring the Kubernetes resources that need to be encrypted; currently, only "secrets" are supported.

9.2.2 Encrypting EKS EBS

EBS is the storage device attached to the EC2 instance, and most compliance frameworks require it to be encrypted. There are two ways in which this can be achieved: either using a custom-generated key or using the AWS-provided key. A custom-generated key will incur cost and also will require additional permissions. Hence, to keep things simple, I am using an AWS-provided key by simply initializing the *kms_key_id* variable as blank.

Using the following block of code in the EKS module, we can configure the EBS device.

Code Block 9-8. Encrypting EBS block volume

File: pgitops/infra/modules/ekscluster/main.tf

```
XXXXXXXXXXXXXXX------SNIPPED-------XXXXXXXXXXXXXXXXXXXX
66:     block_device_mappings = {
67:       xvda = {
68:         device_name = "/dev/xvda"
69:         ebs = {
70:           volume_size          = 75
71:           volume_type          = "gp3"
72:           iops                 = 3000
73:           throughput           = 150
74:           encrypted            = true
75:           kms_key_id           = ""
76:           delete_on_termination = true
77:         }
78:       }
79:     }

XXXXXXXXXXXXXXX------SNIPPED-------XXXXXXXXXXXXXXXXXXXX
```

9.2.3 Enhancing EC2 Metadata Security

AWS provides an internal functionality, using which, EC2 instances can securely obtain privileges to perform actions on behalf of a user/account. This privilege/permission can be obtained by first fetching the IAM Role by performing a GET request to the http://169.254.169.254/latest/meta-data/iam/security-credentials/role-name endpoint. This provides an IAM Role name, which is then used to assume the permissions associated with it.

All was well until someone figured out that using an SSRF (Server-Side Request Forgery), this GET request could be spoofed by attackers with malicious intent. So basically if a web application is vulnerable to SSRF bug, it opens up the possibility of the attacker gaining access to the temporary IAM Role permissions and hence accessing your AWS environment. More on this attack can be read here: https://blog. appsecco.com/getting-started-with-version-2-of-aws-ec2-instance-metadata-service-imdsv2-2ad03a1f3650.

The IMDSv1 service was heavily abused by attackers to launch SSRF attacks, and hence, IMDSv2 was released, which fixes this issue.

The following block of code can be utilized to set up the IMDSv2 (Instance Metadata Service) configuration, which is also a major security requirement.

Code Block 9-9. Configuring all EC2 metadata options for enabling IMDSv2

```
File: infra/modules/ekscluster/main.tf

XXXXXXXXXXXXXXX------SNIPPED-------XXXXXXXXXXXXXXXXXXXXX
81:     metadata_options = {
82:        http_endpoint                = "enabled"
83:        http_tokens                  = "required"
84:        http_put_response_hop_limit  = 2
```

```
85:          instance_metadata_tags      = "disabled"
86:     }
87:   }
XXXXXXXXXXXXXXX------SNIPPED-------XXXXXXXXXXXXXXXXXXXXX
```

Hence, IMDSv2 avoids this by ensuring that a specific header needs to be passed in order to call the IMDS endpoint.

For more information on the attack and IMDSv2, refer to this link: https://blog.appsecco.com/getting-started-with-version-2-of-aws-ec2-instance-metadata-service-imdsv2-2ad03a1f3650.

9.3 Enhancing AWS ALB Security

Any traffic reaching our application first needs to go through the load balancer, and hence, ensuring certain security best practices on the load balancer is very important. In this chapter, we'll look at how we can perform a mandatory HTTPS redirection and dropping of invalid header values to combat specific application attacks. In the next chapter, we'll look at how we can store AWS ALB logs in an S3 bucket.

Allowing the website to be served over HTTP, that is, port 80, renders it vulnerable to man-in-the-middle attacks where attackers can read and tamper with the data in the request. Hence, it's most commonly advisable to have the HTTP port redirect to HTTPS, and the same is achievable by configuring the following annotation in the ingress resource as shown here.

Code Block 9-10. Securing ALB against malformed HTTP headers and HTTPS redirection

File: pgitops/infra/app.tf

```
233:     annotations = {
XXXXXXXXXXXXXXX------SNIPPED-------XXXXXXXXXXXXXXXXXXXXX
```

```
238: "alb.ingress.kubernetes.io/listen-ports" = "[{\"HTTP\":
     80}, {\"HTTPS\":443}]"
239: "alb.ingress.kubernetes.io/actions.ssl-redirect"
     = "{\"Type\": \"redirect\", \"RedirectConfig\":
     { \"Protocol\": \"HTTPS\", \"Port\": \"443\",
     \"StatusCode\": \"HTTP_301\"}}"
240: "alb.ingress.kubernetes.io/load-balancer-attributes" =
     "routing.http.drop_invalid_header_fields.enabled=true"
241:      }
242:   }
243:   spec {
244:     rule {
245:       host = local.url
246:       http {
247:         path {
248:           backend {
249:             service {
250:               name = "ssl-redirect"
251:               port {
252:                 name = "use-annotation"
253:               }
254:             }
255:           }
256:           path = "/*"
257:         }
XXXXXXXXXXXXXXX------SNIPPED-------XXXXXXXXXXXXXXXXXXXXX
274: }
```

L238: Declaring the ingress to open two listener ports in the AWS Load Balancer that will be created.

L239: This is where we declare the annotation that configures the redirection logic and the HTTP redirection code, that is, 301, which needs to be used.

L247–257: The implementation logic of the HTTPS redirection at the root path "/".

L240: Having this configuration that is to disable invalid header fields is very important as it helps in invalidating requests that do not have proper HTTP headers. This helps in mitigating a class of application vulnerabilities called HTTP Request Smuggling, which leverages the desynchronization between the load balancer and its service on acceptance of the content-length vs. transfer-encoding headers.

More information about this attack can be obtained from `https://portswigger.net/research/request-smuggling`.

9.4 Restricting RDS Exposure

Currently, our RDS service is exposed to the entire VPC as the security group that was defined had the entire 10.0.0.0/16 CIDR address. This is now solved by restricting the security group to allow access to the RDS server on port 5432 only from the private subnet as shown here.

Code Block 9-11. Restricting AWS RDS access from the private subnet

File: pgitops/infra/networking.tf

```
53: module "pgsql_sg_ingress" {
54:    source = "./modules/securitygroup"
55:
56:    sg_name        = "pgsql_sg_ingress"
57:    sg_description = "Allow Port 5432 from within the
                        Private Subnet"
```

```
58:    environment      = var.environment
59:    vpc_id           = module.networking.vpc_id
60:    type             = "ingress"
61:    from_port        = 5432
62:    to_port          = 5432
63:    protocol         = "tcp"
64:    cidr_blocks      = var.private_subnets_cidr
65:
66:    depends_on = [module.networking]
67: }
```

L64: This was earlier scoped to the entire VPC and now narrowed down to only the private subnet where our application is currently deployed. Hence, only services deployed in this private network will have access to the RDS database on port 5432.

9.5 Secrets Exposure

Currently, in our application, the most sensitive information is the database password. Let's identify the places where this password can be potentially leaked or visible in clear-text.

9.5.1 Terraform State

If we were to simply grep for the string "password" in our terraform state, it can reveal various different places where the database password string can be found.

CLI Output 9-12. Searching for the password string in terraform state

```
cmd> grep "password" terraform.tfstate
            "module.pgsql.random_password.master_password",
            "module.ssmr-db-password.data.aws_ssm_parameter.
            parameter",
            "module.ssmw-db-password.aws_ssm_parameter.ssm_
            parameter"
            "module.pgsql.random_password.master_password",
            "module.ssmr-db-password.data.aws_ssm_parameter.
            parameter",
            "module.ssmw-db-password.aws_ssm_parameter.ssm_
            parameter"
            "repository_password": null,
        "type": "random_password",
        "name": "master_password",
            "password": "EvlNUope03cXdIlG",
                "value": "password"
```

If we were to now search for the value of the password string in the terraform state, we'll get a better idea of the number of places where the password is stored in clear-text, a total of five locations as shown here.

CLI Output 9-13. Reverse lookup of the password string to know occurrences

```
cmd> grep "EvlNUope03cXdIlG" terraform.tfstate
            "value": "EvlNUope03cXdIlG",
            "result": "EvlNUope03cXdIlG",
            "password": "EvlNUope03cXdIlG",
            "value": "EvlNUope03cXdIlG",
            "value": "EvlNUope03cXdIlG",
```

Hence, it's extremely important that access to terraform state is restricted to select few individuals only.

9.5.2 Kubernetes Deployment Descriptions

In the previous chapter, we implemented restrictions on Kubernetes groups who can read secrets. Other than the administrator, no other group has the privilege to access the Kubernetes Secrets. However, with our secrets being embedded as environment variables in the Kubernetes deployments as shown in the following code on **L70–73,** all groups who have the read-only rights to view the deployment configurations can easily read the database password in clear-text. We shall address this exposure in the next section.

Code Block 9-14. Password in Kubernetes deployment descriptions

File: pgitops/infra/app.tf

```
50:       spec {
51:         container {
52:           image = "salecharohit/practicalgitops"
53:           name  = var.org_name
XXXXXXXXXXXXXXXX------SNIPPED-------XXXXXXXXXXXXXXXXXXXXX
66:           env {
67:             name  = "DB_USERNAME"
68:             value = var.db_user_name
69:           }
70:           env {
71:             name  = "DB_PASSWORD"
72:             value = module.ssmr-db-password.ssm-value
73:           }
XXXXXXXXXXXXXXXX------SNIPPED-------XXXXXXXXXXXXXXXXXXXXX
```

9.6 AWS Secrets Manager

In order to address the problem of database passwords being stored as clear-text in the deployment descriptions, we'll need to make use of the Secrets Store CSI Driver for AWS, more details of which can be found here: `https://github.com/aws/secrets-store-csi-driver-provider-aws`.

9.6.1 Secrets Management Design

Before we explore the new design, let's first understand the old one.

Current Solution

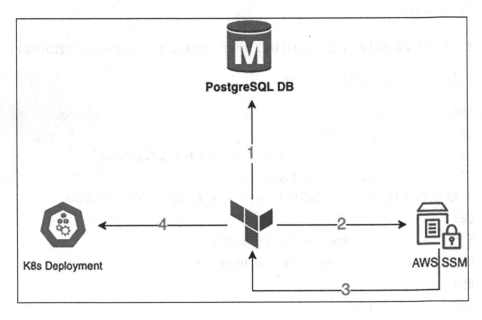

Figure 9-2. *AWS RDS Secrets Storage - Current Solution*

1. Terraform generates a random password and stores
    it in the Database

2. Once the RDS is setup it writes the password as a
    SecureString in AWS SSM

3. Terraform then reads the password from AWS SSM

4. And then writes it into the deployment manifest file
    as an environment variable.

So the database secret is embedded in the terraform Kubernetes
manifest file when terraform apply is running.

New Solution

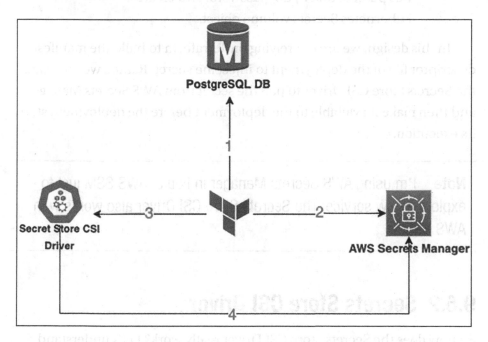

Figure 9-3. *AWS RDS Secrets Storage – New Solution*

1. Terraform generates a random password and stores
   it in the Database.

2. Once the RDS is set up, it writes the password as in
   AWS Secrets Manager.

3. Terraform builds the Kubernetes manifest file
   with the name of the key that is used to store the
   password in the AWS Secrets Manager, for example,
   db_password.

4. Upon successful deployment of the Secrets Store
   CSI Driver, it'll read the password string from AWS
   Secrets Manager using the name of the key that
   was passed, that is, db_password, and create a
   Kubernetes Secrets volume object.

In this design, we are not relying on Terraform to build the manifest
descriptor file of the deployment to inject the secret. Rather, we are using
the Secrets Store CSI Driver to pull the secret from AWS Secrets Manager
and then make it available to the deployment before the deployment starts
its execution.

Note   I'm using AWS Secrets Manager in lieu of AWS SSM just to
explore a new service. The Secrets Store CSI Driver also works with
AWS SSM.

9.6.2 Secrets Store CSI Driver

So how does the Secrets Store CSI Driver really work? Let's understand
using the following diagram.

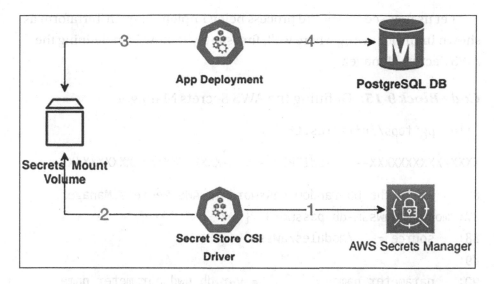

Figure 9-4. *An image showing how Secrets Store CSI Driver works*

1. The Secrets Store CSI Driver is a deployment configuration that will read the secrets from the AWS Secrets Manager from a specified path and location, for example, db_password.

2. Once it reads the value, it will write it to a secret mount volume as an object with a name as db-password-secret.

3. The App deployment will read the db-password-secret object from the secrets volume and obtain the database password, which will be stored as an environment variable. However, this time, since it's a mounted volume from where the data is being read, it won't be shown in clear-text in the deployment descriptor. We'll see this practically when we run the entire application.

4. The deployment then connects to the RDS database using the password.

Let us now see this entire process being implemented in Terraform as shown in the following where we'll first start with how I am defining the AWS Secrets Manager.

Code Block 9-15. Defining the AWS Secrets Manager

File: pgitops/infra/rds.tf

```
XXXXXXXXXXXXXXX------SNIPPED-------XXXXXXXXXXXXXXXXXXXXXX

86: # Write the DB random password in AWS Secrets Manager
87: module "awssm-db-password" {
88:    source = "./modules/awssm"
89:
90:    parameter_name          = var.db_pwd_parameter_name
91:    secret_value            = module.pgsql.db_instance_
                                 password
92:    description             = "DB Password"
93:    environment             = var.environment
94:    deletion_window_in_days = 0
95:
96:    depends_on = [module.pgsql]
97: }

XXXXXXXXXXXXXXX------SNIPPED-------XXXXXXXXXXXXXXXXXXXXXX
```

L87–97: We are defining the module AWS SM or AWS Secrets Manager, which is retrieving the value of the database password on **L91** from the database module. A special note for **L90** where we are defining the parameter name against which the value will be stored as a global variable, which will be used across different modules/files as we'll see ahead.

L94: Just like the AWS KMS, secret deletion can be deferred to a certain period of time; however, for this book, I've defined it as 0 days as it creates issues while destroying the resource. For example, if I set it as 7 days, then this particular resource value cannot be deleted till 7 days, and our terraform will give error while destruction.

Let's now look at how we are installing the Secrets Store CSI Driver.

Code Block 9-16. Installing CSI Secrets Driver

```
File: pgitops/infra/app.tf

XXXXXXXXXXXXXXX------SNIPPED-------XXXXXXXXXXXXXXXXXXXXXX

15: data "kubectl_file_documents" "csi_secrets" {
16:   content = file("modules/csisecretsdriver/aws-secrets-
              csi.yaml")
17: }
18:
19: # Install the CSI Secrets Driver with Secrets Sync Enabled
20: module "csi-secrets-driver" {
21:
22:   source = "./modules/csisecretsdriver"
23:
24:   count_files          = length(data.kubectl_file_documents.
                             csi_secrets.documents)
25:   csi_secrets_version = "1.1.2"
26:   k8s_path             = "modules/csisecretsdriver/aws-
                             secrets-csi.yaml"
27:   namespace            = kubernetes_namespace_v1.app.
                             metadata.0.name
28:
29:   depends_on = [module.eks, resource.kubernetes_
                 namespace_v1.app]
30:
31: }

XXXXXXXXXXXXXXX------SNIPPED-------XXXXXXXXXXXXXXXXXXXXXX
```

L15–17: As discussed earlier, we are using a kubectl provider, which helps in applying Kubernetes manifest files in YAML format. If we've a single manifest file with a single resource definition, we can always declare it in the terraform code itself; however, if there are multiple resources divided by --- (three hyphens), then we need to first count the number of resources and provide that to the kubectl provider, which is what we are doing here, and pass this value on **L24.**

L20–31: Here, we've encapsulated the entire procedure of installing the Secrets Store CSI Driver in a module as it requires installing the driver using helm and then also separately deploying a DaemonSet, which is defined in pgitops/*modules/csisecretsdriver/aws-secrets-csi.yaml* and installed using the kubectl provider.

Next, let's discuss about a custom resource that needs to be created in addition to the CSI driver and the DaemonSet as shown here.

Code Block 9-17. Deploying Kubernetes Secrets custom resource definition

File: pgitops/infra/app.tf

```
XXXXXXXXXXXXXXXX------SNIPPED-------XXXXXXXXXXXXXXXXXXXXX

69: resource "kubectl_manifest" "secrets" {
70:   yaml_body = <<YAML
71: apiVersion: secrets-store.csi.x-k8s.io/v1alpha1
72: kind: SecretProviderClass
73: metadata:
74:   name: aws-secret-application
75:   namespace: ${var.org_name}
76: spec:
77:   provider: aws
78:   secretObjects:
79:     - secretName: db-password-secret
```

```
80:          type: Opaque
81:          data:
82:            - objectName: ${var.db_pwd_parameter_name}
83:              key: db_password
84:      parameters:
85:        objects: |
86:          - objectName: ${var.db_pwd_parameter_name}
87:            objectType: "secretsmanager"
88: YAML
89:
90:    depends_on = [module.pgsql,
91:      module.csi-secrets-driver,
92:      resource.kubernetes_namespace_v1.app
93:    ]
94:
95: }
```

XXXXXXXXXXXXXXX------SNIPPED-------XXXXXXXXXXXXXXXXXXXXXX

L69–70: We are declaring a raw YAML body that needs to be processed where the term YAML is following the HEREDOC syntax ending on **L88**.

L71–72: We are defining the custom resource and the API supporting that resource for Kubernetes.

L74–75: Naming the resource (which will be referenced when mounting the volume in deployment) and scoping it to the same namespace that we are using throughout the code, that is, "gitops".

L78–83: Here, we are declaring the secrets object that will be created with the name of the secret being *db-password-secret* defined on **L79**, which will be referenced in the deployment.

L81–83: Defining the data, that is, the key-value of the secret where the key is defined by us as db_password, which is the same as how it's defined in the AWS Secrets Manager.

L84–87: Here, we need to provide the exact reference of the key with which the value is stored in AWS Secrets Manager, which, as discussed earlier, is defined as a global variable so we don't mess up.

L90–93: Note the dependencies here, especially the CSI Secrets Driver. The custom resource that's defined L72 would error out if Terraform attempted to execute this code before the CSI driver would be set up.

From the preceding code, it's important to note the following definitions, which will be referenced in the deployment file, which we'll explore next:

- aws-secret-application – Name of the custom resource that's defined as SecretProviderClass

- db-password-secret – Name of the Kubernetes Secret resource that will be created by this Secret Provider class

- db_password – Name of the key that'll be used for identifying the secret

Let's now look at the deployment descriptor file with the portion relevant for adding the secrets.

Code Block 9-18. Kubernetes deployment descriptor file for adding secrets

File: pgitops/infra/app.tf

```
099: resource "kubernetes_deployment_v1" "app" {
XXXXXXXXXXXXXXXX------SNIPPED-------XXXXXXXXXXXXXXXXXXXXXX
144:          env {
145:            name = "DB_PASSWORD"
146:            value_from {
147:              secret_key_ref {
148:                name = "db-password-secret"
```

```
149:                    key  = "db_password"
150:                }
151:            }
152:        }
153:
154:        volume_mount {
155:            name       = "db-password-vol"
156:            mount_path = "/mnt/secrets-store"
157:            read_only  = true
158:        }
159:
XXXXXXXXXXXXXXX------SNIPPED-------XXXXXXXXXXXXXXXXXXXXX
186:        volume {
187:            name = "db-password-vol"
188:            csi {
189:              driver    = "secrets-store.csi.k8s.io"
190:              read_only = true
191:              volume_attributes = {
192:                "secretProviderClass" = "aws-secret-
                   application"
193:              }
194:            }
195:        }
XXXXXXXXXXXXXXX------SNIPPED-------XXXXXXXXXXXXXXXXXXXXX
200:  }
```

L154-158: Defining the volume mount *db-password-vol* and loading data from the path */mnt/secrets-store* where the secrets store DaemonSet is storing all the data as Secret Resources.

L186–195: Declaring the volume *db-password-vol* as a CSI driver and referencing the custom resource definition as *aws-secret-application*, which we saw earlier.

L144–152: The environment variable declaration where the DB_ PASSWORD will be populated. The value of the DB_PASSWORD will be populated from the volume mount and retrieved using the name of the secret resource, that is, *db-password-secret*, and the key in that resource whose value needs to be fetched, that is, *db_password*.

Tip   An alternative to this Secrets Store CSI Driver approach is the AWS Secret Sidecar Injector, which follows the sidecar pattern and gets deployed as a sidecar pod along with the application pod (`https://github.com/aws-samples/aws-secret-sidecar-injector`).

9.7 IRSA

9.7.1 Background

In the previous chapter, we looked at the two different authentication/ authorization mechanisms implemented in EKS, and here, we'll be discussing the third type. In AWS, by default, any type of authentication is done by the access keys and authorization using the IAM Roles/Groups and the permissions assigned to them. However, there is another way where the authentication decision can be delegated to a different identity provider by establishing a trust between them.

Currently, AWS supports two such identity providers, that is, OIDC (OpenID Connect) and SAML (Security Assertion Markup Language), which are two different authentication protocols.

By setting up an OIDC/SAML IdP (identity Provider), we can authenticate to these IdPs and then use the authentication token to access any AWS services. While setting up our EKS cluster, we are setting up this OIDC endpoint for establishing the trust relationship.

Within Kubernetes, if a pod needs to access any resource, it needs proper permissions that are defined in the Service Account. A *default* service account is always associated with every Kubernetes resource (pods, deployments, DaemonSets, etc.), which can always be used to authenticate to the Kube API server.

So now the question is, how can a pod running in AWS EKS access AWS services?

This is where IRSA (IAM Roles for Service Accounts) comes into the picture, which is an authentication/authorization architecture for EKS pods to access AWS services by assigning an IAM Role to the service account token that would be mounted on the pods.

9.7.2 Internal Working

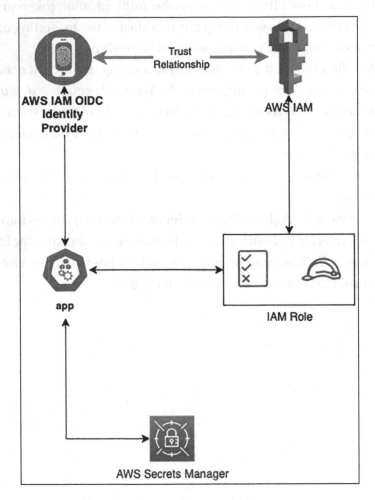

Figure 9-5. *An image showing how IRSA works internally*

- The AWS IAM and OIDC Identity Provider have a trust relationship established between them.

- Kubernetes Service Account is annotated with the ARN of an IAM Role, which is then passed to the OIDC IdP, which validates the IAM Role and provides the authentication token.

- This authentication token is then passed to the AWS service, which needs to be consumed by the pod.

There are two parts to creating a complete IRSA architecture: an IAM Assume Role tied to an IAM permissions policy and a Kubernetes Service account with the ARN of the IAM Role added as an annotation. Let's look at how this would be implemented in Terraform.

9.7.3 IAM Permissions Policy

For our pod to be able to access the Secrets from the AWS Secrets Manager, we need the following permissions policy where we are also restricting the ARN of the secret that we've created. This ensures that this pod is not able to access any secret other than the one that is explicitly defined in the policy document on **L11**.

Code Block 9-19. IAM permissions policy to read a secret from AWS Secret Manager

File: pgitops/infra/data/secrets.json

```
01: {
02:     "Version": "2012-10-17",
03:     "Statement": [
04:         {
05:             "Sid": "SecretsManagerReadOnly",
06:             "Effect": "Allow",
07:             "Action": [
08:                 "secretsmanager:GetSecretValue",
09:                 "secretsmanager:DescribeSecret"
10:             ],
11:             "Resource": "${db_password_arn}"
12:         }
```

```
13:     ]
14: }
```
XXXXXXXXXXXXXXXX------SNIPPED-------XXXXXXXXXXXXXXXXXXXXXX

The IAM permissions policy needs to be created using the resource definition as shown in the following where we are providing the preceding policy as a template and providing the database secret ARN to the policy.

Code Block 9-20. Creating the Policy resource

File: pgitops/infra/app.tf

```
35: resource "aws_iam_policy" "secrets_policy" {
36:    name = "secrets_policy"
37:    path = "/"
38:    policy = templatefile("./data/secrets.json", {
39:      db_password_arn = module.awssm-db-password.arn
40:    })
41: }
```

The following module is used to tie the IAM Permissions to an IAM Role and provide the ARN of this IAM Role as an output, which needs to be annotated on the Kubernetes service account resource.

Code Block 9-21. Creating the IRSA Role

File: pgitops/infra/app.tf

XXXXXXXXXXXXXXXX------SNIPPED-------XXXXXXXXXXXXXXXXXXXXXX

```
43: module "irsa_aws_secrets" {
44:    source = "./modules/irsa"
45:
46:    oidc_url       = module.eks.cluster_oidc_issuer_url
47:    oidc_arn       = module.eks.oidc_provider_arn
```

```
48:    k8s_sa_namespace = kubernetes_namespace_v1.app.
                             metadata.0.name
49:    k8s_irsa_name    = "irsa-aws-secrets"
50:    policy_arn       = resource.aws_iam_policy.secrets_
                             policy.arn
51:
52:    depends_on = [module.eks, resource.kubernetes_
                        namespace_v1.app]
53: }
```

XXXXXXXXXXXXXXX------SNIPPED-------XXXXXXXXXXXXXXXXXXXXXX

Let's dig into this module to understand better how the IAM Role is being created.

Code Block 9-22. Implementing IRSA in Terraform

File: infra/modules/irsa/main.tf

```
02: data "aws_iam_policy_document" "default" {
03:    statement {
04:       actions = ["sts:AssumeRoleWithWebIdentity"]
05:       effect  = "Allow"
06:
07:       condition {
08:          test     = "StringEquals"
09:          variable = "${replace(var.oidc_url, "https://",
                          "")}:sub"
10:          values   = ["system:serviceaccount:${var.k8s_sa_
                          namespace}:${var.k8s_irsa_name}"]
11:       }
12:
13:       principals {
14:          identifiers = [var.oidc_arn]
```

```
15:        type          = "Federated"
16:      }
17:    }
18: }
19:
20: resource "aws_iam_role" "default" {
21:    name                = var.k8s_irsa_name
22:    path                = "/"
23:    assume_role_policy = data.aws_iam_policy_document.
                                default.json
24: }
25:
26: resource "aws_iam_role_policy_attachment" "default" {
27:    role        = aws_iam_role.default.name
28:    policy_arn = var.policy_arn
29: }
```

L02–18: Defining the AssumeRole policy for the Web Identity Provider, which is nothing but our OIDC URL. What this basically states is allow the Kubernetes service account to Assume the web identity by authenticating to the OIDC URL to access the AWS services whose permissions will be attached later.

L20–24: Creating the IAM Role with a specific name and applying the AssumeRole policy.

L26–29: The actual permissions that are allowed by the specific service account and the IAM Role.

Finally, let's look at the last piece of the puzzle that is the Kubernetes service account creation and its attachment to the deployment pod.

Code Block 9-23. Creating a Kubernetes Service Account and attaching in Kubernetes deployment

File: pgitops/infra/app.tf

```
55: resource "kubernetes_service_account" "irsa_aws_secrets" {
56:    metadata {
57:      name     = module.irsa_aws_secrets.role_name
58:      namespace = kubernetes_namespace_v1.app.metadata.0.name
59:      annotations = {
60:        "eks.amazonaws.com/role-arn" = module.irsa_aws_
                                                 secrets.role_arn
61:      }
62:    }
63:    automount_service_account_token = true
64:    depends_on                      = [module.eks,
                                           resource.kubernetes_
                                           namespace_v1.app]
65: }

099: resource "kubernetes_deployment_v1" "app" {
100:    metadata {
101:      name       = var.org_name
102:      namespace = kubernetes_namespace_v1.app.
                       metadata.0.name
XXXXXXXXXXXXXXX------SNIPPED-------XXXXXXXXXXXXXXXXXXXXXX
197:        service_account_name = resource.kubernetes_
                                    service_account.irsa_aws_
                                    secrets.metadata[0].name
198:      }
```

L55–65: Defining the Kubernetes Service Account with the same name as that of the IAM Role that it would be consuming and then deploying in the same namespace as well.

L59–61: This is the key element here where we need to specify the ARN of the IAM Role that would be assumed by this service account.

L197: The service account hence created must be passed to the deployment pod so that it can read the token and authenticate to the OIDC IdP and then access the AWS Secrets Manager.

Tip   You are encouraged to execute the command kubectl get sa -n gitops -o yaml to view the service accounts that are created and the IAM Role ARN annotated.

9.8 Checkov Scanning

It is critically important that the code written by developers be scanned for any security vulnerabilities. However, scanning on Terraform code is a little bit different than the regular code scanning that is employed by various tools as Terraform is a declarative language.

Another challenge is that since developers would be pushing changes quite often, it would be nearly impossible for a single person to scan each and every change manually.

Both these problems are addressed by this tool called *Checkov*, which is a very popular and powerful tool to scan for security bad practices in terraform code. Moreover, the authors of the tool have also created a GitHub Action template, which helps in automated scanning of each change.

The following code shows integration of Checkov into the GitHub Action workflow configured for staging/production and global environments. (Shown here is of only staging; however, the same is applicable for global/production).

Code Block 9-24. Adding Checkov scanning in GitHub Actions

File: pgitops/.github/workflows/staging.yaml

```
XXXXXXXXXXXXXXX------SNIPPED-------XXXXXXXXXXXXXXXXXXXXXX
46:        - name: Run Checkov action
47:          id: checkov
48:          uses: bridgecrewio/checkov-action@master
49:          if: github.event_name == 'pull_request'
50:          with:
51:            directory: global/
52:            quiet: true
53:            soft_fail: true
54:            framework: terraform
55:            output_format: cli
56:          continue-on-error: true
```

L46–48: Declaring the Checkov GitHub Action name

L49: Executing the action only on Pull Requests.

L51: Defining the name of the folder on which the Checkov action needs to be executed. It'll scan all the *.tf files in the specified folder.

L52: Showing only failed results.

L53: A very important configuration. If set as true, it would fail the GitHub Actions pipeline and stop the build/terraform execution.

The following code is used for showcasing the output of the Checkov scan in PR messages.

Code Block 9-25. Spooling Checkov results in PR

File: .github/workflows/infra-staging.yaml

```
XXXXXXXXXXXXXXX------SNIPPED-------XXXXXXXXXXXXXXXXXXXXXX
58:        - name: Checkov Results
59:          uses: actions/github-script@v6
```

```
60:        if: github.event_name == 'pull_request'
61:      env:
62:        CHECKOV: "checkov\n${{ env.CHECKOV_RESULTS }}"
63:      with:
64:        github-token: ${{ secrets.GITHUB_TOKEN }}
65:        script: |
66:          const output = `## Checkov Results
67:          <details><summary>Show Checkov Results</summary>
68:          ${process.env.CHECKOV}
69:          </details>
70:          *Pusher: @${{ github.actor }}, Action: \`${{
             github.event_name }}\`*`;
71:          github.rest.issues.createComment ({
72:            issue_number: context.issue.number,
73:            owner: context.repo.owner,
74:            repo: context.repo.repo,
75:            body: output
76:          })
```

XXXXXXXXXXXXXXX------SNIPPED-------XXXXXXXXXXXXXXXXXXXXXX

9.8.1 Checkov in Action

Let's execute the infra workflow to better understand how Checkov will work as part of the GitHub Actions pipeline and observe the results.

To do this, we'll need to first do some small modification to the code and then create a branch. Then raise a PR into the staging branch to see Checkov in action. We won't actually run the code in staging as we only need to see the PR running all the checks.

For this, I'll modify the value of the instance_types from t3.medium to t3.xlarge and t3.small to t3.large in the *pgitops/infra/terraform.auto.tfvars* file as shown here.

Code Block 9-26. Testing Checkov

```
File: pgitops/infra/terraform.auto.tfvars

XXXXXXXXXXXXXXXX------SNIPPED-------XXXXXXXXXXXXXXXXXXXXXXX

37: instance_types = ["t3.xlarge","t3.large"]
```

Let's now create a feature branch and push the branch.

CLI Output 9-27. Starting Checkov action

```
cmd> git status
On branch main
Your branch is up to date with 'origin/main'.

Changes not staged for commit:
  (use "git add <file>..." to update what will be committed)
  (use "git restore <file>..." to discard changes in working
  directory)
      modified:   infra/terraform.auto.tfvars

no changes added to commit (use "git add" and/or "git
commit -a")
cmd> git checkout -b checkov
Switched to a new branch 'checkov'
cmd(checkov)> git add .
cmd(checkov)> git commit -m "modifying instance types"
[checkov 462cfcc] modifying instance types
 1 file changed, 1 insertion(+), 1 deletion(-)
cmd(checkov)> git push origin checkov
```

Next, let's create a PR into staging as shown here.

435

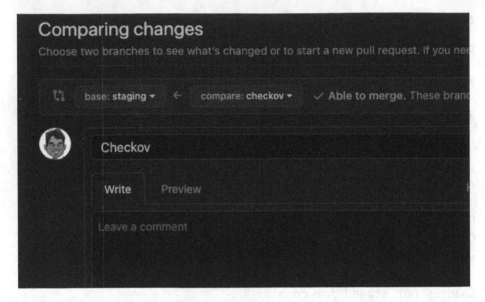

Figure 9-6. *PR for executing Checkov*

Once the PR is created, we can see that the workflow has been initiated as shown here.

Figure 9-7. *Checkov executed in PR*

Once the action has completed its execution, we should be able to see the Checkov results as shown here.

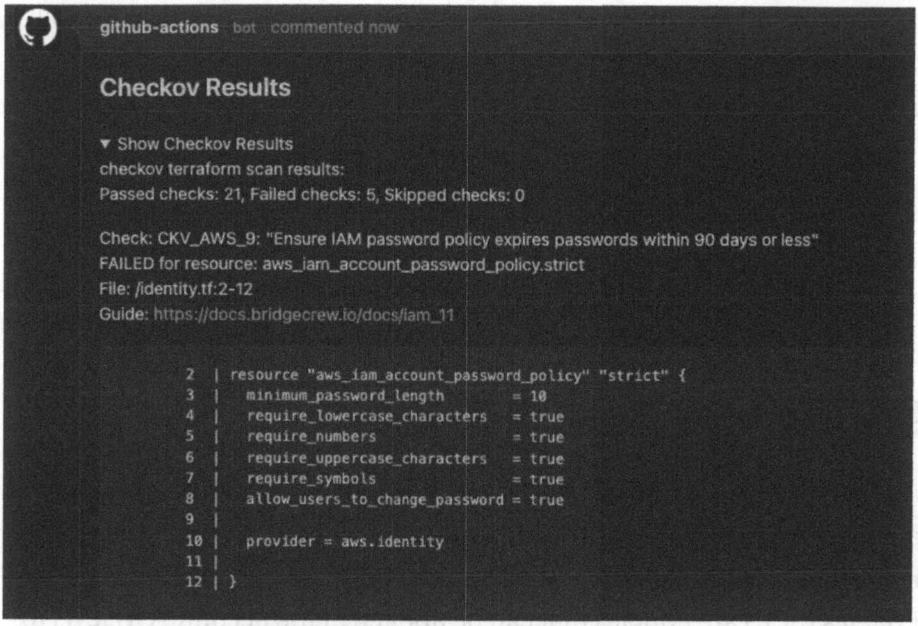

github-actions bot commented now

Checkov Results

▾ Show Checkov Results

checkov terraform scan results:

Passed checks: 21, Failed checks: 5, Skipped checks: 0

Check: CKV_AWS_9: "Ensure IAM password policy expires passwords within 90 days or less"

FAILED for resource: aws_iam_account_password_policy.strict

File: /identity.tf:2-12

Guide: https://docs.bridgecrew.io/docs/iam_11

```
2  | resource "aws_iam_account_password_policy" "strict" {
3  |   minimum_password_length        = 10
4  |   require_lowercase_characters   = true
5  |   require_numbers                = true
6  |   require_uppercase_characters   = true
7  |   require_symbols                = true
8  |   allow_users_to_change_password = true
9  |
10 |   provider = aws.identity
11 |
12 | }
```

Figure 9-8. *Checkov results being spooled*

Another failed compliance is shown in the following.

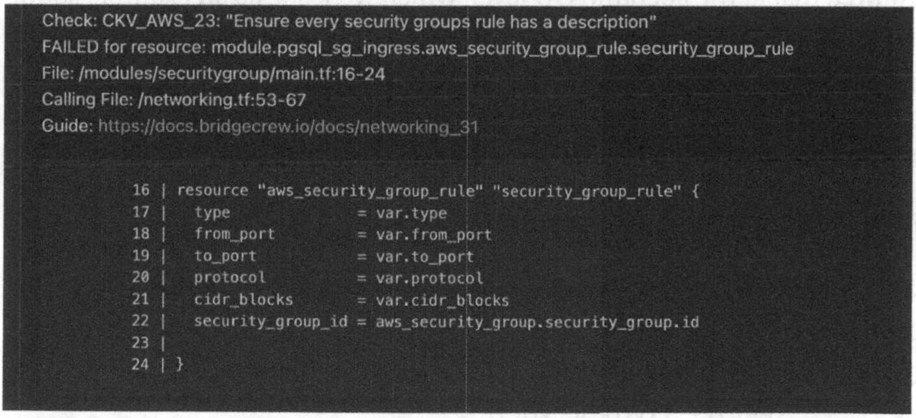

Check: CKV_AWS_23: "Ensure every security groups rule has a description"

FAILED for resource: module.pgsql_sg_ingress.aws_security_group_rule.security_group_rule

File: /modules/securitygroup/main.tf:16-24

Calling File: /networking.tf:53-67

Guide: https://docs.bridgecrew.io/docs/networking_31

```
16 | resource "aws_security_group_rule" "security_group_rule" {
17 |   type              = var.type
18 |   from_port         = var.from_port
19 |   to_port           = var.to_port
20 |   protocol          = var.protocol
21 |   cidr_blocks       = var.cidr_blocks
22 |   security_group_id = aws_security_group.security_group.id
23 |
24 | }
```

Figure 9-9. *Another failed compliance*

In this manner, we can create guardrails around Terraform code that our developers are pushing by reviewing them in PR messages.

Note   I am not merging the PR here as I said earlier that we'll be working on the development environment only in this chapter and the next.

9.9 Service Control Policies

AWS organizations do just help in centralizing billing and management of all the child accounts/organization units but also can help in strategically restraining certain actions at the account/OU level. Service Control Policies (SCP) are policies that can be applied at the account/OU level to restrict/control the usage of AWS resources.

For example, if we want to disallow users from spinning up EC2 instances like t3.xlarge, etc., that can consume a lot of money, then we can enforce that at the account/OU level, which we'll see as an example soon.

Hence, SCPs can help in enforcing compliance centrally through AWS organizations. The following code is used to initialize the SCP using Terraform.

Code Block 9-28. Instantiating Service Control Policies

```
File: pgitops/global/organisations.tf

02: resource "aws_organizations_organization" "root" {
03:
04:    enabled_policy_types = [
05:      "SERVICE_CONTROL_POLICY",
06:      "TAG_POLICY"
07:    ]
08:
```

```
09:    feature_set = "ALL"
10:
11: }
```

XXXXXXXXXXXXXXX------SNIPPED-------XXXXXXXXXXXXXXXXXXXXXX

L04-07: Initializing Service Control Policy and Tag Policies at the AWS Root organization.

SCP enforces resource-level compliance, whereas Tag Policy helps in enforcing proper tags on resources.

I've written four different SCPs in the *pgitios/global/scp.tf* file. Let's look at the InstanceTypeLimitSCP as shown here, which restricts the type of instances that can be launched in staging and development environments.

Code Block 9-29. Creating the Instance Type SCP

```
File: pgitops/global/scp.tf

12: module "instance_type_limit_scp" {
13:    source = "./modules/awsorgpolicy"
14:
15:    policy_name = "InstanceTypeLimitSCP"
16:    description = "Restrict EC2 and DB instance types for
                      dev/staging environments"
17:    policy_file = "data/instance_type_limit.json"
18:
19:    account_ids = [module.staging_account.id, aws_
                      organizations_organizational_unit.
                      development.id]
20:
21:    depends_on = [resource.aws_organizations_
                     organization.root]
22:
23: }
```

XXXXXXXXXXXXXXX------SNIPPED-------XXXXXXXXXXXXXXXXXXXXXX

L12–13: Defining and loading the module, which will create SCPs.

L15–16: Naming and describing the SCP. Describing the SCP is really important as it helps to build context.

L17: The actual JSON policy document that will enforce the restriction. It follows the standard IAM Policy document structure as we'll see in a while.

L19: Account/OU IDs on which this SCP needs to be applied to.

Let's look at the actual policy that is codified for enforcing the EC2 instance types.

Code Block 9-30. The actual policy for restricting instance types

File: pgitops/global/data/instance_type_limit.json

```
01: {
02:     "Version": "2012-10-17",
03:     "Statement": [
04:         {
05:             "Sid": "LimitEC2Instances",
06:             "Effect": "Deny",
07:             "Action": [
08:                 "ec2:*"
09:             ],
10:             "Resource": "*",
11:             "Condition": {
12:                 "ForAnyValue:StringNotLike": {
13:                     "ec2:InstanceType": [
14:                         "*.micro",
15:                         "*.medium",
16:                         "*.small",
17:                         "*.nano"
18:                     ]
19:                 }
```

```
20:                  }
21:             },
XXXXXXXXXXXXXXXX------SNIPPED-------XXXXXXXXXXXXXXXXXXXXXX
39:         ]
40: }
```

L01–03: Standard definition of an IAM Policy.

L04–09: Declaring the name of the policy and the effect and actions on which the effect needs to be performed.

L10-18: Applying this to all resources that do not meet the condition of the EC2 instance being of micro, medium, nano, or small type.

Hence, the policy states that "Deny any EC2 action if the instance type doesn't meet the criteria of being a micro, nano, small, or medium."

Similarly, three more policies have been defined as follows.

Table 9-1. *All the SCPs configured*

Policy Name	Accounts	Description
DenyUserCreationSCP	All except Identity	Deny Creation of Users in all accounts except Identity.
RegionLockSCP	Root account	Restrict AWS services and regions to particular values, that is, "us-east-1", "us-east-2", "us-west-1", and "us-west-2".
EBSRDSEncryptionSCP	Production Account	Enforce encryption on EBS block devices and RDS storage for production account.

9.9.1 SCP in Action

Now that we know what SCP is, let's learn how it practically works.

Note   Our SCPs are already operational since we did the commit for the global folder in the beginning of the chapter.

For this, we'll first merge the changes between the Checkov branch and the main branch since the PR request was not merged in the earlier section.

CLI Output 9-31. Merging Checkov branch for testing the SCP

```
cmd(checkov)> git checkout main
Switched to branch 'main'
Your branch is up to date with 'origin/main'.
cmd> git merge checkov
Updating ffefeb3..6824a6b
Fast-forward
 infra/terraform.auto.tfvars          | 2 +-
 1 file changed, 2 insertions(+), 2 deletions(-)
```

Next, just confirm that in the *pgitops/infra/terraform.auto.tfvars* file, the instance_types is set to t3.large and t3.xlarge.

Now, as per our LimitEC2Instances SCP, the development environment cannot have these instance types. Let's test it out.

CLI Output 9-32. Testing the SCP

```
cmd> export AWS_PROFILE=sita-dev
cmd> cd infra
cmd> terraform init
cmd> terraform apply –auto-approve
```

Terraform would start its execution, and somewhere when it's about to create the EKS Node Groups, that is, the worker nodes, it will throw an error looking something like the following.

CLI Output 9-33. Terraform fails to execute owing to InstanceType
limitation

```
| Error: error creating EKS Node Group (gitops-us-east-1-dev:
app-20220707050520487800000019): InvalidRequestException: You are
not authorized to launch instances with this launch template.
Encoded authorization failure message: jkwlnVZ6DGXkSEoDoi2Qh21i
Dsrp4ZOLdVmolOp1UqcrD3JtkrQmtSQoLirHj1pCgTxTA6hDvCahGWu-f73_gW2
TSBaBLLWV22cMCGyXOef1mPyUSDE32dtJUD824WyFzVOXafE2UlaxM27_9purz
LOvmjP8qDOgQK88dOXXXXXXXXXXXXXXXX------SNIPPED-------
XXXXXXXXXXXXXXXXXXXXXXXXXrHz6qM6MaGB8-B-1ZRSb8P3vPYuCKKuUQn8ImUP_
sezicOWKTvyoSWOXTRHjORPu7MS1gz2BQNROvnvvT8uLq9QfN504l025d2nIuG
GI4GTrVRouOKpAoEWAJ8Z_ei_UP88I3J65fixRGOKHjeUHMMfkkh9JH1uQWHw9c
x1_Yfrvq1reTE4RHOAWafoTncVR-YCbv1CAkY-mdVF9drepeKOy700MSgkQUE4p
80w2p4MlII3CfmfMKUTvyXMADOIlfSO6JhDWCx_qqHTI539PG-s67p1hAigvffMP
| {
|   RespMetadata: {
|     StatusCode: 400,
|     RequestID: "a620ee2c-f788-45a9-857a-90de4b7f452d"
|   },
```

Let's decode the message to better understand what's happening. We'll
need to make use of the following command:

aws sts decode-authorization-message --encoded-message
<encoded-message>

And apply little bit for formatting using *sed 's/\\"/"/g' | sed 's/^"//' | sed
's/"$//'*

as shown here.

CLI Output 9-34. Executing AWS STS decode-
authorization-message

cmd> aws sts decode-authorization-message --encoded-message

jkwlnVZ6DGXkSEoDoi2Qh21iDsrp4ZOLdVmolOp1UqcrD3JtkrQmtSQoLirHj1p
CgTxTA6hDvCahGWu-f73_gW2TSBaBLLWV22cMCGyXOef1mPyUSDE32dtJUD824
WyFzVOXafE2UlaxM27_9purzLOvmjP8qDOgQK88dOz7waPgIObTxOFYxLNak7U
LjfYQPtFzwzGN5SDpIgOcw_YwTgFZBXmcEA9tHXXXXXXXXXXXXXXX------
SNIPPED-------XXXXXXXXXXXXXXXXXXXXXXXQfN504lO25d2nIuGGI4GTrVRouO
KpAoEWAJ8Z_ei_UP88I3J65fixRGOKHjeUHMMfkkh9JH1uQWHw9cx1_Yfrvq1re
TE4RHOAWafoTncVR-YCbv1CAkY-mdVF9drepeKOy7OoMSgkQUE4p8Ow2p4MlII3
CfmfMKUTvyXMADOIlfSO6JhDWCx_qqHTI539PG-s67p1hAigvffMP |

sed 's/\\"/"/g' | sed 's/^"//' | sed 's/"$//'

{
    "DecodedMessage": "{"allowed":false,"explicitDeny":true,"ma
tchedStatements":{"items":[{"statementId":"LimitEC2Instances","
effect":"DENY","principals":{"items":[{"value":"AROA5JNUXXXXXXX
XXXXXX"}]},"principalGroups":{"items":[]},"actions":{"items":[{
"value":"ec2:*"}]},"resources":{"items":[{"value":"*"}]},"
conditions":{"items":[{"key":"ec2:InstanceType","values":{"i
tems":[{"value":"*.micro"},{"value":"*.medium"},{"value":"*.
small"},{"value":"*.nano"}]}}]}}]},"failures":{"items":[]},"c
ontext":{"principal":{"id":"AROA5JNUXXXXXXXXXXXXXX:aws-go-sdk-
1657169654646371000","arn":"arn:aws:sts::91XXXXXXXX7:assumed-
role/AssumeRoleAdmindev/aws-go-sdk-1657169654646371000"},"act
ion":"ec2:RunInstances","resource":"arn:aws:ec2:us-east-1:91
XXXXXXXX7:instance/*","conditions":{"items":[{"key":"ec2:Metad
ataHttpPutResponseHopLimit","values":{"items":[{"value":"2"}]}
},{"key":"ec2:InstanceMarketType","values":{"items":[{"value":
"on-demand"}]}},{"key":"aws:Resource","values":{"items":[{"val

ue":"instance/*"}]}},{"key":"aws:Account","values":{"items":[{
"value":"91XXXXXXXX7"}]}},{"key":"ec2:AvailabilityZone","value
s":{"items":[{"value":"us-east-1c"}]}},{"key":"ec2:ebsOptimize
d","values":{"items":[{"value":"true"}]}},{"key":"ec2:IsLaunch
TemplateResource","values":{"items":[{"value":"true"}]}},{"ke
y":"ec2:InstanceType","values":{"items":[{"value":"t3.large"}
]}},{"key":"ec2:RootDeviceType","values":{"items":[{"value":"
ebs"}]}},{"key":"aws:Region","values":{"items":[{"value":"us-
east-1"}]}},{"key":"ec2:MetadataHttpEndpoint","values":{"items"
:[{"value":"enabled"}]}},{"key":"ec2:InstanceMetadataTags","val
ues":{"items":[{"value":"disabled"}]}},{"key":"aws:Service","v
alues":{"items":[{"value":"ec2"}]}},{"key":"ec2:InstanceID","v
alues":{"items":[{"value":"*"}]}},{"key":"ec2:MetadataHttpToke
ns","values":{"items":[{"value":"required"}]}},{"key":"aws:Type
","values":{"items":[{"value":"instance"}]}},{"key":"ec2:Tenanc
y","values":{"items":[{"value":"default"}]}},{"key":"ec2:Region
","values":{"items":[{"value":"us-east-1"}]}},{"key":"aws:ARN",
"values":{"items":[{"value":"arn:aws:ec2:us-east-1:91XXXXXXXX7
:instance/*"}]}},{"key":"ec2:LaunchTemplate","values":{"items"
:[{"value":"arn:aws:ec2:us-east-1:91XXXXXXXX7:launch-template/
lt-007064a3db6d169af"}]}}]}}}
}

The preceding error message clearly mentions the SCP that blocked the creation of our t3.large EC2 instance! It truly shows the power of policy enforcement!

Of course, there is one drawback here: that this message is shown a little later when almost half of the infrastructure is almost already set up.

9.10 Clean-Up

Since our infrastructure was only partially set up, it's best to destroy it using the usual terraform destroy command as shown here.

CLI Output 9-35. Destroying the Dev environment

```
cmd> export AWS_PROFILE=sita-dev
cmd> cd infra
cmd> terraform destroy -auto-approve
```

Note   At any point, if terraform is unable to destroy, please check Annexure A where steps have been presented to delete the resources manually.

We still are not destroying the global folder as it's needed in the next chapter.

Also we need to revert back the instance_type configuration for the development environment, without which, we won't be able to set up the development environment. Let's revert the values back to t3.small and t3.medium as shown here.

Code Block 9-36. Reverting back the configuration

```
File: pgitops/infra/terraform.auto.tfvars

XXXXXXXXXXXXXXX------SNIPPED-------XXXXXXXXXXXXXXXXXXXXXX

37: instance_types = ["t3.small","t3.medium"]
```

Once this configuration has been reverted, you are strongly advised to run the terraform apply to set up the entire infrastructure and then check the following:

- Is HTTP being redirected to HTTPS?

- Can you view the database credentials when viewing the deployment manifests in Kubernetes? *kubectl describe deploy gitops -n gitops*

- Which service-account-token is mounted on gitops deployment?

9.11 Conclusion

In this chapter, we saw how certain security features can be introduced using Terraform to make our infrastructure a tidy bit more secure like secrets being stored in AWS KMS and synced real time. Our website is no longer serving on a clear-text port; rather, it is redirected to a secure connection, that is HTTPS. We looked at how individual pods can securely communicate with the AWS services using IRSA, implemented guardrails with Checkov to better understand the security hygiene of our terraform code, and finally enforced policy compliance centrally to ensure certain best practices using SCPs.

In the next chapter, we'll look at the logging, monitoring, and observability aspects of this infrastructure that we've set up.

CHAPTER 10

Observability

Observability is the science of observing a running infrastructure through various metrics and data points that the tools provide. While an entire book can be written on how to actually observe your infrastructure, this chapter's focus is more on how to set up the supporting infrastructure that can help us drive decisions based on the behavior of the application that is observable through various metrics and data points.

In this chapter, we'll look at setting up an OpenSearch cluster to view all Kubernetes and application logs in real time, observing performance metrics using Prometheus and Grafana stack, centralizing CloudTrail of all accounts into a single account, capturing ALB logs in an S3 bucket, installing Karpenter (a horizontal node scaling tool to scale the nodes based on pod requirements), upgrading the Kubernetes version from 1.20 to 1.21, and observing the changes happening in real time and finally creating CloudWatch alerts based on events like root login.

10.1 Code Update

Before diving into the code, let's first ensure that we've updated the pgitops directory with the code from the Chapter 10 folder. To do this, follow these steps:

- First, copy the contents of the Chapter 10 folder into the pgitops folder.

- Get inside the pgitops directory and then check which files/folders are changing.

- We shall commit only the global directory as we need the changes to be reflected in the global environment.

- Changes done in the infra folder can be committed, and the CI can be skipped as we'll be testing the changes only in the development environment for this chapter.

CLI Output 10-1. Updating Chapter 10 code

```
cmd> cp -a chapter10/. pgitops/
cmd> cd pgitops
cmd> git status
On branch main
Your branch is up to date with 'origin/main'.

Changes not staged for commit:
  (use "git add <file>..." to update what will be committed)
  (use "git restore <file>..." to discard changes in working
  directory)
        modified:   README.md
        modified:   global/README.md
        modified:   global/data/padma.pub.old
        modified:   global/data/raadha.pub.old
        modified:   global/data/sita.pub.old
        modified:   global/identity.tf
        modified:   global/organisations.tf
        modified:   global/outputs.tf
        modified:   global/prod/main.tf
        modified:   global/staging/main.tf
        modified:   global/terraform.auto.tfvars.old
        modified:   global/variables.tf
        modified:   infra/README.md
        modified:   infra/app.tf
```

```
    modified:    infra/eks.tf
    modified:    infra/modules/acm/main.tf
    modified:    infra/modules/alb/iam_policy.json
    modified:    infra/modules/alb/main.tf
    modified:    infra/modules/alb/variables.tf
    modified:    infra/modules/csisecretsdriver/aws-
    secrets-csi.yaml
    modified:    infra/modules/ekscluster/main.tf
    modified:    infra/modules/ekscluster/output.tf
    modified:    infra/modules/vpc/main.tf
    modified:    infra/terraform.auto.tfvars.old

Untracked files:
  (use "git add <file>..." to include in what will be
  committed)
    global/data/rds_encryption_check.json
    global/logging.tf
    global/logging/
    global/modules/cwalarm/
    global/modules/snsemail/
    infra/modules/alb/s3_log.json
    infra/modules/karpenter/
    infra/modules/logging/
    infra/modules/monitoring/
    infra/observability.tf

no changes added to commit (use "git add" and/or "git
commit -a")
```

The changes can summarized as follows:

– We are creating an Organization Trail that centralizes
  CloudTrail from all accounts into the master account and
  archiving it in an S3 bucket.

– Creating a CloudWatch rule that sends an email alert
  whenever a root user logs into the accounts.

– Creating an Admin IAM Role in the master account and
  allowing a Sita user to access the master account by
  assuming this IAM Role.

– Creating an S3 bucket that stores all ALB access logs.

– Deploying Karpenter, a horizontal node scaler by AWS.

– Creating an OpenSearch cluster that will have application
  and Kubernetes logs pushed into using Fluent bit.

– Creating a Monitoring stack using Prometheus and
  Grafana, obtaining metrics using Metrics Server.

10.1.1 Committing Only Global

For the sake of simplicity and for ensuring that the global folder is
committed, let's execute the following commands. However, there is a
small addition that needs to be done to the *pgitops/global/terraform.auto.
tfvars* file before pushing the code. There is an additional variable, *alert_
email*, that needs to be initialized without which our code will not run.
Ensure to add an appropriate value to it before pushing the code.

Code Block 10-2. Comitting only global changes

```
File: pgitops/global/terraform.auto.tfvars

XXXXXXXXXXXXXXX------SNIPPED-------XXXXXXXXXXXXXXXXXXXXXX
```

```
39: org_name = "gitops"
40: domain   = "gitops.rohitsalecha.com"
41: alert_email = "alert@example.com"
```

Of course, the ideal way to push this code would be to create a branch, raise a PR, and then merge it. However, for sake of simplicity, let's push it directly into the main branch as shown here.

CLI Output 10-3. Pushing Global changes

```
cmd> git add .
cmd> git commit -m 'committing only global for chapter10
-- global
cmd> git push
```

Once we fire *git push*, it can be observed that only global changes have gone live.

With these, the following items have been created:

- Organization Trail spooling all logs in CloudWatch of the master account

- An S3 bucket archiving all CloudTrail data as backup since CloudWatch has a limit of only 30 days of storage

- An IAM Role created in the master/root account for Admin to access

- A CloudWatch Alarm with an SNS topic

10.1.2 Committing Infra

The other changes, for example, infra, etc., are still in staging in our local system as shown in the following. Let's push these changes as well but without triggering the GitHub Actions, that is, by adding [skip ci] in our commit message.

CLI Output 10-4. Committing infra changes

```
cmd> git status
On branch main
Your branch is up to date with 'origin/main'.

Changes to be committed:
  (use "git restore --staged <file>..." to unstage)
        modified:   README.md
XXXXXXXXXXXXXXX------SNIPPED-------XXXXXXXXXXXXXXXXXXXXX
        modified:   infra/modules/alb/s3_log.json
        new file:   infra/modules/karpenter/
        modified:   infra/variables.tf

cmd> git commit -m '[skip ci] committing infra'
cmd> git push
```

10.2 Executing Infra

Unlike the previous chapters, this time, let's first start executing the infra in the development environment to view all the different changes that we've made as we progress through the code.

One small prerequisite for our infra code to run is an additional variable ***alb_s3_bucket*** in the *pgitops/infra/terraform.auto.tfvars* file that needs to be instantiated as shown in the following. Please add an appropriate value to this variable before executing the infra terraform files. This variable holds the name of the S3 bucket, which will hold our ALB Access Logs.

Code Block 10-5. Executing infra

```
File: pgitops/infra/terraform.auto.tfvars
```

```
XXXXXXXXXXXXXXX------SNIPPED-------XXXXXXXXXXXXXXXXXXXXXXX
36: eks_version    = "1.20"
37: instance_types = ["t3.medium","t3.small"]
38: alb_s3_bucket  = "gitops-logs-s3-bucket-5"
```

Standard process now to execute our infra terraform files.

CLI Output 10-6. Executing infra changes in the dev environment

```
cmd> export AWS_PROFILE=sita-dev
cmd> cd pgitops/infra
cmd> terraform init
cmd> terraform apply --auto-approve
```

10.3 Organization Trail

AWS records all activities performed by a user/IAM Role through the console as well as programmatically as events. These events are then stored as records in a service called CloudTrail.

In order to get these records, CloudTrail needs to be enabled in all accounts that are operational. When working with AWS organizations and using various different accounts, it's not feasible to go ahead and enable CloudTrail in all accounts. Moreover, if you ever manage to do so, you'll always need to log into that account to view the CloudTrail logs under the Logs section.

However, AWS in 2018 introduced a feature called Organization Trail, which can be launched from the master account. Once enabled, this feature enables CloudTrail in all existing accounts as well as new accounts and most importantly gets all the CloudTrail logs from the member accounts into the master account for central logging purpose.

Let's explore how this feature can be enabled through Terraform, and in the Master Account Login section, we'll actually log in and view the CloudTrail records from other accounts.

Code Block 10-7. Enabling CloudTrail

```
File: pgitops\global\organisations.tf

2: resource "aws_organizations_organization" "root" {
3:
4:   aws_service_access_principals = [
5:     "cloudtrail.amazonaws.com"
6:   ]
XXXXXXXXXXXXXXXX------SNIPPED-------XXXXXXXXXXXXXXXXXXXXXX
```

L4-6: When creating a service role in AWS IAM - that is, a role that can be assumed by an AWS Service - you need to specify the service by a unique identifier. That unique identifier is known as a service principal. This service principal now allows access to CloudTrail service for all accounts.

Tip   Unofficial List of Service Control Principals

```
https://gist.github.com/shortjared/4c1e3fe52bd
fa47522cfe5b41e5d6f22
```

Code Block 10-8. Configuring Organization Trail

```
File: pgitops\global\logging.tf

XXXXXXXXXXXXXXXX------SNIPPED-------XXXXXXXXXXXXXXXXXXXXXX
10: resource "aws_cloudtrail" "central_cloud_trail" {
```

```
11:
12:    name                           = "CentralCloudTrail"
13:    s3_bucket_name                 = module.logging.s3_bucket_id
14:    s3_key_prefix                  = "trails"
15:    enable_log_file_validation     = true
16:    enable_logging                 = true
17:    include_global_service_events  = true
18:    is_multi_region_trail          = true
19:    is_organization_trail          = true
20:    cloud_watch_logs_role_arn      = module.logging.cw_logs_
                                        role_arn
21:    cloud_watch_logs_group_arn     = "${module.logging.cw_
                                        logs_arn}:*"
22:    depends_on = [module.logging,
23:    aws_organizations_organization.root]
24:    tags = {
25:      terraform-managed = "true"
26:    }
27: }
XXXXXXXXXXXXXXX------SNIPPED-------XXXXXXXXXXXXXXXXXXXX
```

L10: This is the standard way of enabling a CloudTrail in AWS using Terraform.

L13: This S3 bucket is created in the master account and is primarily used for archiving.

L17-19: These are the actual flags that distinguish a local CloudTrail from an Organization Trail. If set to true, the resource becomes an Organization Trail enabling CloudTrail in all member accounts.

L20-21: Specification of the CloudWatch Group that is needed to view the CloudTrail logs by default. This CloudWatch group is created in the master account.

Code Block 10-9. Adding logging configurations in the
master account

```
File: pgitops\global\logging.tf

2: module "logging" {
3:    source              = "./logging"
4:    account             = "master"
5:    identity_account_id = module.identity_account.id
6:
7: }
XXXXXXXXXXXXXXXX------SNIPPED-------XXXXXXXXXXXXXXXXXXXXXX
```

In the preceding module, the following things are getting created in the
master account:

- CloudWatch Group for storing Organization Trail logs

- S3 bucket for Organization Trail with necessary IAM
  Permissions such that CloudWatch can push the data

- IAM Admin Role for the master account

10.4 CloudWatch Alarm

In this section, we'll look into how we've set up the CloudWatch Alarm for
root login by first creating a subscription using the AWS SNS and an alarm
on specific conditions using CloudWatch Alarm. Before we move on, let's
first understand CloudWatch and SNS because this is one of the most
powerful combinations in AWS infrastructure as it helps in creating an
EDA (Event-Driven Architecture).

CloudWatch keeps a track of all the events like bucket creation, new file added to a bucket, EC2 creation, etc. You can attach a filter of your choice to fish out the events that you are interested in like filter all events when an EC2 is destroyed.

SNS can be used to send email or text notifications to end users. In this case, you can trigger a notification based on an event that matches the filter criteria that you have set inside CloudWatch; for example, if we create a filter for the preceding use case that an EC2 is being destroyed, then it'll trigger an SNS notification, which in turn will trigger an SMS or an email to the user.

10.4.1 Configuring AWS SNS

Once the terraform code in the global folder is executed successfully, you should receive an email on the value specified in the *alert_email* variable as shown here.

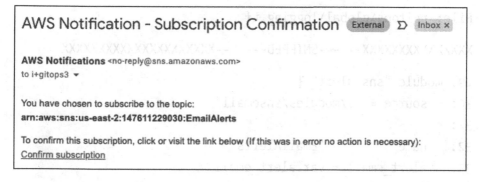

Figure 10-1. *AWS SNS Subscription confirmation for Alert Email*

Warning   Ensure to click Confirm subscription to have the following confirmation.

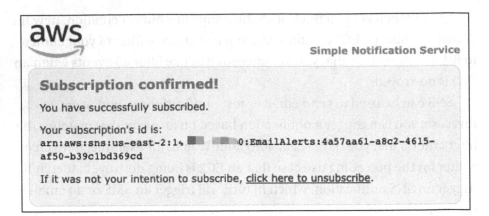

Figure 10-2. Subscription confirmation

The following is the code that is responsible for doing the same. It creates an AWS SNS (Simple Notification Service) subscription with the email specified in the variable.

Code Block 10-10. Configuring SNS notification

```
File: pgitops\global\logging.tf

XXXXXXXXXXXXXXX------SNIPPED-------XXXXXXXXXXXXXXXXXXXXXX

29: module "sns_alert" {
30:    source = "./modules/snsemail"
31:
32:    name        = "EmailAlerts"
33:    alert_email = var.alert_email
34:
35: }
```

10.4.2 Configuring CloudWatch Alarm

Code Block 10-11. Configuring CloudWatch Alarm

File: pgitops\global\logging.tf

```
XXXXXXXXXXXXXXX------SNIPPED-------XXXXXXXXXXXXXXXXXXXXXX
39: module "root_user_login_alarm" {
40:    source                          = "./modules/cwalarm"
41:    name                            = "RootLogin"
42:    cw_group_name                   = module.logging.cw_log_
                                         group_name
43:    pattern                         = "{ ($.userIdentity.
                                         type = \"Root\") &&
                                         ($.userIdentity.
                                         invokedBy NOT EXISTS)
                                         && ($.eventType !=
                                         \"AwsServiceEvent\") }"
44:    metric_filter_count             = "1"
45:    metric_filter_namespace         = "CloudTrailMetrics"
46:    description                     = "A CloudWatch Alarm that
                                         triggers if a root user
                                         is logging in."
47:    metric_alarm_statistic          = "Sum"
48:    metric_alarm_period             = "60"
49:    metric_alarm_threshold          = "1"
50:    metric_alarm_evaluation_periods = "1"
51:    metric_alarm_comparison_operator = "GreaterThanOrEqualTo
                                          Threshold"
52:    metric_alarm_treat_missing_data = "notBreaching"
```

```
53:    sns_topic_arn                    = module.sns_alert.arn
54:
55:    depends_on = [aws_cloudtrail.central_cloud_trail]
XXXXXXXXXXXXXXX------SNIPPED-------XXXXXXXXXXXXXXXXXXXX
```

L39–41: Invoking the CloudWatch Alarm module and configuring the name of this alarm as RootLogin.

L42: The CloudWatch group that will be monitored to raise the alarm, basically the input to the alarm.

L43: Most important configuration, which is checking if the root user is performing any AWS Activity, then please flag!

L47–51: Configuring the alarm to check for the CloudWatch data every 60 seconds for any breach.

L52: Configuring the default condition when there is no data.

L53: Configuring the SNS Topic created earlier where in case of a breach or alarm being triggered, a notification will be sent to the AWS SNS topic, and subsequently an email will be sent.

10.4.3 Root Login Alarm in Action

Let's test this alarm by simply logging in using the root email address and observing the email as shown in the following.

Note   Wait for about two minutes after logging into the account to get the email.

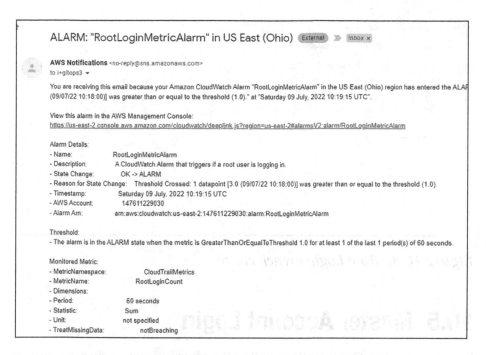

Figure 10-3. *Root Login Alarm in Action*

We can also see the Alarm being breached in the CloudWatch console. Search for CloudWatch in the search bar and then open the RootLoginCount Alarm as shown here.

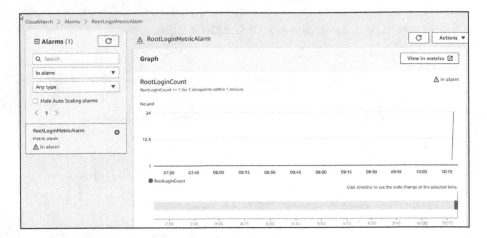

Figure 10-4. *Root Login breach count*

10.5 Master Account Login

So we created an Organization Trail in the master account, and the only way to access the master/root account is to use the root credentials or the credentials of the "gitops" admin user, which was the very first user that we created. Both these credentials must be locked down and used only for emergency purposes. Then how do we access the management account to view the CloudTrail logs?

Very simple, create an IAM Role with administrator privileges and then allow the Sita user to assume that role, which is what is being done as shown in the following.

Note   Of Course, you could use a lesser privilege role rather than an Administrator role like a simple CloudTrailsAdmin role as an example.

Code Block 10-12. Updating Admin role privileges

```
File: pgitops\global\identity.tf

XXXXXXXXXXXXXXX------SNIPPED-------XXXXXXXXXXXXXXXXXXXXXX

87:      admin = [
88:        module.staging.assume_admin_role_arn,
89:        module.prod.assume_admin_role_arn,
90:        module.dev.assume_admin_role_arn,
91:        module.logging.assume_admin_role_arn
92:      ],

XXXXXXXXXXXXXXX------SNIPPED-------XXXXXXXXXXXXXXXXXXXXXX
```

Earlier we logged into the master account using the root credentials; let's login into the master account now using this newly created IAM Role assumed by user Sita.

1. Firstly, we need the account ID of the master account in order to log in; hence, from the CLI, fire the following commands.

CLI Output 10-13. Login using GitOps user credentials

```
cmd> export AWS_PROFILE=gitops
cmd> aws sts get-caller-identity
{
    "UserId": "AIDASEXSQTNTGAEZIZL3P",
    "Account": "14XXXXXXX30",
    "Arn": "arn:aws:iam::14XXXXXXX30:user/gitops"
}
```

Make a note of this account ID.

2.   Let's log in into the console of the identity account
using the Sita user's credentials and click Switch role
as shown here.

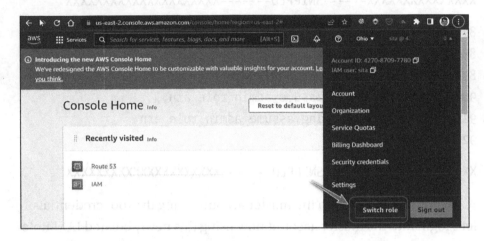

Figure 10-5. *Switch role through Console*

3.   Now in the Switch role console, enter the Account
ID obtained earlier and name of the IAM Role,
which can be obtained from the Terraform Cloud
Global workspace outputs as shown here.

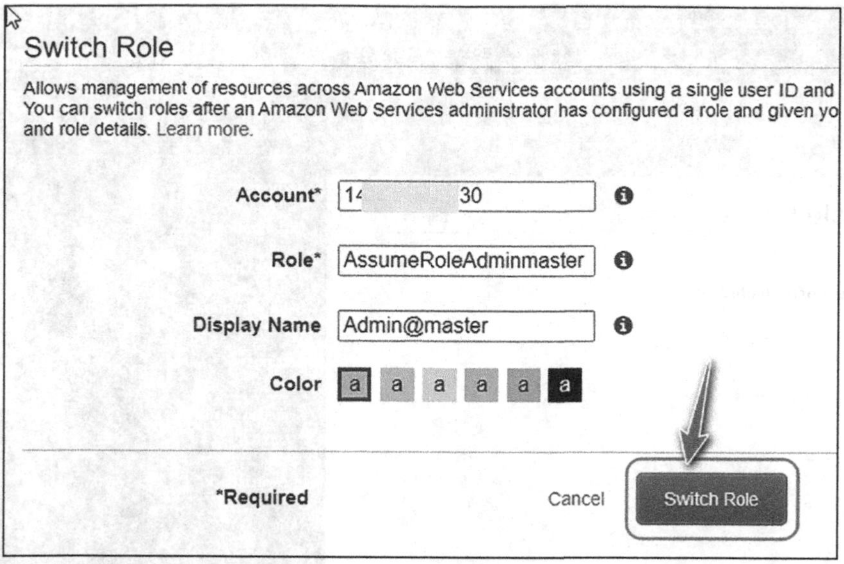

Figure 10-6. *Switch Role details*

4. If everything is correctly entered, you should be
    navigated to the master account as shown here.

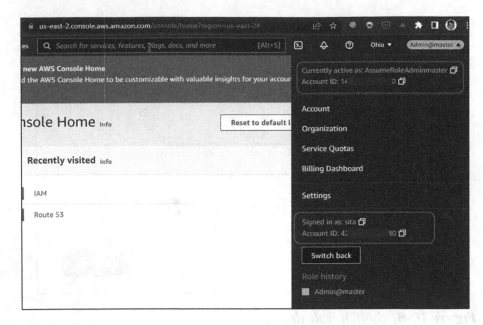

Figure 10-7. *Switched Role to master account*

5.   Navigate to the CloudWatch Console and view the
CloudTrail group as shown in the following. Ensure
you are in the correct region, that is, (us-east-2).

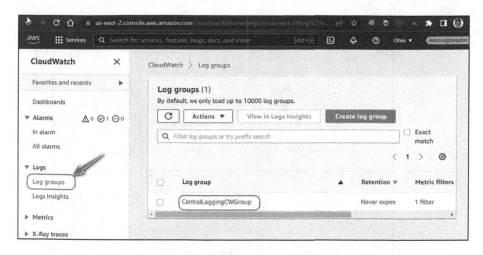

Figure 10-8. *Navigating to the CloudWatch console*

6.   Streams from different accounts can be seen.

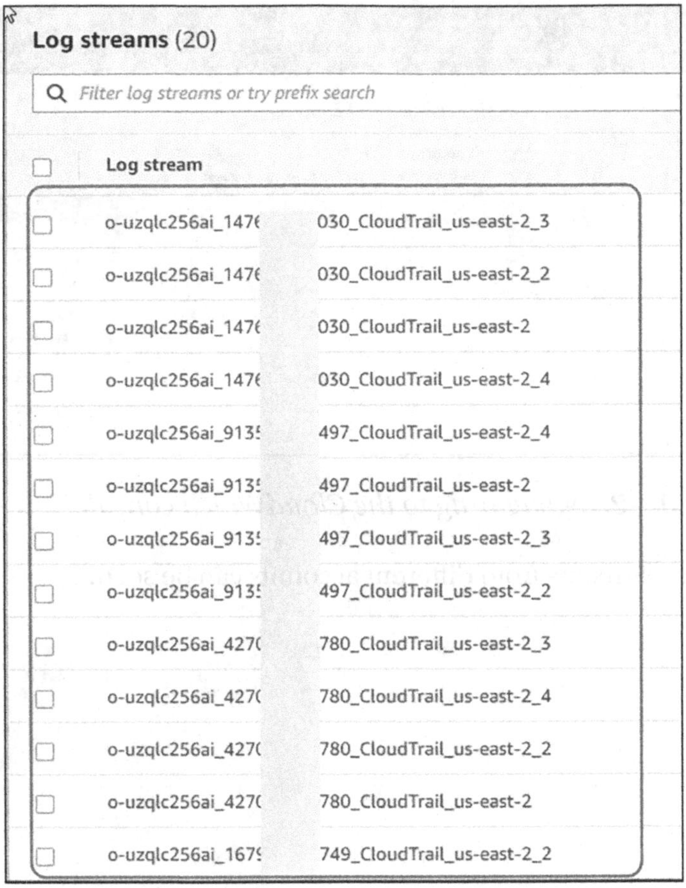

	Log stream	
☐	o-uzqlc256ai_1476	030_CloudTrail_us-east-2_3
☐	o-uzqlc256ai_1476	030_CloudTrail_us-east-2_2
☐	o-uzqlc256ai_1476	030_CloudTrail_us-east-2
☐	o-uzqlc256ai_1476	030_CloudTrail_us-east-2_4
☐	o-uzqlc256ai_9135	497_CloudTrail_us-east-2_4
☐	o-uzqlc256ai_9135	497_CloudTrail_us-east-2
☐	o-uzqlc256ai_9135	497_CloudTrail_us-east-2_3
☐	o-uzqlc256ai_9135	497_CloudTrail_us-east-2_2
☐	o-uzqlc256ai_4270	780_CloudTrail_us-east-2_3
☐	o-uzqlc256ai_4270	780_CloudTrail_us-east-2_4
☐	o-uzqlc256ai_4270	780_CloudTrail_us-east-2_2
☐	o-uzqlc256ai_4270	780_CloudTrail_us-east-2
☐	o-uzqlc256ai_1679	749_CloudTrail_us-east-2_2

Log streams (20)

Figure 10-9. *Streams from different accounts*

10.6 ALB Access Logs

The load balancer is the first point of entry into our application, and hence, access logs need to be maintained and stored as per many compliance frameworks. These logs can help in identifying any unusual activity or debug an issue.

Also, setting this up is relatively easy; we only have to set up an S3 bucket and reference the bucket in an annotation of the ingress resource as shown here.

Code Block 10-14. Updating Kubernetes ingress resource for ALB Logging

File: pgitops\infra\app.tf

```
229: resource "kubernetes_ingress_v1" "app" {
230:    wait_for_load_balancer = true
231:    metadata {
232:      name       = var.org_name
233:      namespace = kubernetes_namespace_v1.app.
          metadata.0.name
234:      annotations = {
235:        "kubernetes.io/ingress.
class"                          = "alb"

XXXXXXXXXXXXXXX------SNIPPED-------XXXXXXXXXXXXXXXXXXXXXX

241:        "alb.ingress.kubernetes.io/load-balancer-attributes"
           = "access_logs.s3.enabled=true,access_logs.
           s3.bucket=${var.alb_s3_bucket},access_logs.
           s3.prefix=gitops,routing.http.drop_invalid_header_
           fields.enabled=true"
242:        "alb.ingress.kubernetes.io/group.name"
= "gitops"
```

L241: An additional annotation that has been added, "alb.ingress. kubernetes.io/load-balancer-attributes", which holds the name of the S3 bucket and its prefix where the logs will be stored.

L242: Another annotation that has been added to group ingress rules within the same resource. As we'll see in Section 10.8, when we set up Grafana, this same annotation will be added to Grafana's ingress resource.

471

Thereby we avoid setting up two different AWS ALBs, which is the default behavior as discussed in Section 7.6.

10.7 Logging

Setting up a logging infrastructure is extremely important as any debugging if needed has to be done by sifting through the logs we have. Logging infrastructure gives us feedback of what's really happening, what data is coming in, and how the application is processing the data.

The EFK or the Elastic, Fluent Bit, and Kibana is one of the most popular stacks for setting up the logging infrastructure. AWS has set up its own stack called OpenSearch, which was forked out of Elastic Stack v 7.10 onward.

It is an onerous and a mammoth task to set up a logging infrastructure because of the two most important factors that need to be considered, namely, scalability and security.

A logging infrastructure needs to be scalable as application usage can go up during certain periods and down during certain ones. Hence, a standard production-grade EFK stack will have multi-node clusters.

It also has to maintain top-notch security because plenty of sensitive information like credit card numbers, passwords, etc., that would be part of HTTP requests/responses could be stored/processed in this infrastructure.

AWS through OpenSearch provides both scalability and security; hence, it's prudent to use this service.

The entire logging infrastructure setup has been encapsulated in a single module in Terraform as shown in the following.

Code Block 10-15. Creating the OpenSearch Stack

File: pgitops\infra\observability.tf

```
06: module "logging" {
07:    source = "./modules/logging"
08:
09:    es_instance_type     = "t3.medium.elasticsearch"
10:    es_instance_count    = 1
11:    es_version           = "OpenSearch_1.2"
12:    fb_version           = "2.23.3"
13:    oidc_url             = module.eks.cluster_oidc_issuer_url
14:    oidc_arn             = module.eks.oidc_provider_arn
15:    acm_arn              = module.acm.acm_arn
16:    url                  = local.url
17:    zone_id              = data.aws_route53_zone.
                              domain.zone_id
18:    environment          = var.environment
19:    fluentbit_count_yaml = length(data.kubectl_file_
                              documents.fluentbit_yaml_count.
                              documents)
20:
21:    depends_on = [
22:       module.eks,
23:       resource.kubectl_manifest.aws_auth
24:    ]
25: }
```

L09–11: Important prerequisites that need to be provided to set up the OpenSearch cluster. It has its own instance naming convention like *t3.medium.elasticsearch*. Cluster count is important, and for production purposes, this should be a minimum of 3.

L12–14: Providing information to set up Fluent Bit, which is a tool that ships the logs to the OpenSearch cluster. It'll run as a DaemonSet on each node, and an IRSA (hence sharing OIDC information) setup has to be made so that it can write to the OpenSearch cluster.

L15-17: The OpenSearch corresponds to Elasticsearch, and for Kibana, we have OpenDashboard provided by AWS, and it can be accessible over the Internet. Hence, providing it the requisite information to set up on a customer domain taking the format as logging.<environment>.<domain>. For example, for the development environment, it'll be accessible on the FQDN as **logging.dev.gitops.rohitsalecha.com** where **gitops. rohitsalecha.com** is the main domain and **dev** is the environment.

10.7.1 Exploring OpenSearch

The full URL for accessing our OpenSearch cluster in the dev environment is as follows:

```
https://logging.dev.gitops.rohitsalecha.com/_dashboards/
app/login
```

and the credentials are elastic:Elastic@123, which are currently hard-coded in *pgitops\infra\modules\logging\main.tf*, and it is strongly recommended that they are changed and also make use of a secrets managing service to store them.

Figure 10-10. *Login Console of OpenSearch*

Post authentication, two options are provided; select "Add data" as shown here.

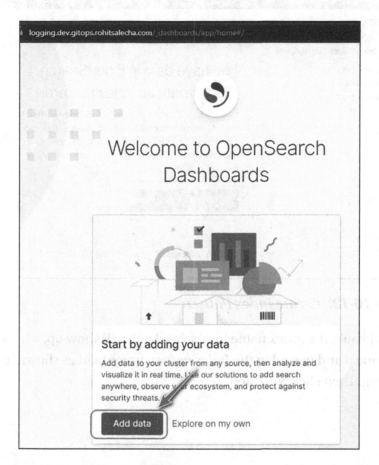

Figure 10-11. *Add data after login*

Next, we need to create an Index in the OpenSearch cluster as shown here.

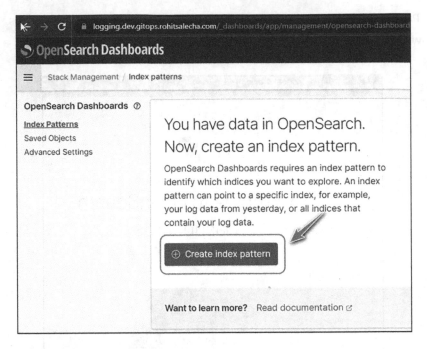

Figure 10-12. *Create Index Pattern*

By default, the index name logstash-<date> will show up, which needs to be copied and pasted in the *Index pattern name* field as shown in the following. Then click Next step.

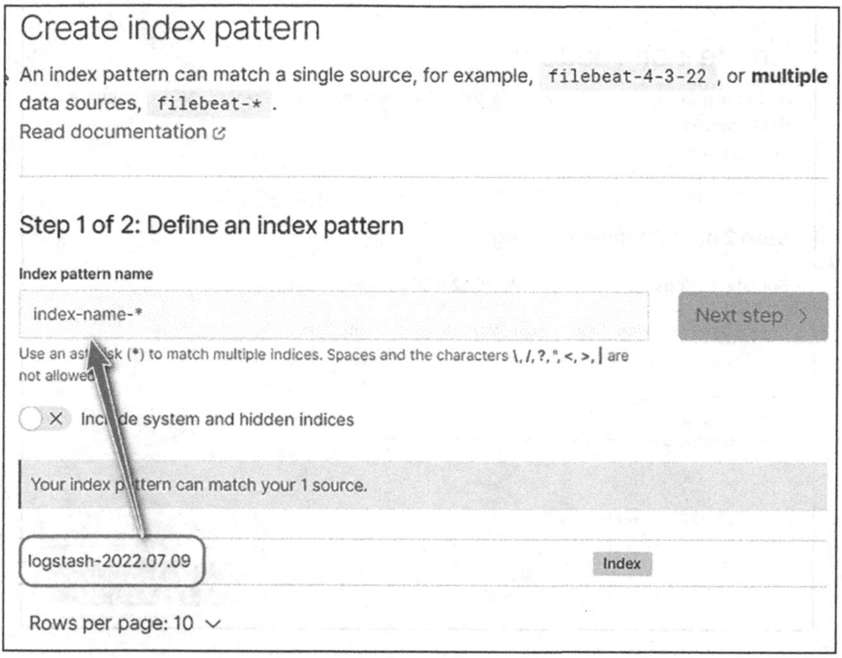

Create index pattern

An index pattern can match a single source, for example, `filebeat-4-3-22`, or **multiple** data sources, `filebeat-*`.

Read documentation ⤤

Step 1 of 2: Define an index pattern

Index pattern name

index-name-*	Next step >

Use an asterisk (*) to match multiple indices. Spaces and the characters \, /, ?, ", <, >, | are not allowed

◯ ✕ Include system and hidden indices

Your index pattern can match your 1 source.

logstash-2022.07.09	Index

Rows per page: 10 ∨

Figure 10-13. Add logstash pattern

Select timestamp and then click "Create index pattern" as shown here.

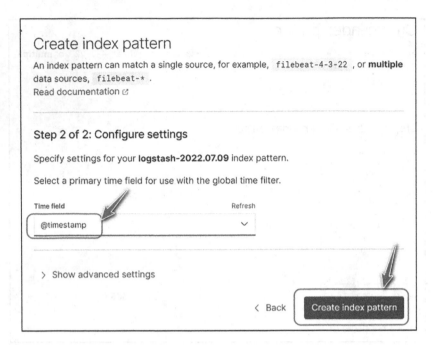

Figure 10-14. *Selecting timestamp*

Once the index pattern is created, click on the hamburger menu and then click Discover.

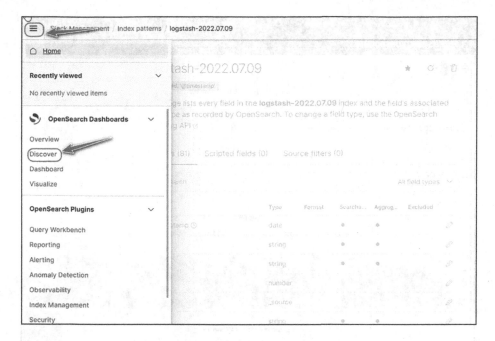

Figure 10-15. *Navigating to the Discover page*

In this page, we can now see all our Application as well as Kubernetes logs as shown in the following pictures.

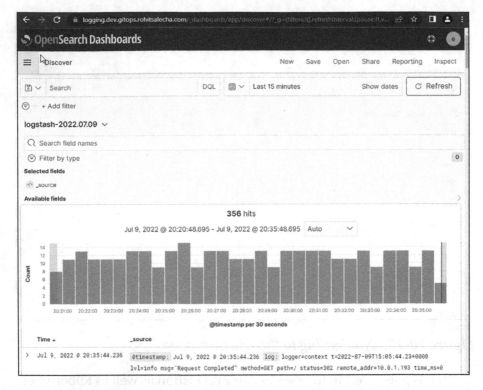

Figure 10-16. Application as well as Kubernetes logs

Kubernetes logs can be seen by default.

Time ▾	_source
> Jul 9, 2022 @ 20:35:4⋅ ⊕ ⊝	@timestamp: Jul 9, 2022 @ 20:35:44.236 log: logger=context t=2022-07-09T15:05:44.23+0000 lvl=info msg="Request Completed" method=GET path=/ status=302 remote_addr=10.0.1.193 time_ms=0 size=29 referer= stream: stdout time: Jul 9, 2022 @ 20:35:44.236 kubernetes.pod_name: grafana-5c75ccc866-j5c94 kubernetes.namespace_name: monitoring kubernetes.pod_id: 4de85848-5276-486c-a14b-bceb71334e72 kubernetes.labels.app_kubernetes_io/instance: grafana
> Jul 9, 2022 @ 20:35:38.563	@timestamp: Jul 9, 2022 @ 20:35:38.563 log: ERROR: logging before flag.Parse: E0709 15:05:38.563852 10 memcache.go:147] couldn't get resource list for metrics.k8s.io/v1beta1: the server is currently unable to handle the request stream: stderr time: Jul 9, 2022 @ 20:35:38.563 kubernetes.pod_name: aws-node-4bwbs kubernetes.namespace_name: kube-system kubernetes.pod_id: ccb49e60-f6b7-46cb-a75e-7fa132f0dbae
> Jul 9, 2022 @ 20:35:35.275	@timestamp: Jul 9, 2022 @ 20:35:35.275 log: logger=context t=2022-07-09T15:05:35.27+0000 lvl=info msg="Request Completed" method=GET path=/ status=302 remote_addr=10.0.2.133 time_ms=0 size=29 stream: stdout time: Jul 9, 2022 @ 20:35:35.275 kubernetes.pod_name: grafana-5c75ccc866-j5c94 kubernetes.namespace_name: monitoring kubernetes.pod_id: 4de85848-5276-486c-a14b-bceb71334e72 kubernetes.labels.app_kubernetes_io/instance: grafana
> Jul 9, 2022 @ 20:35:34.345	@timestamp: Jul 9, 2022 @ 20:35:34.345 log: logger=context t=2022-07-09T15:05:34.34+0000 lvl=info msg="Request Completed" method=GET path=/ status=302 remote_addr=10.0.3.42 time_ms=0 size=29 referer= stream: stdout time: Jul 9, 2022 @ 20:35:34.345 kubernetes.pod_name: grafana-5c75ccc866-j5c94 kubernetes.namespace_name: monitoring kubernetes.pod_id: 4de85848-5276-486c-a14b-bceb71334e72 kubernetes.labels.app_kubernetes_io/instance: grafana

Figure 10-17. *Kubernetes logs*

To see the application logs, visit the application and then create a user with test, test@test.com and 000000000 data as shown in the following. Click Add User.

Figure 10-18. *Adding test data*

Now go back to the OpenDashboard Discover page, and in the query box, search for "test" as shown in the following, and we can see our application logs being shown.

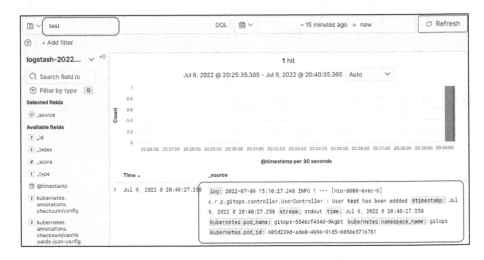

Figure 10-19. *Viewing test data in the OpenSearch console*

Thus, this sets up our logging infrastructure where we can view all our logs in a single place.

10.8 Monitoring

Monitoring our infrastructure is very critical especially when we are having so many moving parts like pods, ingresses, nodes, etc. How do we know how many pods are running or how many nodes are currently there without actually accessing the Kubernetes API?

Kubernetes dashboard provides a one-stop solution for logging as well as monitoring; however, Prometheus and Grafana stack are one of the most popular as they can be used to monitor not just Kubernetes but also EC2 instances and many more types of infrastructure that Prometheus supports.

Hence, the monitoring infrastructure in this book has been set up using Prometheus, Grafana, and the default metrics server provided by Kubernetes. Installation of this entire stack has been encapsulated in the following module:

File: infra\observability.tf

```
28: module "monitoring" {
29:   source = "./modules/monitoring"
30:
31:   grafana_version    = "6.26.0"
32:   prometheus_version = "15.8.0"
33:   ms_version         = "3.8.0"
34:   acm_arn            = module.acm.acm_arn
35:   url          = local.url
36:   zone_id           = data.aws_route53_zone.domain.zone_id
37:
38:   depends_on = [
39:     module.eks,
40:     resource.kubectl_manifest.aws_auth
41:   ]
42: }
```

Figure 10-20. *Setting up monitoring using Prometheus, Grafana, and Metrics Server*

L31–33: Grafana, Prometheus, and Metrics Server are being set up using Helm charts, and their specific versions have been provided here. All three are being set up on our Kubernetes Nodes and Grafana exposed to the Internet.

L34–36: These details are needed to expose Grafana over to the Internet as monitoring.<environment>.<domain-name>. For example, for our case, it would be monitoring.dev.gitops.rohitsalecha.com.

10.8.1 Exploring Grafana

Let's access our Grafana application located at `https://monitoring.dev.gitops.rohitsalecha.com/login`

Credentials are grafana:Gr@fAna123, hard-coded in *pgitops\infra\modules\monitoring\main.tf.*

Figure 10-21. *Logging into Grafana*

It is strongly recommended to change these credentials and also implement a Secrets Management strategy as discussed in Chapter 9 using AWS Secrets Manager.

Post authentication, the default screen of Grafana can be seen. Since no dashboard has been set up, let's import one by clicking Import as shown here.

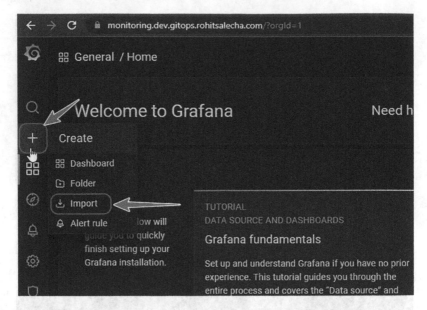

Figure 10-22. *Importing a Grafana dashboard*

Enter the ID 14623 as shown in the following and click Load.

Figure 10-23. *Enter the ID 14623*

Select the Datasource as Prometheus, leaving everything else as default. Then click Import.

Figure 10-24. *Selecting Prometheus as the default data source*

And our super cool Grafana dashboard is ready for monitoring almost all metrics: CPU usage, RAM usage, number of pods, number of nodes, etc.

Figure 10-25. *Grafana dashboard showing all monitoring metrics*

10.9 Karpenter Autoscaler

One of the biggest advantages of using Kubernetes is the ability to scale based on various factors. We can scale up pods based on the incoming network traffic and also scale up nodes to accommodate the rising number of pods. The former is also called vertical scaling, and the latter is called horizontal scaling.

This chapter will discuss horizontal scaling, that is, scaling nodes based on the increasing/decreasing number of pods.

For AWS EKS, AWS has an open source project called Karpenter that can be installed using Helm charts, and the entire configuration has been encapsulated in a module as shown here.

Code Block 10-16. Installing Karpenter

```
File: pgitops\infra\eks.tf

58: module "karpenter" {
59:    source = "./modules/karpenter"
60:
61:    node_group_role_arn     = module.eks.eks_managed_node_
                                 groups["app"].iam_role_name
62:    eks_cluster_id          = module.eks.cluster_id
63:    eks_cluster_endpoint_url = module.eks.cluster_endpoint
64:    oidc_url                = module.eks.cluster_oidc_
                                 issuer_url
65:    oidc_arn                = module.eks.oidc_provider_arn
66:    karpenter_version       = "v0.6.0"
67:
68:    depends_on = [module.eks, module.networking]
69: }
```

L61: The EKS module creates a role that has permissions to create/
delete EC2 nodes, and that Role name is being passed on to Karpenter so
that it can also get the same permissions to create EC2 instances and join
them into the EKS cluster.

L62–66: Details about the cluster are needed so that Karpenter can
join the correct cluster.

10.9.1 Karpenter in Action

Let's view Karpenter in action. As per the Grafana dashboard we saw
earlier, only two nodes were configured. Let's now increase the number
of deployment replicas from 1 to 10 as shown below and then perform
terraform apply.

Code Block 10-17. Updating deployments to view Karpenter in action

File: pgitops\infra\app.tf

```
099: resource "kubernetes_deployment_v1" "app" {
100:    metadata {
101:       name      = var.org_name
102:       namespace = kubernetes_namespace_v1.app.
          metadata.0.name
103:       labels = {
104:         app = var.org_name
105:       }
106:    }
107:
108:    spec {
109:       replicas = 10
```

XXXXXXXXXXXXXXX------SNIPPED-------XXXXXXXXXXXXXXXXXXXXXX

L109: Add a zero.

Let's run terraform apply and observe the nodes and metrics in Grafana.

CLI Output 10-18. Executing changes of ten deployments

```
cmd> export AWS_PROFILE=sita-dev
cmd> cd pgitops/infra
cmd> terraform apply --auto-approve
```

Before Apply

Figure 10-26. *Before applying the changes*

After Apply

Ten minutes after applying the changes, CPU usage is high, the number of nodes is 3, and the number of pods shots up to 40!

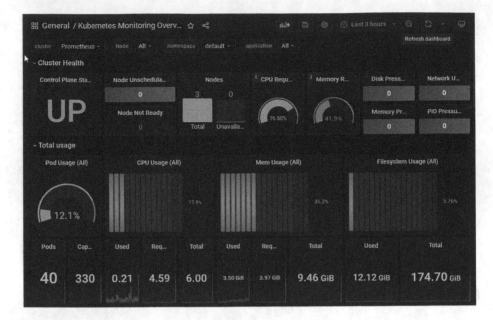

Figure 10-27. *After applying changes*

Let's view the change from the console.

CLI Output 10-19. Viewing changes from the console

```
cmd> aws eks update-kubeconfig --name gitops-us-east-1-dev
--region us-east-1
cmd> kubectl get nodes -o wide
```

Output shows three nodes; however, if carefully observed, the runtimes of the three nodes are different as shown here.

CLI Output 10-20. Three nodes are up, one by Karpenter

```
CONTAINER-RUNTIME
containerd://1.4.13
docker://20.10.13
docker://20.10.13
```

That is because when Karpenter launches a node, it builds it with the default runtime as **containerd://1.4.13**

Hence, setting up the nodes with Karpenter is an easy task; however, if the infrastructure was to be destroyed at this stage, Terraform would error out as it doesn't have the capability to delete a node set up using Karpenter. This is a known issue captured here:

https://github.com/aws/karpenter/issues/1134

Hence, if a Karpenter launched node needs to be deleted, then an instance with the name "karpenter.sh/provisioner-name/default" needs to be searched in the EC2 home page and manually deleted.

To avoid such a scenario, let's revert back the setting from ten replicas to one and apply terraform apply.

CLI Output 10-21. Reverting the changes

```
cmd> export AWS_PROFILE=sita-dev
cmd> cd pgitops/infra
cmd> terraform apply --auto-approve
```

The Grafana dashboard should now show the reduced numbers as it was earlier once terraform apply is completed.

10.10 Upgrading Kubernetes

Upgrading Kubernetes infrastructure is challenging for any administrator. However, with AWS EKS and Terraform, it is quite simple where we only need to modify the version (and also ensure that the deployment resources are compatible with that version) in the *pgitops\infra\terraform.auto.tfvars* from 1.20 to 1.21 and then perform terraform apply!

Code Block 10-22. Upgrading to version 1.21

```
File: pgitops\infra\terraform.auto.tfvars

36: eks_version     = "1.21"
```

CLI Output 10-23. Executing the change

```
cmd> export AWS_PROFILE=sita-dev
cmd> cd pgitops/infra
cmd> terraform apply --auto-approve

XXXXXXXXXXXXXXXX------SNIPPED-------XXXXXXXXXXXXXXXXXXXXX

Plan: 0 to add, 20 to change, 0 to destroy
```

The apply operation will take approximately 40–45 minutes as the following actions will be undertaken:

1. AWS Master node will be upgraded which is totally abstracted from us which would take about 10 minutes as shown below. New TLS certificates being generated shows a new cluster has been created.

CLI Output 10-24. New cluster being created

```
module.eks.module.eks.aws_eks_cluster.this[0]: Still modifying... [id=gitops-us-east-1-dev, 9m20s elapsed]
module.eks.module.eks.aws_eks_cluster.this[0]: Modifications complete after 9m21s [id=gitops-us-east-1-dev]
module.eks.module.eks.data.tls_certificate.this[0]: Reading...
module.eks.module.eks.data.tls_certificate.this[0]: Read complete after 1s [id=2022-07-09 16:37:40.09521 +0000 UTC]
```

2.   New nodes with the new version will be created first.

CLI Output 10-25.   New nodes being created

```
module.eks.module.eks.module.eks_managed_node_group["app"].aws_eks_node_group.this[0]: Still modifying... [id=gitops-us-east-1-dev:app-2
02207091101002404000001b, 3m50s elapsed]
module.eks.module.eks.module.eks_managed_node_group["system"].aws_eks_node_group.this[0]: Still modifying... [id=gitops-us-east-1-dev:sy
stem-20220709110100248100000019, 4m0s elapsed]
module.eks.module.eks.module.eks_managed_node_group["app"].aws_eks_node_group.this[0]: Still modifying... [id=gitops-us-east-1-dev:app-2
02207091101002404000001b, 4m0s elapsed]
```

The Grafana dashboard at this point shows six nodes.

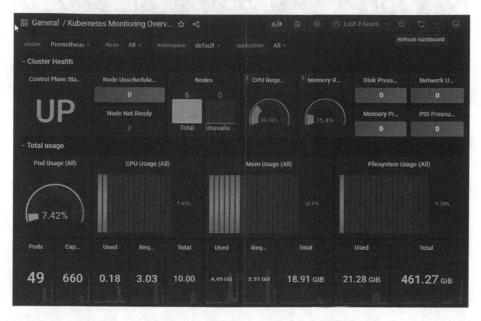

Figure 10-28.   *Grafana dashboard showing six nodes*

3.   Once new nodes are created, pods from the old nodes will be cordoned off and consequently will be installed in new nodes. At this point, Grafana will sign you out, and you'll need to re-log in and re-import the dashboard. Once done, it should show around nine nodes as shown here.

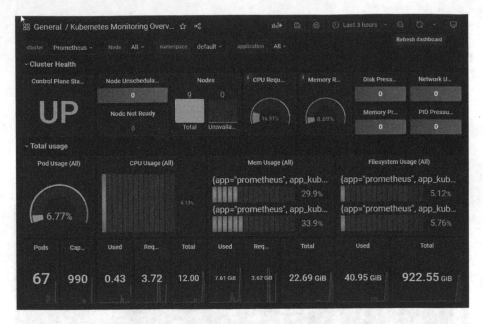

Figure 10-29. *Grafana dashboard showing nine nodes*

4. Old nodes will be destroyed/unscheduled once
    the pods are cordoned off. The following Grafana
    dashboard shows one node is unschedulable,
    meaning old nodes are now being destroyed.

Figure 10-30. *One node is unschedulable*

5. Finally, the entire cluster will fall back to normalcy
    with 2 nodes and 25 pods as shown here.

Figure 10-31. *Cluster back to normal*

In this entire process, the application never goes down! It's always up. Kubernetes has now been upgraded to 1.21 as shown here!

```
NAME                        STATUS  ROLES    AGE  VERSION
ip-10-0-11-132.ec2.internal  Ready   <none>   30m  v1.21.12-eks-5308cf7
ip-10-0-13-164.ec2.internal  Ready   <none>   30m  v1.21.12-eks-5308cf7
```

Figure 10-32. *New cluster is up*

10.11 Clean-Up

While cleaning the infra folder is quite easy and straightforward as in this chapter, only the development environment was set up. So a simple terraform destroy would do the work as shown here.

CLI Output 10-26. Destroying the environment

```
cmd> export AWS_PROFILE=sita-dev
cmd> cd pgitops/infra
cmd> terraform destroy--auto-approve
```

Note   At any point, if Terraform is unable to destroy, please check Annexure A where steps have been presented to delete the resources manually.

However, cleaning up the global folder is a bit challenging as there are plenty of dependencies involved. These steps are totally optional, and the only cost that is being incurred if the global folder is not destroyed is the three Route53 Zones that have been set up. The rest is all nonchargeable.

The very first thing that needs to be done is that each user needs to first delete their access keys by manually logging into the AWS console and then deactivating and deleting the keys.

However, for us since Sita is the IAMAdmin in the Identity account we can login into the account and delete the keys of all users.

Once the access keys have been deleted, browse to the Global workspace of the Terraform Cloud application and destroy the plan as shown here.

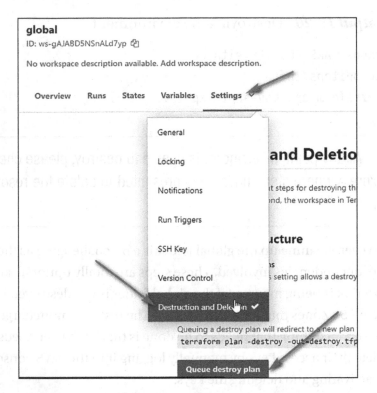

Figure 10-33. *Destroy Global in Terraform Cloud*

Terraform destroy will run effectively and destroy all the resources except the AWS accounts and will show the following error.

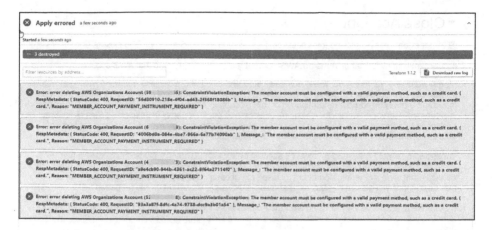

Figure 10-34. *Terraform account deletion error*

AWS accounts cannot be deleted using Terraform, and hence, the only way to delete them is to follow these steps:

- Reset the password of the root user for each of the preceding accounts using the forgot password functionality. Please set a strong password and enable 2FA if possible.

- You can now close your account by simply navigating to the Accounts section here: https://us-east-1.console. aws.amazon.com/billing/home?region=us-east-1#/ account. Scroll down and click Close Account.

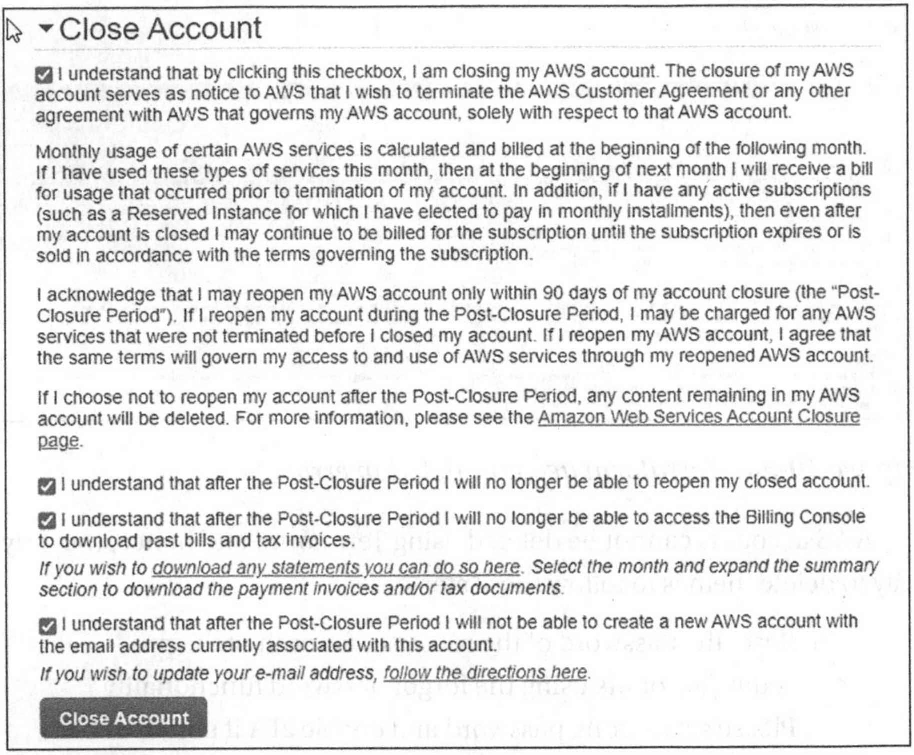

> ☐⃝ ▾ Close Account
>
> ☑ I understand that by clicking this checkbox, I am closing my AWS account. The closure of my AWS account serves as notice to AWS that I wish to terminate the AWS Customer Agreement or any other agreement with AWS that governs my AWS account, solely with respect to that AWS account.
>
> Monthly usage of certain AWS services is calculated and billed at the beginning of the following month. If I have used these types of services this month, then at the beginning of next month I will receive a bill for usage that occurred prior to termination of my account. In addition, if I have any active subscriptions (such as a Reserved Instance for which I have elected to pay in monthly installments), then even after my account is closed I may continue to be billed for the subscription until the subscription expires or is sold in accordance with the terms governing the subscription.
>
> I acknowledge that I may reopen my AWS account only within 90 days of my account closure (the "Post-Closure Period"). If I reopen my account during the Post-Closure Period, I may be charged for any AWS services that were not terminated before I closed my account. If I reopen my AWS account, I agree that the same terms will govern my access to and use of AWS services through my reopened AWS account.
>
> If I choose not to reopen my account after the Post-Closure Period, any content remaining in my AWS account will be deleted. For more information, please see the Amazon Web Services Account Closure page.
>
> ☑ I understand that after the Post-Closure Period I will no longer be able to reopen my closed account.
>
> ☑ I understand that after the Post-Closure Period I will no longer be able to access the Billing Console to download past bills and tax invoices.
> *If you wish to download any statements you can do so here. Select the month and expand the summary section to download the payment invoices and/or tax documents.*
>
> ☑ I understand that after the Post-Closure Period I will not be able to create a new AWS account with the email address currently associated with this account.
> *If you wish to update your e-mail address, follow the directions here.*
>
> **Close Account**

Figure 10-35. *Closing the AWS account*

Once the account is closed, you can no longer use the email address associated with the closed account to create a new account.

Tip   If you ever plan to re-run the terraform code in the global folder, ensure to use new email addresses like instead of email+prod@ somedomain.com, use email+prod1@somedomain.com.

Also do remove the NS mapping in your hosted zone records that were created in Chapter 8.

10.12 Conclusion

This concludes the chapter and this book where we saw how cloud and cloud-native resources can be spun up and teared down with the power of Infrastructure as Code all the while with full automation and guardrails in place.

I hope by reading this book, the reader can get a better understanding and insight into Terraform, AWS, and GitHub Actions, the three main pillars of discussion throughout this book, and how all of them can be tied together to bring forth a completely automated system that is version controlled in Git, making it practical GitOps. :-)

10.12 Conclusion

ANNEXURE A

Manually Delete Resources

In order to delete resources from a specific account, first, we need to assume a role into that account, namely, prod, staging, and dev, where the resources are stuck.

The same can be done by logging into the identity account and then clicking Switch role as shown here.

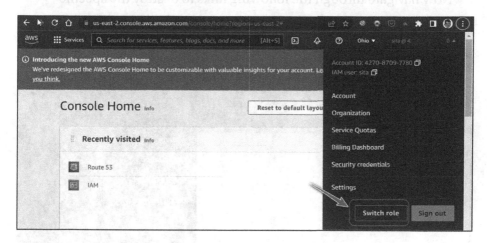

Assume the role by entering the requisite information. All the information is available in the Global workspace of the Terraform cloud application.

R. Salecha, *Practical GitOps*, https://doi.org/10.1007/978-1-4842-8673-9

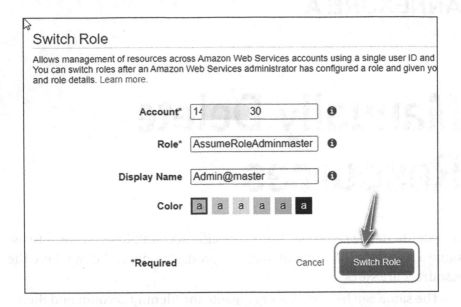

Now navigate through the following links to destroy the specific resources.

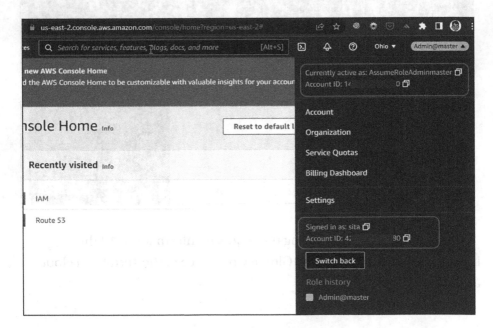

Ensure that the resources are destroyed in this specific order. Also ensure you are in the correct region.

1) Delete RDS – `https://console.aws.amazon.com/rds/home?region=us-east-1#databases:`

2) Delete RDS Subnet Group – `https://console.aws.amazon.com/rds/home?region=us-east-1#db-subnet-groups-list:`

3) Delete SSM Parameter – `https://us-east-1.console.aws.amazon.com/systems-manager/parameters/?region=us-east-1&tab=Table#`

4) Delete EKS – Click on the EKS Cluster configured: `https://console.aws.amazon.com/eks/home?region=us-east-1#/clusters`

   a) Delete NodeGroups – Click on each Node Group as shown here.

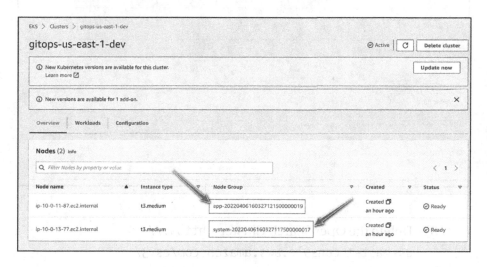

   b) Delete the App NodeGroup.

c) Navigate back. Select the System NodeGroup and then delete the System NodeGroup.

d) Wait for about five minutes and then delete the EKS Cluster as shown in the following once the NodeGroup is shown empty.

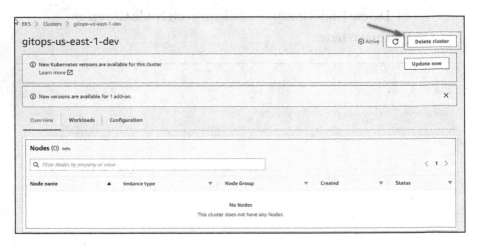

5) Delete the OpenSearch Cluster – https://us-east-1.console.aws.amazon.com/esv3/home?region=us-east-1#opensearch/domains

6) Disable and delete KMS keys – All KMS keys with alias as "eks" need to be first disabled and then deleted. `https://us-east-1.console.aws.amazon.com/kms/home?region=us-east-1#/kms/keys`

7) Delete Identity Provider – `https://us-east-1.console.aws.amazon.com/iamv2/home?region=us-east-1&skipRegion=true#/identity_providers`

8) Delete LB – `https://console.aws.amazon.com/ec2/v2/home?region=us-east-1#LoadBalancers:sort=loadBalancerName`

9) Delete ACM Certificates – `https://console.aws.amazon.com/acm/home?region=us-east-1#/certificates/list`

10) Delete Secret from Secrets Manager – `https://us-east-1.console.aws.amazon.com/secretsmanager/home?region=us-east-1#!/listSecrets/`

11) Delete CloudWatch Log Groups (All) – `https://us-east-1.console.aws.amazon.com/cloudwatch/home?region=us-east-1#logsV2:log-groups`

12) Detach VPC Gateways – First, select the VP Gateway and then detach it. Once detached, delete it: `https://us-east-1.console.aws.amazon.com/vpc/home?region=us-east-1#VpnGateways:`

13) Delete NAT Gateway – `https://us-east-1.console.aws.amazon.com/vpc/home?region=us-east-1#NatGateways:`

14) Release Elastic IPs – (Wait for NAT Gateway to be deleted before trying) `https://us-east-1.console.aws.amazon.com/ec2/home?region=us-east-1#Addresses:`

15) Delete any residual Network Interfaces(if any) – `https://us-east-1.console.aws.amazon.com/ec2/home?region=us-east-1#NIC:`

16) Delete the VPC - `https://us-east-1.console.aws.amazon.com/vpc/home?region=us-east-1#vpcs:`

17) Delete Customer-Created Policies – AWSLoadBalancerControllerIAMPolicy1,secrets_policy and AmazonEKS_EFS_CSI_Driver_Policy `https://us-east-1.console.aws.amazon.com/iamv2/home?region=us-east-1&skipRegion=true#/policies$customer`

18) Delete the following IAM Roles – app-eks-node-group-2**************** , aws-load-balancer-controller,gitops-us-east-1-dev-cluster-2*************,system-eks-node-group-20*****************,irsa-aws-secrets,efs-csi-controller-sa `https://us-east-1.console.aws.amazon.com/iamv2/home?region=us-east-1&skipRegion=true#/roles`

ANNEXURE B

Terraform Cloud Destroy Problem

While destroying the staging/production environment from the Terraform Cloud, you may encounter an error like as follows.

In this scenario, we need to download the state file from the terraform cloud, add it in the location where the source code for the development environment is located, modify the variables, and then run terraform destroy as shown in the following.

1. Download the state file.

© Rohit Salecha 2023
R. Salecha, *Practical GitOps*, https://doi.org/10.1007/978-1-4842-8673-9

2. Move the state file to the code location.

    ```
    cmd> ls -al
    total 4064
    -rw-r--r--@  1 rohit   rohit     974819 Jul  8 18:45
    sv-1JTUXEs2GQTWoU3D.tfstate
    cmd> mv sv-1JTUXEs2GQTWoU3D.tfstate terraform.tfstate
    cmd> mv terraform.tfstate pgitops/infra
    ```

3. Update the default variables to reflect the staging/
    prod environment.

    File: pgitops/infra/variables.tf

    ```
    4: variable "environment" {
    5:   description = "The Deployment environment"
    6:   type        = string
    7:   default     = "staging"
    8: }
    9:
    15: variable "region" {
    16:   description = "AWS region"
    17:   type        = string
    18:   default     = "us-east-1"
    19: }
    ```

4. Update the account of the staging/prod environment that needs to be destroyed.

   File: infra/terraform.auto.tfvars

   43: assume_role_account_id = "16XXXXXXXXX9"

5. Finally, run terraform destroy.

```
cmd> export AWS_PROFILE=sita-staging
cmd> terraform destroy --auto-approve
```

ANNEXURE C

Code Compatibility on OS

C.1 Mac M1

All chapters have been thoroughly tested, and code is working fine on Mac M1.

C.2 Windows Native (cmd.exe)

Code works absolutely fine on all chapters except for Chapter 10.

In Chapter 10, I am making use of a local-exec as shown in the following where curl needs to be used. This local-exec is not working on Windows even after installing curl on the Windows path. Hence, Chapter 10 doesn't work on Windows native.

File: pgitops\infra\modules\logging\main.tf

```
156: resource "null_resource" "fluentbit-role" {
157:   provisioner "local-exec" {
158:     command = <<EOT
159:       curl -sS -u "${local.es_username}:${local.es_
             password}" -X PATCH \
```

© Rohit Salecha 2023
R. Salecha, *Practical GitOps*, https://doi.org/10.1007/978-1-4842-8673-9

```
160:            https://${aws_elasticsearch_domain.es.endpoint}/_
               opendistro/_security/api/rolesmapping/all_
               access?pretty \
161:            -H 'Content-Type: application/json' \
162:            -d'
163:            [
164:              {
165:                "op": "add", "path": "/backend_roles",
                   "value": ["'${aws_iam_role.irsa_
                   fluentbit.arn}'"]
166:              }
167:            ]
168:            '
169: EOT
170:    }
171:    triggers = {
172:      endpoint = aws_elasticsearch_domain.es.endpoint
173:    }
174:
175:    depends_on = [resource.aws_elasticsearch_domain.es]
176: }
```

C.3 WSL2 (Ubuntu)

Tested the code on WSL2 for all chapters and it works absolutely fine till Chapter 6. However, from Chapter 7 onward, you might get this error:

```
| Error: Kubernetes cluster unreachable: Get "https://
B29481B1D200A05798E568DCF979DE62.gr7.us-east-1.eks.amazonaws.
com/version": getting credentials: decoding stdout: no
kind "ExecCredential" is registered for version "client.
```

```
authentication.k8s.io/v1alpha1" in scheme "pkg/runtime/
scheme.go:100"
|
|    with module.alb_ingress.helm_release.lbc,
|    on modules/alb/main.tf line 73, in resource "helm_
     release" "lbc":
|    73: resource "helm_release" "lbc" {
```

To resolve this error on WSL (Ubuntu), modify

api_version = "client.authentication.k8s.io/v1beta1" to **v1alpha1** as shown below

```
provider "helm" {
  kubernetes {
    host                   = module.eks.cluster_endpoint
    cluster_ca_certificate = base64decode(module.eks.cluster_
                             certificate_authority_data)
    exec {
      api_version = "client.authentication.k8s.io/v1alpha1"
      command     = "aws"
      args = [
        "eks",
        "get-token",
        "--role-arn",
        local.assume_role_arn,
        "--cluster-name",
        module.eks.cluster_id
      ]
    }
  }
}
```

This issue has been reported (https://github.com/hashicorp/terraform-provider-helm/issues/913).

Index

A, B

Amazon Web Services (AWS), 1
  access control, 390–393
  account creation
    access keys screen, 37
    cost explorer, 35
    email address, 33
    final screen, 37
    IAM dashboard, 34
    policy/permissions screen, 36
    user screen, 35
  authentication/authorization
    (authz), 372–385
  cloud computing, 33
  documentation, 31
  EC2 machine, 40
  Elastic Compute Cloud, 33
  historical overview, 32
  identity and access
    management
    (IAM), 338–355
  infrastructure resources, 32
  login information
    access keys file, 38
    CLI profile configuration, 39
    sign-in screen, 39
  organization trail, 455
  organization units, 326–338
  production environment, 240
  profiles, 385–387
  Route53 Zone, 355–357
  scalability, 32
  secrets management
    design, 414–424
  security/secrets management,
    397, 408–418
  Spring Boot app, 263
  terraform, 68
Application Load Balancer (ALB)
  access logs, 470–472
  security/secrets
    management, 408–410
Application programming
    interface (API)
  actions tab, 213
  driven terraform workspace,
    210, 211
  environment variables, 211, 212
  pushing workflow, 212
  workflow execution
    apply stage, 215–217
    configuration, 213
    execution, 215
    logs streaming, 218
    trigger, 214
    triggering workflow, 214

C

G, H

P, Q

V, W, X, Y, Z

Printed in the United States
by Baker & Taylor Publisher Services